# GREEK TRAGIC THEATRE

*Greek*
know
in pe
encou
ing th

Emph
the *p*
which
matte
practi
prom
whose

The s
*Orest*
*Wom*
traged
the ch

**Rush**
at Sta

# THEATRE PRODUCTION STUDIES
## General Editor: John Russell Brown
### University of Michigan

There has long been a need for books which give a clear idea of how the great theatre of the past worked and of the particular experiences they offered. Students of dramatic literature and theatre history are increasingly concerned with plays in performance, especially the performances expected by their authors and their audiences. Directors, designers, actors and other theatre practitioners need imaginative, practical suggestions on how to revive plays and experiment with rehearsal and production techniques.

*Theatre Production Studies* fills this need. Designed to span Western theatre from the Greeks to the present day, each book explores a period, or genre, drawing together aspects of production from staging, wardrobe and acting styles, to the management of a theatre, its artistic team, and technical crew. Each volume focuses on several texts of exceptional achievement, and is well illustrated with contemporary material.

*Already published:*

SHAKESPEARE'S THEATRE (second edition)          *Peter Thomson*
JACOBEAN PUBLIC THEATRE          *Alexander Leggatt*
BROADWAY THEATRE          *Andrew Harris*

# GREEK TRAGIC THEATRE

Rush Rehm

London and New York

First published 1992
Reprinted in hardback 1994
First published in paperback 1994
by Routledge
11 New Fetter Lane, London EC4P 4EE

Simultaneously published in the USA and Canada
by Routledge
29 West 35th Street, New York, NY 10001

Typeset in Garamond by
Falcon Typographic Art Ltd, Fife, Scotland
Printed and bound in Great Britain by
TJ Press (Padstow) Ltd, Padstow, Cornwall

*British Library Cataloguing in Publication Data*
Rehm, Rush
Greek tragic theatre. – (Theatre production series)
I. Title II. Series
882.0109

*Library of Congress Cataloging in Publication Data*
Rehm, Rush.
Greek tragic theatre / Rush Rehm.
p. cm. – (Theatre production studies)
Includes bibliographical references and index.
1. Greek drama (Tragedy) – History and criticism. 2. Political
plays, Greek – History and criticism. 3. Theatre – Greece – History.
I. Title. II. Series.
PA3131.R38    1992
882'.0109 – dc20    91–33611

ISBN 0–415–11894–8

# CONTENTS

# PREFACE

Greek tragedy is read, studied, written about, lauded, and occasionally reviled, and yet the plays are rarely performed. When they are, the productions are usually disappointing. The style is too staid, or too wild; the translations are too stilted, or too hip; the mood is too then, or too now. And yet those of us who come in contact with tragedy in performance have recognized moments of sheer theatrical greatness, experiences of such astounding power that they beggar description, speaking as they do over centuries of cultural and historical difference. Perhaps in these moments of rediscovery something of the complex simplicity of Greek tragedy finds us out – the dance of the language, the agonizing passion of the characters, the surge of the chorus, or simply the sound of an incomparable name, evoking its story of pain and insight.

Enthusiasms such as these are important in drawing us into the theatre, but they don't get us very far once we are there. For the challenge of the stage, as the Greeks well knew, is to wed ideas and insights to their concrete realization, incarnating words and actions in performance, giving the tale to be told a specific shape before a particular audience. With that in mind, this book addresses the question of how Greek tragedy *worked*, focusing on what the plays do rather than what can be extracted from them. My hope is that the reader – student, classicist, playgoer, theatre professional – catches some sense of the excitement of engaging Greek tragedy, and comes away with a better idea of how its theatrical challenges can be met by understanding how they once were.

Part I emphasizes the political nature of Greek theatre, in the sense that it was a theatre of, by, and for the *polis* ('city'), the social institution that bound Greeks together as a human community. In this light, I discuss Athens as a *performance culture*, one in which the theatre stood alongside other public forums as a place to confront matters of import and moment. Individual chapters follow on specific aspects of fifth-century tragic performance: the festival context, participation in and responsibility for dramatic production, the constraints and opportunities presented by the theatre of Dionysus, and important conventions of tragic staging. My aim is to show how the generic

vii

elements of production cohered around a vision of the theatre as integral to the life of the city – a theatre, in short, whose focus was on the audience.

In Part II, I examine four exemplary tragedies – in the case of the *Oresteia*, a connected trilogy – as they might have been realized in original performance. My choice of the *Oresteia* and *Oedipus Tyrannus* may appear unadventurous, but the towering status of these works has kept critics from approaching them as plays enacted before an audience. Two tragedies by Euripides are probably too few, since his work is so diverse and much more of it has survived. By examining *Suppliant Women* and *Ion*, radically different in subject and form, I focus on works virtually unknown to the theatre, and yet plays of clear theatrical genius.

The discussion of individual plays skirts the critical tradition, focusing instead on how each tragedy unfolds in performance, generating different relationships between the characters (and chorus) on-stage and the audience in the theatre.[1] Such a sequential approach runs the risk of alienating those readers closely familiar with the texts, but a certain amount of 're-telling' is unavoidable if we are to engage imaginatively in the dynamics of performance.

By following the path that each play lays out, I shift perspectives between that of a director staging a production and that of an audience helping to make the production come to life. The audience is a virtual one, 'we', although I do differentiate fifth-century spectators from their modern counterparts when issues of cultural and historical specificity are paramount. We need to keep in mind that, as Adrian Poole puts it, 'the power of Greek tragedy to outlive the local conditions of its original production depends on the quality of the challenge which it once offered to those local conditions'.[2]

The book eschews any general comments about the differences between the three great tragedians, concentrating instead on the dramatic and imaginative integrity of the particular play under discussion. Generalizations about the nature of Aeschylean and Sophoclean tragedy are particularly dangerous, given that our sample is so small. On the basis of Sophocles' seven extant plays, can we confidently pronounce the nature of the more than 100 others that we have lost? Let us simply admit that the fifth century was a time of extraordinary theatrical production, and appreciate that all three playwrights were innovators, theatrical experimentalists, beneficiaries of the tradition even as they challenged and reshaped it.

# ACKNOWLEDGEMENTS

To acknowledge fully, and with full grace, the many people who have influenced my approach to Greek tragedy and its theatrical life is – like aspects of the plays themselves – simply beyond me. Preliminary work was undertaken at the American School of Classical Studies in Athens, and my thanks go to the Secretary of the School, Bob Bridges, and the School Librarian, Nancy Winters. The photographs are courtesy of the Deutsches Archäologisches Institut-Athen. I had a splendid year as a Junior Fellow at the Center for Hellenic Studies in Washington, DC, and I owe a debt of gratitude to Zeph and Diana Stewart. My special thanks to Ron Davies, Laurence Maslon, Geoffrey Reeves, Bonna Wescoat, Dianne Wood, and the series editor John Russell Brown.

# A NOTE ON TRANSLATIONS AND EDITIONS

In discussing individual passages, I have followed (where possible) the lineation of the most recent Oxford edition:

AESCHYLUS:
*Aeschyli: Septem Quae Supersunt Tragoedias*, D. Page (ed.), 1972.
*Agamemnon*, J.D. Denniston and D. Page (eds), 1957, rpt 1972.
*Choephori*, A.F. Garvie (ed.), 1986, rpt with corrections 1988.
*Eumenides*, A.H. Sommerstein (ed.), Cambridge, Cambridge University Press, 1989.

SOPHOCLES:
*Sophoclis Fabulae*, H. Lloyd-Jones and N.G. Wilson (eds), 1990.

EURIPIDES:
*Euripidis Fabulae*, J. Diggle (ed.), vol. 1, 1984, rpt with corrections 1989; vol. 2, 1981, rpt with corrections 1986; vol. 3, G. Murray (ed.), 1909, the last supplemented by the editions of *Helen*, R. Kannicht (ed.), Heidelberg, 1969; *Orestes*, C.W. Willink (ed.), 1986; and *Bacchae*, E.R. Dodds (ed.), 2nd edn, 1960.

Unless otherwise noted, all translations are my own. Those of Aeschylus' *Oresteia* can be found in *Aeschylus' Oresteia: A Theatre Version*, Melbourne, Hawthorn Press, 1978. The translations of *Ion* are by W.S. DiPiero and Rush Rehm.

All dates are BC unless otherwise noted.

# Part I

# THE SOCIAL
# AND THEATRICAL
# BACKGROUND

# 1

# THE PERFORMANCE CULTURE
# OF ATHENS

In the culture of fifth-century Athens, Greek tragic theatre was one kind of performance among many, drawing its strength (and often its material) from the greater and lesser public occasions that surrounded it. The areas of politics, law, religion, athletics, festivals, music, and poetry shared with the theatre an essentially public and performative nature, so much so that one form of cultural expression merged easily with another. Important aspects of family life – including various rites of passage, weddings, and funerals – also 'went public' in a theatrical fashion. Gatherings for wine, food, and entertainment called *symposia* developed into occasions for performance, especially music and solo poetry. Although barred from these drinking parties (unless present as musicians, dancers, or prostitutes), women sang and told stories when they worked at the loom, and their participation in various religious cults also included songs and dances of a more sober nature.

We find references to, and enactments of, these ritual and artistic practices in every tragedy, as if the overtly performative genre of theatre acknowledged its debt to the other manifestations of Athenian performance culture. We may compare the Elizabethan and Jacobean playwrights who were drawn to particularly *theatrical* metaphors, viewing life as a dramatic role, as in Jaques' 'All the world's a stage' lament, or Macbeth's despairing conclusion that 'Life's but a walking shadow, a poor player/ who struts and frets his hour upon the stage/ and then is heard no more'. The ancient sense of the theatrical seems to have been more generalized, transitive, all-encompassing. Far from singling out the stage as a metaphor, Athenian society as a whole was imbued with a sense of *event*, of things said and done in the context of a conventional frame, so that participation entailed both a commitment to the moment and a critical distance from it. Today, for example, we perceive a great difference between participating in a ritual where issues of belief are paramount, and attending a theatrical performance where suspension of disbelief is at issue. Ancient Athenians seem to have viewed these events as a continuum of performance rather than as opposed attitudes to the world.

There is no better example of the pervasiveness of performance in

3

ancient Greece than the political system of participatory democracy by which Athenians governed themselves. At least once every month (but usually two, three, or even four times) the citizens of Athens (free-born males over 18) gathered on the hill called the Pnyx for the meeting of the Assembly. Through the power of the spoken word, and by various appeals to reason, emotion, and morality, the Assembly speakers swayed the citizen body, much like actors in a large outdoor theatre. Here, however, anyone present was free to speak, although the size of the audience – 6,000 or more – made such a prospect daunting. In this egalitarian public gathering, a speaker's performance would be judged critically and knowledgeably, for the Assembly was *the* means of formulating state policy, determined year in and year out by simple majority vote.

The large concavity of the Pnyx established a relationship between the (changing) speakers and their audience that mirrored the relationship between actors and spectators at the great theatre of Dionysus, discussed in Chapter 4. The same situation applied in the smaller political forums, such as the Council (a group of 500 who set the agenda for the Assembly), the assemblies of local districts (*demes*), and the meetings of kinship and neighbourhood organizations. For example, when the Council chamber was rebuilt at the end of the fifth century, the seating banks were set around the speaker's platform on the model of the cavea surrounding the orchestra in the Athenian theatre. Reporting an act of sacrilege by anti-democratic elements that took place in this very chamber, Xenophon describes the forceful removal of the suppliants as if it were a scene in a Euripidean tragedy – only the actions were staged to terrify the Council members rather than a theatre audience.[1]

We get a sense of the eloquence and power of political speeches from Thucydides' *History*, an account of the Peloponnesian War fought between Athens and Sparta in the last third of the fifth century. The confrontation between opposing speakers in various Thucydidean debates has all the vitality and imaginative life of a dramatic scene, with the assembled citizenry as audience, alternately swept up in the rhetoric of the moment and then reflecting critically on its ramifications. An even closer analogue to the verbal life of a Greek tragic performance was found in the Athenian lawcourts. After hearing speeches offered by the litigants, the jury (ranging from 100 to 1,500 members) reached its verdict by simple majority vote, taken without consultation.[2] As with the decisions of the Assembly that could be overturned at a subsequent meeting, the trial-by-jury process was ongoing and open-ended. The loser of a case one day could file a counter-charge the next and try his opponent before a different set of jurors, a process that fully acknowledged the autonomy and individuality of any given audience.

Many lawcourt speeches have survived, composed by professional writers to be delivered by litigants, since there were no lawyers present at the trial. The legal system converted both plaintiff and defendant into actors interpreting their lines for the benefit of their jury-audience.[3] The speechwriter's task was to establish the good character of his client and attack that of his opponent. Was this the kind of man who would bring harm to the city? Would this sort of citizen do that sort of thing? Whom should I believe? Histrionics from the sublime to the ridiculous operated in these forensic displays – one minute a speaker claims that he has observed all the duties owed his dead forebears, and in the next he mounts an attack on the legitimacy of his opponent's mother.

The creation and interpretation of a 'character' for a single lawcourt performance drew on, as it influenced, the comparable work of the dramatist in the theatre. The litigiousness of the Athenians provided a bottomless source of material for Greek comedy. It also left its mark on tragedy, in the genre's rich legal vocabulary and the frequency of 'courtroom scenes', ranging from the momentous trial of Orestes in Aeschylus' *Eumenides* to the arraignment of Polymnestor in Euripides' *Hecuba*, where the verdict is reached *after* the accused has been brutally punished.[4]

There were countless other occasions for forensic display and rhetoric in the city, reflecting the spontaneous and theatrical flair of her citizens. Athens was animate with debate and argument, and public life was a kind of lived performance in which a community of interested (or simply curious) parties could form at any moment. Lectures by philosopher-teachers known as sophists became popular during the fifth century, and the rhetoricians captured the imagination and custom of the sons of the Athenian elite, who developed their skills in persuasive argument in order to influence political events. Informal debates in the agora (market place) were common fare, as we know from the Platonic dialogues where Socrates prods some arrogant soul into revealing he has no rational basis for his most cherished opinions. The dialogue structure that Socrates adopts owes much to the tragedies staged in Athens, although the philosopher remained suspicious of the relationship between speaker and audience, between performer and 'performed upon', that operated in the theatre and other public forums:

> Isn't it the public themselves who are sophists [educators] on a grand scale, and give a complete training to young and old, men and women, turning them into just the sort of people they want ... when they crowd into the seats in the assembly, or lawcourts, or theatre?[5]

Furthermore, the Athenian state devoted over a hundred days in the calendar year to public festivals, organized around religious cults that were sanctioned by the city. In recreating what these 'performances' were like, we should keep in mind the differences between pagan and modern attitudes towards religion. As Sir Kenneth Dover puts it, 'to the ordinary Greek, festive and ceremonial occasions were the primary constituent of religion; theology came a very bad second'.[6] Unlike the political forums of the city, most civic festivals were open to everyone – men, women, slaves, children, resident aliens, visiting foreigners. There were exceptions – men were excluded from the all-women festivals associated with Demeter, for example – but generally speaking the city gathered in all its variety, providing both performers and audience for the various events.

A basic ritual pattern characterized most festival worship, and the form it took included many recognizable theatrical elements. A procession involving an array of participants made its way to the temple where the cult-image of the deity was housed. The parade included priests wearing sacral robes, underlings who carried various ritual objects, attendants who led the beasts to be sacrificed, common folk who marched or simply watched as the others passed by. The Parthenon frieze gives a rich impression of what the grandest of these Athenian processions, the Panathenaia, may have been like.

Assembled before the altar outside the temple, the crowd then witnessed the performance of the sacrifice itself. Looking out from the altar steps over the gathered throng, the priest uttered prayers and formulae, and after a series of actions to signal the victim's consent, the dramatic moment arrived. The first animal was struck, the women raised a ritual cry, and the smoke of burnt flesh rose to the heavens. At large-scale festivals such as the City Dionysia and the Panathenaia, the ritual slaughter had less of a sacred character than one might suppose, since an enormous number of victims were offered (an excessive 240 cattle at the City Dionysia in 333 BC). It was customary that only the inedible parts of the animal were dedicated and burnt to the gods; the rest was cooked and distributed to the crowd in a city-sponsored feast. A similar practice was followed at local sacrifices and those made in private households, allowing the participants to enjoy meat that was far too expensive to be consumed on less than special occasions.[7]

After the feast, the other festival events occurred, and these frequently included performances organized as contests. There were athletic events, instrumental competitions on the *kitharode* (lyre) and *aulos* (a reed instrument comparable to a clarinet), solo songs with the singer accompanying himself on the lyre, choral singing and dancing, and so on. Many of the songs and choral odes make reference to their actual performance, reminding us that they were rehearsed, sung, and danced under the direction of the poet as choirmaster and choreographer.[8] Although the contestants officially offered their various performances to the divinity, their efforts were directed primarily to the tastes and interests of the people who gathered as celebrants to watch and listen, to judge and reward. This was certainly the case at the City Dionysia, the main festival where comedies and tragedies were performed, as we shall see in the following chapter.

In addition to the festivals in Athens, great pan-Hellenic (all-Greek) gatherings were celebrated at Olympia, Nemea, and Isthmia, renowned for their athletic competitions, and at Delphi, famed for contests in poetry and music. Athens sent an ambassador to each of these festivals, and her citizens entered the competitions as individuals – the ancient games lacked some of the nationalistic zeal that dominates the modern Olympic movement. Victories at these prestigious competitions could generate their *own* performances, for the victors would commission poets such as Pindar to compose victory-odes, called *epinicians*, that were sung and danced by a chorus in the victor's home town, and possibly on other public occasions as well. The genre of encomiastic, or 'praise', poetry found its way into many tragedies, a means for the playwright to bring the contemporary world to the stage, and a further example of the pervasive modality of performance in fifth-century Athens.

Leaving the enormous crowds of the pan-Hellenic games, let us briefly consider performances of a more intimate nature, the rituals of weddings and funerals. These rites played a *central* role in the life of the Greek family, and, as such, constitute a recurring motif in Greek tragedy. Since neither ritual was conceived as a single event, but rather as an ongoing series of performed activities, they offered the playwright a variety of possible points of reference. On their wedding day, an Athenian bride and groom were given (separately) a ritual bath, and then dressed in white with a crown or garland to mark the occasion. The evening began with a banquet offered by the bride's father, where the gathered company danced and sang wedding hymns, followed by a nocturnal procession as the groom conveyed the bride to her new home. If circumstances allowed, the journey was made by horse- or mule-cart, accompanied by torch-bearers and friends who played music and sang. The groom's parents met the couple at the threshold of their new home, and during the night, the parties who accompanied the procession sang *epithalamia*, songs 'outside the marriage chamber'. In the morning more songs awakened the couple, who later received gifts in a ceremony that led up to a final wedding banquet. References to these rites are found in almost every extant tragedy, from the nuptial bath that Polyxena will never have in *Hecuba* to the wedding procession Admetus remembers in *Alcestis*, from the wedding hymn that Sophocles' Antigone sings en route to her 'burial', to the poisoned wedding gifts that convert Glauke into her own nuptial torch in *Medea*.

At the other end of the ritual spectrum, funerals constituted a performance for and about the dead. The ritual tasks of preparing the corpse – washing, anointing, dressing, crowning, adorning with flowers, and covering it for burial – fell to the female members of the family. The body was laid out in the courtyard where mourners paid their respects, and the women wailed dirges and other lamentations. When the time came for burial, the funeral party dressed in black, and the men led the funeral cortège while the women followed behind the bier, reciting the ritual lament, occasionally accompanied by professional musicians and dirge-singers. As with the wedding, no priest officiated the rites, for the funeral was organized and performed solely by the family and friends of the deceased. After the inhumation or cremation, a final dirge was performed, offerings were poured, and the mourners departed. That evening a banquet was held where the funeral party delivered eulogies for the deceased and sang funeral hymns. As in the case of weddings, such theatrical features as costuming, singing, dancing, and making speeches constituted a good part of Greek burial custom. And tragedy is replete with funeral activity – the lamentations and threnodies that resound through Aeschylus' *Persians*, the focus on burial in Sophocles' *Ajax* and *Antigone*, the procession of corpses in Euripides' *Suppliant Women*. In fact, aspects of the funeral ritual occur so frequently in tragedy that scholars once thought the earliest drama sprang from laments at the grave-site.

Both the Athenian wedding and funeral rites were conceived as performances where the participants moved back and forth between the roles of actor and spectator, conjoining public and private worlds in a way that is hard for us to imagine. This is not to romanticize life in fifth-century Athens, where slavery was practised, where women had extremely limited opportunities, where living conditions were primitive, where disease was poorly understood. But in grappling with the performance culture out of which tragedy grew, we must realize that it operated radically differently from our professional, pre-packaged society, where everything is marketed for consumers – from peanuts to sidearms, from sex to salvation, from care for the elderly to care for the dead. To be sure, Athenians bought and sold in their market place, the agora in the centre of the city, but as they haggled over prices they also talked of the Assembly, the latest case in the lawcourts, a nephew's initiation, the upcoming festivals, a friend's wedding, the theatre – events that took place within a short walk of the fish stalls, as we can see in the aerial photograph of the city (Plate 1).

One such event deserves our closer attention, for it played an important role in the development of tragedy – the contests for reciting the great epic poems of Homer, the *Iliad* and *Odyssey*. Although unofficial performances of Homer went back many years, official competition among rhapsodes was included in the Panathenaic festival sometime between 566 and 514 BC, with the odds on an earlier rather than a later date. Unlike other pre-tragic contests, epic recitation was not based on music, spectacle, or lyric poetry, but on the semi-dramatic presentation of a complex narrative. We learn from Plato that a rhapsode was similar to an actor, interpreting from memory the lines of a great poet, combining the technical demands of verse and vocal production (the crowds were large) with the emotional expression and sympathy required to play several different roles in the course of a performance.[9] Roughly two-thirds of the *Iliad* is in direct speech, and the rhapsodes must have varied their delivery, volume, and tone to convey the different characters and their response to changing situations. Although composed long before the first tragedy, the poems are highly theatrical, and the most compelling sections read like scenes written for the stage – the great quarrel between Agamemnon and Achilles in Book 1 of the *Iliad*; the encounters in Book 6 between Hector and his mother Hecuba, his sister-in-law Helen, and his wife Andromache (a scene much admired by

Pnyx

Agora

Acropolis

Theatre of Dionysus

*Plate 1* Aerial view of the city of Athens

the tragedians); the great embassy in Book 9, where Odysseus, Phoenix, and Ajax try to persuade Achilles to rejoin the battle; the unprecedented encounter between Priam and Achilles in Book 24, where mortal enemies momentarily unite in the communality of grief.[10]

The oral and aural qualities of Homeric poems remind us of their intimate connection with performance. Eric Havelock points out that 'we read as texts what was originally composed orally, recited orally, heard acoustically, memorized acoustically, and taught acoustically in all communities of early Hellenic civilization'.[11] We get some sense of what oral performance might have been like not only from Plato's account of the later rhapsodes, but also from the Homeric epics themselves. In the *Iliad* (3.216–20), Odysseus impresses the Trojans by the stillness and control with which he delivers his speech, ancient testimony to the value of playing against the audience's expectations. In the *Odyssey* (4.271–89), Helen disguises her voice to mimic the wives of the Greek soldiers hidden in the Trojan horse, so effectively that the men almost betray their presence by answering. The bard Demodocus sings of the fall of Troy, and the unrecognized Odysseus responds so emotionally that he is forced to divulge his identity (*Od.*, 8.485–9.20). In a later Homeric hymn to Delian Apollo (149–64), the island girls of Delos imitate the speech of others so convincingly that 'each one would say that he himself was singing'. The power of the spoken word to create a credible fiction of another's presence lies at the core of ancient theatrical performance, and Plato was surely right to call Homer 'the supreme master of tragic poetry'.[12]

The epic poems unfold not simply via speaking characters, but through the alternation of their direct speech with more conventional narration, a pattern similar to the shift between rhetoric (actors' speech) and lyric (choral song and dance) in Greek tragedy. In particular, epic narrative is distinguished by the presence of extended similes that introduce radically different perspectives on the action, drawing the audience into a new relationship with what went before and what is to come. As we shall see in Chapter 5, the 'epic simile' may have had an impact on the placement and function of lyric sections in tragedy as the dramatic genre developed.

In addition to the epic's formal influence, it would be hard to exaggerate the importance of the Homeric poems on the spirit, sensibility, and ethos that gave rise to Greek tragedy. The *Iliad* and *Odyssey* provide, respectively, the prototypes for many plots and character types that appear in Attic tragedy and comedy. The Iliadic Hector, Achilles, Patroclus, Priam, Hecuba, and Andromache are clearly the ancestors of the great heroes of tragedy, and the clever inventiveness of Odysseus in the *Odyssey* finds its counterpart in the comic heroes of Aristophanes. As regards ethical and normative influence, 'it is hardly possible to overestimate the importance for Western literature of the *Iliad*'s demonstration that the fall of an enemy, no less than of a friend or leader, is tragic and not comic', as Northrop Frye puts it.[13]

The recitations of Homeric epic brought home to sixth-century Athenians in general, and to the future tragedians in particular, the power of words to animate the dramatic imaginations of the audience until they join the performer-poet in creating living characters. The ability to draw an audience imaginatively and critically into this process is not the least of the 'slices' that the tragedians took from the 'banquet of Homer',[14] part of the ongoing feast offered by the performance culture of ancient Athens.

# 2

# THE FESTIVAL CONTEXT

'There is much that is uncertain here.'

Sir Arthur Pickard-Cambridge

Formal dramatic productions in Athens were associated with festivals dedicated to the god Dionysus, and we can understand how tragedy worked only by viewing the performances in their festival context. However, the association of tragedy with Dionysus leads inexorably to the problem of tragic origins. Although there is no simple answer to the question 'whence tragedy?', a brief review of the evidence will clear up some persistent misconceptions about the way tragedy was (and, by extension, ought now to be) approached.[1] We then will examine the nature of Dionysiac worship, and trace out the organization and schedule of the greatest dramatic festival, the City (or Great) Dionysia, held every spring in Athens.

Explanations for the rise of tragedy and the incorporation of tragic performances into the civic and festival life of Athens tend to focus on the following influences: contemporary ritual, including funeral lamentation, hero cults, and initiation rites; earlier forms of artistic performance, including song, dance, poetry, and Homeric recitation (discussed in the previous chapter); Dionysiac worship, ranging from folkdances linked with the harvest to ritualized impersonation, from drunken revels to formal initiation into the Dionysiac mysteries; anthropological paradigms, such as the worship of a cyclical 'year-god' who suffers, dies, and comes back to life with the changing seasons; intellectual, spiritual, and creative energies cohering in a 'tragic' vision, epitomized in Nietzsche's brilliantly speculative *The Birth of Tragedy*; or political and cultural forces aimed at promoting civic loyalty, democratic ideology, and social cohesion.

Although little can be claimed with confidence, it seems that a combination of these influences – ritual, artistic, Dionysiac, folkloric, political – rather than any single element in isolation gave rise to Greek tragic theatre. The performance culture of ancient Athens included rural celebrations in honour of Dionysus where the agricultural cycle of planting and harvesting played an important role. The worship of the god is attested in Greece back into the Bronze Age, and over time Dionysus came to be associated with a wide array of powers and interests. Above all the god of wine (both its cultivation and enjoyment), Dionysus seems to have represented the 'sap' of life, a deity of natural, animate forces that were well worth celebrating, but also needed pacifying. Perhaps the intensity with which the Greeks felt the forces of nature led them to view Dionysus as the embodiment of contradictory tendencies, a fundamental paradox inherent in the world, life-giving but potentially destructive. As a modern scholar puts it, 'More than any other Greek god, Dionysus lacks a consistent identity. Duality, contrast and reversal are his hallmark.'[2] If a numinous force lies behind the theatrical impulse, then most theatre artists would agree that the ever-changing Dionysus is well cast for the role.

The most notorious activity associated with the god was ritual maenadism, but here the horrific excesses depicted in Euripides' *Bacchae* have displaced in the popular imagination what we know about the actual practice of this female cult. A far cry from anarchic frenzy, maenadism was characterized by a fixed periodicity, a defined regional location, and the organization of women celebrants into local congregations.[3] Every two years the women gathered in specified mountainous areas (the Athenian congregation joined others on Mt Parnassos above Delphi) where they dressed in special array (possibly animal skins), carried a thyrsos (a wand wreathed in ivy and vine-leaves topped by a pine cone), sacrificed to Dionysus, and performed ecstatic dances in his honour. We cannot know what the experience of maenadism was like, but its organized nature militates against the popular notion of mass hysteria and uncontrolled violence. The maenads were a small group of women (the cult was not 'popular' in the fifth century) who celebrated Dionysus in a difficult, but liberating, way, translating physical exhaustion into spiritual well-being and merging their individual consciousnesses into that of the group.

By leaving their homes and going to the mountains, activities associated with male hunters, the maenads participated in the kind of sexual role reversal found in other cults linked to Dionysus. For example, at the Oschophoria (a September festival celebrating the grape harvest) a sacrificial procession made its way from a temple of Dionysus in Athens to the seaside shrine of Athena Skiras, an aspect of the goddess connected with the vintage. Two men carrying grapes on the vine and dressed in female robes led the procession. Hardly encouraged in everyday society, cross-dressing found its way into various festivals as part of their ritual licence, and the practice seems to have been associated with the transition of young men into adults. In the case of the Oschophoria, the female clothing may have recalled a trick by which the Athenian hero Theseus smuggled in a pair of young warriors for two of the girls meant to be sacrificed to Minos (of Minotaur fame) on Crete.[4]

Costumes, masking, and disguise played a part in one of the oldest Athenian festivals to Dionysus, the Anthesteria. Celebrating the opening

13

of the new wine in the early spring, the festivities included dances and other activities around a mask of Dionysus affixed to a pillar or hanging from a tree. In a more formalized part of the celebrations, the wife of the annually elected archon basileus (the city official in charge of religious activities) celebrated a 'sacred marriage' with Dionysus, spending the night with the god in the building that served as the archon's headquarters. As far as we can tell, the archon *himself* impersonated the god, wearing a large mask and lavish robes, and so allowing the wedding night to stay 'within the family'. The Athenian celebrants escorted the god and his bride in a great torchlight procession, symbolizing the fertility of the entire city, a pageant similar to that which took place on a smaller scale at a normal wedding.[5] Again we observe how the performance culture of Athens brought together domestic ritual and public festival, Dionysiac worship and play-acting, agricultural rites and civic identity.

The earliest pre-dramatic celebrations in honour of Dionysus were known as *komoi* or 'revels', the root of the word 'comedy'. Some of these revels included a traditional refrain called the dithyramb, and our earliest reference is from a fragment of the seventh-century poet Archilochus: 'I know how to lead [*exarchai*] the fair song of [in honour of?] Lord Dionysus, the dithyramb, when my wits are fused with wine.'[6] The poet seems to imply that he acted as the leader (*exarchos*) who sang an improvisation, followed by the conventional response given by a group of revellers. We find parallels of a less festive sort in the funeral lamentation in Homer's *Iliad*, where women selected as leaders sing a dirge and then are joined in ritual wailing by the other female mourners.

Viewing the question of tragic origins from his fourth-century perspective, Aristotle credits those who 'led off' (*exarchontôn*) the dithyrambs – the poets themselves? – with taking the key step in the development of tragedy, emerging out of the group as proto-actors. From this early, improvised stage, dithyrambs gradually evolved into more formal compositions intended for choral performance. The mode was narrative rather than dramatic, focusing on a divine or heroic legend at least tangentially connected with Dionysus. Performances usually were accompanied by the *aulos* (clarinet), an instrument associated with Dionysiac cult.[7] Eventually dithyrambs were included in the City Dionysia along with tragedies and comedies, developing into large choral performances of fifty men or fifty boys dressed in simple robes and without masks. Unlike the tragic and comic playwrights who were primarily Athenian, the most famous composers of contest dithyrambs were foreign-born – Pindar of Thebes, and Simonides and Bacchylides of Keos.

The inevitable questions arise – when were the first productions of *tragedy*, and at what point were tragic performances incorporated in the festival life of the city? The standard textbooks confidently assert that the first tragic competitions at the City Dionysia took place in 534 BC and included plays by the tragedian Thespis, that dithyrambs were added in 508 BC, and that comedies followed in 486 BC. This scenario has been repeated so often that it has become one of the few fixed points in the otherwise shifting sands of fragmentary evidence, legend, and hypothesis that constitute what we know of early tragic performances. Based on a probable misreading of an inscription on a marble slab called the Marmor Parium (found on the Greek island of Paros and shipped to London in 1627 AD), the conclusion that the Great Dionysia was instituted in 534 BC by the tyrant Peisistratus hardly seems secure. To understand why, we need to consider some particulars of the festival itself.

The specific cult honoured at the City Dionysia was that of Dionysus Eleuthereus, the god 'having to do with Eleutherae', a town on the border between Boeotia and Attica that had a sanctuary to Dionysus. At some point Athens annexed Eleutherae – most likely *after* the overthrow of the Peisistratid tyranny in 510 and the democratic reforms of Cleisthenes in 508–07 – and the cult-image of Dionysus Eleuthereus was moved to its new home.[8] Athenians re-enacted the incorporation of the god's cult every year in a preliminary rite to the City Dionysia. On the day before the festival proper, the cult-statue was removed from the temple near the theatre of Dionysus and taken to a temple on the road to Eleutherae. That evening, after sacrifice and hymns, a torchlight procession carried the statue *back* to the temple, a symbolic re-creation of the god's arrival into Athens, as well as a reminder of the inclusion of the Boeotian town into Attica. As the name Eleutherae is extremely close to *eleutheria*, 'freedom', Athenians probably felt that the new cult was particularly appropriate for celebrating their own political liberation and democratic reforms.

More evidence comes from an inscription called 'the Fasti' that lists the victories in the festival, beginning with *komoi* to Dionysus, then adding tragedies, and finally comedies. Although the inscription is fragmentary and requires restoration, the scholarly consensus is that the record for tragedies goes back only to 501 BC. Those who associate the first tragic performances with the legendary playwright Thespis, the tyrant Peisistratus, and the year 534 BC argue that the Fasti refers to a *reorganization* of the City Dionysia. However, it seems that 501 BC is a perfect date for the initial incorporation of tragedy into the festival. As the Fasti indicates, earlier performances consisted of *komoi* (eventually leading to competitions in the dithyramb) and then branched out to include tragedies. By 488–87 (the date seems secure from the inscription) the performance of comedies was added to the festival.

If this interpretation is correct, then tragic performances linked to Thespis must have been part of older, *country* celebrations honouring Dionysus. Thespis is associated with the rural *deme* of Ikaria in Attica, and certain features attributed to his theatre (such as performances on carts) are at home

15

in a rustic setting.[9] Similarly, the etymological connection between tragedy and 'goat singers', *tragoi + aoidoi*, may imply that early competitions offered a goat as prize, also befitting a rural context. It stands to reason that some such dramatic prototype preceded the inclusion of state-sponsored tragedies at the Great Dionysia, a festival of signal importance in the cultural and political life of fifth-century Athens.

The City Dionysia took place in the Greek month of Elaphebolion, middle to late March, which coincided with the opening of the sailing season. This meant that foreigners could visit Athens, since travel by sea was the preferred method even between points on the mainland (overland journeys were arduous and slow). The last reluctant olive in the Attic countryside would have been gathered in February, and the grain crop would not be ready to harvest until late May. The biggest event on the Athenian horizon was the season for military campaigns, April and May (before the barley and wheat harvests) if Athens were – as so often – at war. The timing of the City Dionysia enabled tragedies and comedies to have a particularly strong political impact, since the annual election of the ten *stratêgoi* (military commanders chosen by tribe) followed soon after the festival, as did the Assembly meetings that would decide on military campaigns and strategies, or on initiatives for peace.

Although precise correlation between festival days and specific events is difficult to determine, the following order was probably in place until the outbreak of the Peloponnesian War in 431 required changes in the schedule.[10] After the torchlight procession of the cult-statue the previous night (discussed above), the first day of the festival proper seems to have been spent preparing for the bigger, sacrificial procession to come. The *proagôn* (the 'pre-contest') also took place, during which the playwrights and actors (without masks or costumes) mounted a wooden platform and introduced the plays they would be performing over the next few days. These theatrical 'teasers' may have taken a more formal tone with the construction of Pericles' Odeion (c. 444 BC) to the east of the theatre, a roofed concert hall that housed the *proagôn* as well as musical competitions for the Panathenaic festival.

On the following day the great procession (called the *pompê*) wound its way to the temple of Dionysus near the theatre. Men and women bore various ritual vessels and offerings, resident aliens wore scarlet robes, citizens carried leather wine-skins (for what reason we do not know), the *chorêgoi* (citizen-producers) of the various performances dressed in gorgeous robes to mark their status, and other participants bore phalloi in honour of the god. Typical of many Dionysiac cults, everyone was included – there were no prohibitions against women, children, or slaves – and we can be fairly confident that there also were no restrictions on attending the performances.[11]

We get a sense of the excitement of the onlookers during the *pompê* from a passage in Euripides' *Bacchae*:

> Those in the road, those in the road, make way!
> Who stays inside? Come out! and on all lips
> let there be good words, holy words. Our custom
> for Dionysus, I will sing always for the god.
>
> (68–71)

In *Acharnians* Aristophanes offers a comic version of the procession as it might have been practised at a rural Dionysia, with celebrants carrying a basket of offerings and a phallos, making their way to the sacrifice. As noted in Chapter 1, the offerings for the City Dionysia were on a massive scale and, following the sacrifices, the meat was cooked and distributed in a state-sponsored feast of national proportions. These two events – the *pompê* and the sacrifice at the altar of the temple of Dionysus – were the *sine qua non* of the City Dionysia, for without them there was no cult worship and no basis for the contests and other festivities.

Before the competitions began on the third day, the theatre was purified by killing a piglet and carrying its corpse around the performance space. Similar purification rites were practised for the Athenian Assembly and Council, as well as for temples and various public buildings. Other pre-performance practices of a more secular nature set the dramatic competitions squarely in the context of fifth-century civic and political life. The annual tribute paid to Athens by her allies in the Delian League fell due just before the City Dionysia, and the wealth was displayed in the theatre orchestra.[12] During the second half of the fifth century, much of the tribute was destined for Pericles' great building programme on the Acropolis, so the display in the orchestra was linked directly to the glorification of Athens. Similarly, when an Athenian fell in battle, his male orphans were raised at state expense and given full hoplite armour when they reached manhood. Before the commencement of the tragic performances, the orphans who had come of age paraded through the orchestra in their new armour and then took complimentary seats in the audience. A herald announced honours that the city had conferred on citizens and foreigners over the course of the year, and he read out the names of slaves who had been freed. The last activity helped protect the newly liberated by converting the theatre audience into potential witnesses of their manumission.[13]

Even the performances themselves shared a public and political function. In the dithyrambic competitions (ten choruses of boys and ten of men), each chorus consisted of fifty members drawn from the same tribe. In 508–07 the Athenian leader Cleisthenes had reformed the political organization of Attica into ten tribes, a democratic and egalitarian move intended to undermine the influence of old familial clans and local power bases. The dithyrambic competitions reflected these reforms, since their tribal organization helped to solidify new civic loyalties.[14]

On the fourth, fifth, and sixth days came the tragic contests, each day reserved for a tetralogy (three tragedies and a satyr-play) by one of the three competing tragedians. We will deal with the specifics of tragic production in the next chapter. On the seventh day five comedies were performed, each written by a different playwright, although at some point during the Peloponnesian War the day reserved for comedies may have been eliminated and the number of comic productions reduced to three. By adding a comedy to the end of each day's tragic performances, the festival could save time and the expense of two comic productions. At the close of the festival, the archon in charge held a meeting of the Assembly in the theatre to evaluate the proceedings and to review the conduct of festival officials.

The City Dionysia was not the only opportunity to see tragedy performed in Athens, although on all occasions productions were connected with Dionysiac cult. The Lenaia festival, held annually in January, included a procession (without phallic elements) and sacrifice to the god, much like the larger City Dionysia. Here, however, comedy was king. Comic performances were instituted around 440 BC, and five poets competed with a single comedy each, although the number may have been reduced to three during the Peloponnesian War. Tragedies were introduced some eight years later, two plays each by two different playwrights, with no satyr-play. The Lenaia generally did not attract the cream of the tragic playwrights, serving more as a proving ground for younger talent, although Sophocles seems to have competed here occasionally (with a total of over 120 plays to his credit, this is not surprising). The performances may have taken place in the theatre of Dionysus, or in the area of the agora called the *orchêstra*, or more probably in the (yet undiscovered) sanctuary known as the Lenaion that lay just outside the city walls. Foreigners could not attend the Lenaian performances, but resident aliens of Athens were allowed to serve as the producers (*chorêgoi*) of comedies and tragedies, and also could perform in the choruses, aspects of production we will discuss in the next chapter.

Athenians also attended tragedies at the various rural Dionysia that took place on the local (*deme*) level. With the initial success of the dithyrambic and dramatic performances at the City Dionysia in the early fifth century, it seems likely that the less formal productions in the country dropped off in number and quality, reflecting the concentration of talent, energy, and financial support in the city proper. However, as the popularity of the city festivals grew, so did Athenian hunger for theatre, and performances returned to the neighbourhoods. Most of our evidence for these rural Dionysia comes from the fourth century, supporting the idea that tragedy first moved from the country to the city and then, after flourishing in town, returned to the country in a more developed state.

We know little of the various rural festivals, save that they seem to have been held in the winter (roughly our December). Some communities held processions on the model of the City Dionysia, like the one parodied in Aristophanes' *Acharnians* discussed above. Out of 139 *demes* in Attica, we know of fourteen that had theatres, and there were probably many more. Plato describes Athenian theatrephiles going from *deme* to *deme* during the various rural Dionysia to catch different productions, and it seems likely that acting troupes toured with a repertory of plays. The local crowd could see revivals of successful tragedies, and 'rural' productions at Piraeus (the port of Athens) and Eleusis (the home of the Mysteries) were important affairs. We hear of Socrates walking to Piraeus to see a performance of Euripidean tragedies, and Sophocles and Aristophanes directed revivals of their plays at Eleusis near the end of the fifth century.[15]

This brief look at the festival context should make us wary of viewing dramatic performances primarily as religious worship, or of conceiving tragedy as a form of 'high art' divorced from the social and political life of its audience. Least of all should we succumb to the fashion of analysing Greek drama as a language game spinning out conundrums for the delectation of an interpretive elite. Although elevated in style, and frequently in character and setting, Greek tragedy was grounded in a festival context integral to the ongoing life of the city. No one who has struggled with a Greek text would deny that tragedies have a complex verbal dimension, but the complexities serve ends that have characterized all great popular theatre – the exploration of the concerns, tensions, and aspirations of the society from which they grew. In the foundation of the City Dionysia and its close connection with the development of democracy, we find that the festival context for tragic performances implies an engagement with political, religious, and social questions, part of the 'classical' Athenian impulse to clarify, challenge, and change.

# 3

# PRODUCTION AS PARTICIPATION

As with all theatre production, mounting Greek tragedies at the City Dionysia involved the participation of many different parties who brought their talents, interests, money, and time to bear on the project. The process was a far cry from what we are accustomed to in the modern theatre, and it rewards closer examination. Given the city's integral involvement with dramatic festivals, let us begin with the administrative role before moving into the financial, creative, performance, and appreciative aspects of tragic production.

In charge of the City Dionysia – the procession, the opening and closing ceremonies, and the dithyrambic and dramatic competitions – was the archon eponymous, one of nine annually selected city leaders. Associated with secular matters, the archon eponymous served as one of three senior magistrates, along with the polemarch (military commander) and the archon basileus (overseer of religious festivals like the Eleusinian Mysteries, and also in charge of the Lenaia). As many of these offices were filled by lot, scores of different Athenians exercised control over the great theatrical performances at the City Dionysia during the fifth century, a festival that was viewed from an administrative standpoint as a secular, and not a religious, affair.

Shortly after taking his position in July, the archon eponymous nominated wealthy citizens to serve as financial producers, called *chorêgoi*, for the festival. A total of eight were required for the dramatic performances, one for each tragedian (responsible for producing three tragedies and a satyr-play) and one for each of the five comic playwrights (who entered a single comedy each). The *chorêgoi* for the dithyrambs were selected at the tribal level, presumably one or two from each of the ten tribes, to cover the costs of the ten boys' and ten men's choruses.[1] Since expenses were tied largely to personnel and not to sets and scenery, the cost of producing a dithyramb with fifty performers probably was greater than a tragic tetralogy with a chorus of twelve to fifteen, plus three actors, or a single comedy with a chorus of twenty-four singer-dancers and three or four actors.

The selection of *chorêgoi* was part of the Athenian institution of 'liturgies', a form of service based on *noblesse oblige* by which wealthy individuals

20

were selected to support specific public activities.[2] Following the festival calendar, civilian liturgies occurred on a regular basis, and could involve paying for a chorus (the liturgist as *chorêgos*) or underwriting the cost of festival games (a *gymnasiarchos*). There were also military liturgies that called for donations to build a warship, or trireme (a *trierarchos*). Only the well-off were compelled to contribute, and not more often than once every two years. In actuality, citizens frequently volunteered, since liturgies provided the means of gaining social status and launching a political career. For example, at the end of the fifth century a client of the speechwriter Lysias served as *chorêgos* eight times in nine years. Alcibiades, the mercurial leader who played such a chequered role in the Peloponnesian War, liked to boast of his liturgies. We have lawcourt speeches where defendants point to their frequent liturgical sponsorship as evidence of their importance to the city, and of their innocence in the face of charges from less generous plaintiffs.[3]

In a case where a citizen felt put-upon at being selected as liturgist, he could find a voluntary replacement or ask another citizen to answer the call. If that person refused, the original draftee could bring a legal charge called *antidosis*, whereby he offered to exchange property with his counterpart and then undertake the liturgy![4] At the Lenaia, non-citizens who were resident aliens called 'metics' could serve as *chorêgoi*, an important opening into the life of the city and one that reflected the metics' growing economic importance. Lowering the number of comedies performed at the City Dionysia and Lenaia during the Peloponnesian War freed members of the elite to provide needed military liturgies, and for a single year near the end of the war (406–05) the city instituted a *synchorêgoi* at the City Dionysia whereby two citizens combined to fund a single set of tragedies or a comedy. To get some idea of the expenses involved, a tragic *chorêgos* in 411–10 spent 3,000 drachmas on his tetralogy, and a comic *chorêgos* in 403–02 spent 1,600 drachmas on his comedy, at a time when a sculptor-mason working on the Erechtheum temple on the Acropolis was paid a drachma a day.

The lengths to which some liturgists might go to secure victory reveal the competitive nature of dramatic performances in Athens. In the mid-fourth century, Demosthenes delivered a speech in court against a certain Meidias, who purportedly interfered with a dithyrambic chorus under Demosthenes' choregic sponsorship:

> The sacred apparel – for all apparel provided for use at a festival I regard as sacred until after it has been used – and the golden crowns, which I ordered for the decoration of the chorus, he plotted to destroy ... by a nocturnal raid on the premises of my goldsmith .... But not content with this, he actually corrupted the trainer of my chorus; and if Telephanes, the *aulos*-player, had not proved the staunchest of friends, if he had not seen through the fellow's game and sent him about his business, if he had not felt it his duty to train the chorus

21

and weld them into shape himself, we could not have taken part in the competition ... the chorus would have come in untrained and we should have been covered with ignominy. Nor did his [Meidias'] insolence stop there. It was so unrestrained that he bribed the crowned archon himself; he banded the chorus members against me; he bawled and threatened, standing beside the judges when they took the oath; he blocked off the side entrances.[5]

Demosthenes evidently had a rough day in the theatre. Allowing for rhetorical exaggeration characteristic of the genre, the passage still gives a sense of the efforts (financial and otherwise) that a liturgist might make to ensure that his participation in the production led to victory.

But what of the deeper civic and political interests that dramatic liturgies could inspire? Consider a set of fascinating correspondences that scholars have pieced together about the early days of tragic performances. The playwright Phrynichus, an older contemporary of Aeschylus, produced one of the few tragedies based directly on a contemporary historical event, *The Capture of Miletus* (now lost). Based on the Persian sack in 494 BC of a Greek city in Asia Minor, the play so distressed the Athenians (who had done little at the time to help their distant countrymen) that Phrynichus was fined a thousand drachmas. Although the date is uncertain, *The Capture of Miletus* may have been produced in 492 when Themistocles was the archon eponymous and oversaw the play selection for the City Dionysia. It seems that Themistocles had supported the Ionian revolt in Asia Minor, setting himself in opposition to reactionary forces in Athens, just as he later persuaded the Athenian Assembly to build ships as the 'wooden walls' that would save the city against the Persians. As it turns out, Themistocles also served as *chorêgos* for Phrynichus' *second* tragedy on a contemporary theme, *Phoenician Women*, produced in 476. The body of the play has not survived, but we know that it included a messenger speech relating the defeat of the Persians at Salamis, a victory for which Themistocles deserved much credit. Celebrating a triumph rather than Athenian shame, *Phoenician Women* met with the response denied to *The Capture of Miletus* – Phrynichus and Themistocles won first prize as playwright-director and *chorêgos* respectively.

Here the plot thickens, for Themistocles was ostracized in 472 for alleged collusion with the Persians, a charge trumped up by rival Athenian politicians opposed to other aspects of his policy. Earlier that spring at the City Dionysia, Aeschylus achieved his first victory with the *third* tragedy on a contemporary theme, *Persians*. As with Phrynichus' *Phoenician Women*, Aeschylus tells of the defeat of the Persian navy at Salamis, and by emphasizing Themistocles' contribution to that great victory, *Persians* constituted subtle but tacit support for the beleaguered leader. The successful *chorêgos* of Aeschylus' play was none other than the young Pericles, who at the outset of his political career positioned himself as Themistocles' successor. The subject is fascinating, and ancient historians have worked out many variations;[6] it is sufficient for our purposes to appreciate the close interconnection that could obtain in the production process between archon, *chorêgos*, playwright, and the tragedies themselves.

The *sine qua non* for dramatic productions was, of course, the playwright. We have little secure information about these men, but it does not seem likely that a fifth-century playwright made his living solely in the theatre. The purported epitaph of Aeschylus (525–456) highlights his role in the battle against the Persians at Marathon and fails to mention that he wrote tragedies. We know that Sophocles (496–06) was involved deeply in the political and religious life of Athens, serving at various periods as state treasurer, as one of the elected generals (*stratêgoi*), and as a priest in the cult of the healer Asclepius. Generally speaking, however, the ancient biographical tradition is unreliable, converting details drawn from individual tragedies and comedies into facts about the poet's life: Euripides (480–06) was torn apart by dogs (like Pentheus torn asunder by maenads in *Bacchae*), Aeschylus was chased from the stage for revealing the Mysteries (probably drawn from a joke in a lost comedy), Sophocles' election as one of the ten generals of Athens in 441–40 (attested by a reliable source) resulted from his victory with *Antigone* which must then date to 442–41 (a conclusion reached on virtually no evidence, although often repeated as if it were certain). Even the generally accepted idea that Euripides spent his last years in self-exile at the court of Archelaus in Macedonia may have been conjured from a few references in *Bacchae* to those regions in the north.[7]

One thing we know with confidence is that each of the tragedians began a theatrical tradition within his own family. Two sons of Aeschylus wrote tragedies, and one of them, Euphorion, won first prize in 431 BC against Sophocles and Euripides (whose *Medea* was one of his group of plays that placed third in the competition). Euphorion's triumphant tetralogy may have included the revival of one or more of his father's plays. Revivals of earlier masterpieces are attested for the City Dionysia in the fourth century, but the intimate knowledge of Aeschylus' plays in the later fifth century strongly suggests that revivals of Aeschylus were instituted earlier. In addition to his sons, Aeschylus' nephew Philocles, purported author of over 100 plays, defeated Sophocles in the year that he produced *Oedipus Tyrannus*. Philocles himself had a son who wrote tragedies and is the butt of several Aristophanic jokes. Sophocles' son Iophon won several victories, and even competed against his father (given Sophocles' longevity, this isn't surprising), and he may have fathered an illegitimate son who also wrote tragedies. Either a son or nephew of Euripides directed his posthumous tetralogy that included *Bacchae* and *Iphigenia in Aulis* in 405, and that relative may have written tragedies himself. So, too, in comedy, Araros directed some of the later plays of his father, Aristophanes. The presence of this familial

23

tradition may have contributed to the situation whereby playwrights worked in only one genre, either tragedy or comedy, but never both.[8]

We have fairly reliable information that Aeschylus wrote eighty-two plays (seven extant, with the names of sixty-eight others), Sophocles 123 (seven surviving and the titles of [all?] 116 others), and Euripides ninety-two (nineteen surviving and sixty-one other titles). Although the least successful of the three great tragedians in terms of prizes (winning only five victories, one of them posthumous), Euripides seems to have been granted a chorus every year that he proposed a tetralogy to the archon. It is both a testimony to his later popularity and a happy accident of history that so many of his plays have survived. Ten of his tragedies were selected c. 200 AD for use in schools, and copies of their texts survived; in addition, a Byzantine manuscript has come down to us with these same plays (only *Trojan Women* is missing), as well as nine *other* plays in a quasi-alphabetical grouping (Greek letters E, H, I, K). Without this manuscript, we would be missing such Euripidean masterpieces as *Heracles, Helen, Suppliant Women [Iketides], Iphigenia in Aulis, Ion*, and the only fully extant satyr-play *Cyclops [Kyklops]*.

These three tragedians dominated the fifty-century theatre. In Aristophanes' *Frogs*, they are the only playwrights deemed worthy to compete for the right of returning from Hades to save the city, and later ancient literary historians refer to them collectively as the 'Three Tragic Poets'. But the names of other tragic playwrights and the titles of their lost plays have survived. In addition to the aforementioned Phrynichus and the half-legendary Thespis, Choerilus and Pratinas lived in the half-generation before Aeschylus and both may have produced tragedies at the rural Dionysia before the inauguration of the City festival, where they competed as well. There were many contemporaries of Sophocles and Euripides – the playwrights Ion, Achaeus, and Agathon stand out in the ancient tradition, but the names of dozens of others have come down to us. The presence of foreign names among the victory-lists for playwright-directors indicates that non-Athenians and metics could compete as tragedians. We have the text of only 3 per cent of the tragedies produced in the fifth century, perhaps 10 per cent of the titles, reminding us not only of how much we have lost, but also of how productive the theatre was in classical Athens.[9] Just as we understand Shakespeare's plays as part of the vital Elizabethan and Jacobean theatrical scene in England, so the mastery of tradition and innovative brilliance of Aeschylus, Sophocles, and Euripides reflect the lively theatrical culture in which, as fifth-century Athenians, they were fortunate to live.

We know little about the selection process for plays at the City Dionysia, save that a playwright would apply for a chorus by reading/reciting a part of his work before the archon eponymous. As a tragedian's reputation grew, it became easier for his work to be selected, and the author of the winning productions any given year was entitled automatically to a chorus the following year if he so desired. Once the archon assigned the three successful tragedians their respective *chorêgoi* and the playwrights chose their *aulos*-player (probably drawing lots for first pick), the production process was under way.

The first meetings probably involved the playwright and *chorêgos* working out the parameters of the production based on budgetary concerns. They would determine not only material outlay – costumes, properties, exceptional stage equipment, and special effects – but also the rehearsal period, since the *chorêgos* was responsible for paying a salary of some sort to the chorus members and the *aulos*-player, and also for providing a banquet after the production closed. We can imagine the meeting between Aeschylus and Pericles in the summer of 473, where the playwright outlined his *desiderata* for *Persians* – a full chariot entrance for the queen, regal garments for her and rich robes for the chorus to set off the rags of the defeated Xerxes, the effects (if any) required for raising the ghost of Darius. We only can guess at the many compromises that must have been made between a poet's original conception and the actual performance. Similarly, we have no way of knowing what ideas may have found their way into a production (and even into the text) thanks to a *chorêgos* who was drawn into the project and eager for its success.

The playwright himself almost always served as stage director, or *didaskalos* ('teacher'), and the Greek phrase for directing a play was *didaskein choron*, 'to teach a chorus'. The list of victors was called the *didaskaliai*, indicating that the prizes were given for directing and not for writing. In the early days of the theatre, therefore, a play was conceived more in terms of its production than as an artistic creation on its own. For example, at the Lenaia of 425, Aristophanes' *Acharnians* won for best comedy, but the prize went to Kallistratos who directed the play and not the 23-year-old Aristophanes who wrote it.

The playwright-director also served as choreographer, and he composed the music that was sung by the chorus, and occasionally by one or more of the actors. In the years before the institution of the actor's prize in 449 BC, he seems to have been his own leading actor as well. As far as we can tell, the tragedian also designed the sets (such as they were), costumes, and possibly the masks, always working with the *chorêgos* who had to meet the expenses. We must wait for Shakespeare and Molière before we meet again such consummate men of the theatre, playwright-directors who had all artistic aspects of production under their control, and whose task was to mould those elements into a performance that would bring over fully and powerfully the dramatic texts they had written.

The term for directing, 'to teach a chorus', underlines the importance of choral training in the production process. Here lay the major expense and the most time-consuming rehearsals, working with a group of players to bring together music, movement, and a highly literate and demanding text. A good deal of learning took place via oral repetition, since it cannot be

25

assumed that the performers could read; the oral curriculum in fifth-century Athenian schools was handled in similar fashion. The choral melodies also were taught by ear, and we have ancient testimonia of Euripides singing one of his odes to his chorus at a rehearsal. So, too, the patterns of the dance must have been worked out with the chorus members and playwright 'on their feet', much as choreography is developed today.

The same twelve performers (the number may have grown to fifteen during the fifth century) played the chorus in all four plays – three tragedies and a satyr-play – composed by a given tragedian.[10] To get a sense of what this meant in practice, consider Aeschylus' production of the *Oresteia* in 458 BC. The same group of performers appeared as a chorus of Argive elders in *Agamemnon*, a group of captured slave-women in *Choephori*, the terrifying spirits of vengeance called the Furies in *Eumenides*, and a band of (presumably) randy satyrs in the lost satyr-play *Proteus*. Not only were masks, costumes, and personae different, but the style of movement, the music, the level and quality of emotion, and countless other factors shifted from play to play. Since there was only one performance, the chorus were compelled to master a wide range of material without the benefit of preview audiences, although we must assume that the final rehearsals (at least) were held in the theatre itself.

Given what must have been a long and involved rehearsal process, the notion that the text and lyric metres that have survived were ever purely those of Aeschylus or Sophocles or Euripides is extremely unlikely. Much of what was performed in the orchestra resulted from the give and take between the tragedian (juggling his input as playwright, lyricist, composer, choreographer, and director) and his chorus, with the aulos-playing accompanist making his contributions as well. As with every new script, changes surely were introduced during rehearsal, demanding flexibility on the part of playwright and performers alike. It is probable that the dramatist viewed his original script as a starting point, and then spent the early rehearsals adjusting the play to the performers. Although the fifth-century playwright possessed extraordinary artistic autonomy, his work on the production was essentially collaborative.

About the selection of the chorus members we know nothing. It seems reasonable to assume that there was some kind of audition for interested parties, with the specifics of the playwright's project and the remuneration offered by the *chorêgos* as the twin incentives to participate. At the City Dionysia the chorus consisted of male citizens, not professional actors, although it is certainly possible that remuneration was sufficient to constitute a second income. A group of choral semi-pros might find themselves called upon for a rural revival of a play they had performed at the City Dionysia, or might balance their schedule between the Lenaia one year and the Dionysia the next.

A recent theory that has generated much interest links the teaching of the chorus to the military training of ephebes, male youths on the point of maturity.[11] Proponents adduce ancient evidence that tragic choruses were divided into ranks and files, suggesting strict rectilinear patterns of movement based on the military analogy with marching and drill. However, the source is late, a theatre historian named Pollux who was a professor in Athens in the Roman period and dedicated his work to the emperor Commodus (161–92 AD). Pollux's conclusions reflect the theatre and the theatrical conventions of his day, over 600 years after Aeschylus, and we should be wary of assuming that his views on staging, theatre space, and choral movement reflect the situation in fifth-century Athens. How many lyric sections in the *Oresteia*, for example, can we imagine danced in ordered rank and file like a march or military drill? The great *kommos* between the chorus of women, Orestes, and Electra? The binding song of the Furies around Orestes, or their final benedictions over the city of Athens? The visionary lyrics of Cassandra that eventually draw the chorus into the dance? The evocation of the sacrifice of Iphigenia, or the choral lament over the slain Agamemnon? We could multiply examples, but the point is clear – the thesis that tragic choruses provided ersatz military training fails where it matters most, in performance. Better to conclude that participation in a Greek tragic chorus was open to male citizens generally (and to male metics at the Lenaia), and was not restricted to boys on the verge of a beard.

In the earliest tragic performances, the playwright himself acted the most important roles and procured the services of fellow-actors to fill out his cast. Given that the performers were masked (a convention discussed in Chapter 4), an actor could play several parts in any given tragedy. So, for example, in *Persians*, the earliest surviving tragedy, only two actors are needed – the playwright Aeschylus probably played the Messenger (much the biggest part) and the ghost of Darius, and another actor played the queen and her son Xerxes. At some point a third actor became available, and we know that Aeschylus took advantage of the addition in his *Oresteia* of 458.

In 450–49, the city assumed responsibility for procuring and paying actors, initiating a prize for best tragic actor at the City Dionysia, followed by a similar contest at the Lenaia (around 432 BC). As with comic and tragic playwrights, actors performed in one genre only, and prizes for comic performers also were awarded – in the fifth century at the Lenaia and in the fourth century at the City Dionysia. Although we have no direct evidence for the reasons behind this development, the state sponsorship of actors speeded up a process that had been in train for some time, namely the division of labour between playwriting and acting. There is ancient testimonia that Sophocles stopped performing because of the weakness of his voice, dubious in its specifics but credible as a sign of a general trend. We have no indication that Euripides ever acted; he first competed at the City Dionysia in 455 BC, only five years before it became impossible for playwrights to perform leading roles in their own plays. And it is difficult to imagine Aeschylus at age 67 undertaking the role of Clytemnestra in the *Oresteia*, produced three years before Euripides' debut.

Whatever the reason for the change to city-sponsored acting, one result was the more even-handed participation of the best actors in the annual festival. No longer could a financially committed *chorêgos* simply buy up the most accomplished performers in any given year. With the institution of the prize for acting, the three tragic playwrights would draw lots to pick one of the three actors chosen that year, who in turn would provide the other actors needed to perform the tetralogy. Each group invariably included two additional men capable of playing a variety of speaking roles, and also might involve a fourth mute actor who took on such parts as the silent Pylades in Euripides' *Electra*, as well as other supernumeraries. The situation gave rise to diminutive acting companies, a master-actor and his (small) band of apprentices, competing for public support each year and ready to serve the playwright who was allotted them.

Only the leading actor of each of the competing tetralogies was eligible for the acting prize, although we cannot be sure if it honoured the best set of performances over the course of a given tetralogy, as seems likely, or if it rewarded the best performance in any single play. In either case, the character(s) played by the lead actor (called the protagonist or 'primary competitor') would have been scrutinized with special interest and, for that reason, could establish a privileged relationship with the audience. Although it seems likely that the theatre public would recognize the leading actors even in masks, one of the purposes of the *proagôn* early in the festival may have been to announce the roles to be played by each of the three protagonists. After the annual competitions, the winning actor's name was inscribed on the official list of victors, alongside that of the victorious playwright-director and the *chorêgos*. That the public record of contributions to the *polis* included the names of actors is a remarkable tribute to the importance of performance in Athens, given the low status associated with actors throughout most of the history of theatre.

The celebration of acting and actors had its negative side as well, reaching its nadir in the late fourth century, when the tragedies of Aeschylus, Sophocles, and Euripides were revived as star-vehicles and may have been performed without their choruses. Interpolations by actors were so prevalent that the texts became more and more contaminated. Finally the politician Lycurgus (c. 330) passed a law establishing an official copy of the plays of the three great tragedians and requiring that all city-sponsored revivals conform to those scripts.

The selection of the three leading actors must have been based on their previous public performances (both in major and in minor festivals), supplemented when necessary by auditions before the archon eponymous. Although the random selection process seems to have prohibited playwrights from writing plays with specific actors in mind, there is counter-evidence to suggest that tragedies were tailored to a certain actor, or at least a certain kind of actor. Ancient testimonia associate Aeschylus with two actors, Cleander and Mynniscus; Sophocles is singled out for having written parts for specific actors, where the names Cleidemides and Tlepolemus come up; and Euripides' later plays often require acting skills that may not have been generally available. Among extant tragedies, only three – Euripides' *Andromache*, *Ion*, and *Trojan Women* – require that *two* actors sing, and the monodies of Andromache and Peleus, Ion and Creusa, and Hecuba and Cassandra are central to their respective plays.[12] Unless performers were available who could handle these difficult lyric sections, Euripides would not have included them.

On the model of the great Elizabethan playwright–actor teams of Marlowe and Alleyn, of Shakespeare, Kempe, and Burbage, some form of ongoing collaboration between playwright and actor must have been possible in fifth-century Athens, although the specifics escape us. We do know that the prize for acting did not have to go to the protagonist in the tetralogy that won best play for the tragedian and *chorêgos*. Since both the victorious playwright-director and actor were guaranteed a place in the following year's competition, perhaps one or the other was allowed first pick, or some other mechanism enabled the tragedians to write parts for specific actors after the institution of the actor's prize. Whatever the circumstances of selection and rehearsal, the state sponsorship and public recognition of acting make it clear that the art was recognized as central to Athenian tragic drama.

In total, some 1,250 artists and performers participated annually at the City Dionysia. The dithyrambic competitions required ten to twenty poets and as many *chorêgoi*, 500 men and 500 boys who made up the twenty choruses, and twenty *aulos*-players. For the tragic contests, there were three poets, three *chorêgoi*, three *aulos*-players, thirty-six to forty-five chorus members, and nine actors (plus supernumeraries and supplemental choruses when necessary); for the comedies, five playwrights, five *chorêgoi*, five *aulos*-players, 120 chorus members and fifteen comic actors for the five comedies. To this number we should add the various trainers, builders, costumers, rehearsal assistants, and others who worked behind the scenes.

As impressive a figure as this is, it remains small when compared to the most essential participants in the theatre of Dionysus, the crowds who gathered in the audience. We will discuss the physical nature of the theatre in the next chapter, but a fair estimate of the crowd at tragic performances in fifth-century Athens is 12,000–14,000 on each of the three days. It seems likely that Athenian men, women, and children, resident aliens, slaves, and foreigners alike came to watch the plays, in keeping with the inclusionary nature of the festival and of much Dionysiac cult. We are unsure when admission began to be charged and what the price was, but it seems that during at least part of the fifth century the audience paid two obols (one-third of a drachma) per seat. At some point a *theoric* fund was

29

established to subsidize tickets for the poor, but the evidence suggests that this practice began in the fourth century.

To provide judges for the contests, each of the ten tribes had a jar filled with names of male citizens in attendance, and one was drawn from each jar just before the performances began. The random drawing of judges was aimed at avoiding bribery and partisanship, and the process resembled that for choosing jurors and filling political offices by lot. At the conclusion of each set of performances, the judges marked their ballots anonymously and placed them in the voting urn; they were drawn out one by one, until a majority (or plurality) for a given contest was achieved.[13]

Judging the plays and the actors was only the most formal way in which an Athenian spectator participated at the City Dionysia. The lively accounts in comedy make it clear that theatre was no church service – the audience laughed, applauded, and hissed; they raised a din by kicking the wooden benches with their feet; when the plays bored them they ate the food they brought, and if things got deadly, they threw it as well. Surely the tragedies elicited a more decorous response than the satyr-plays and comedies, but we must not imagine the hushed crowds that follow the dimming of the lights in a modern indoor theatre or the programmed response of a 'live' audience in a television studio. After all, the city had gathered to see itself represented in, and challenged by, the dramatic competitions. Production as participation meant that the audience, no less than the playwrights, producers, and performers, were central to what was happening, part and parcel of the energies gathered and released in the theatre.

# 4

# THE THEATRE OF DIONYSUS

At some point early in the fifth century an area on the south slope of the Acropolis became home to the performances of the City Dionysia. Located just above the temple of Dionysus Eleuthereus in the precinct dedicated to the god, the hillside gradually assumed the recognizable form of a Greek theatre. However, we must keep in mind that the remains visible today – primarily the greatly altered theatre of the Roman emperor Nero (first century AD) and a certain Phaedrus (third or fourth century AD) – bear a problematic relationship to the performance area as it appeared in the fifth century BC. The nature of the evolution in the shape and function of the theatre from that early period has generated much speculation, and not a little controversy. However, to understand what classical Athens looked for in a theatre we first should consider the situation of tragic productions *before* there was a theatre of Dionysus at all.

The original city performances of dithyrambs and tragedies took place in the *orchêstra* (dancing place) located in the central, open area of the agora, or market area.[1] Sloping gently down from the foot of the Acropolis that lies to the southeast, the agora developed into the hub of the city, the site of political, judicial, commercial, and religious activities. Here were located the meeting places for the Council, the lawcourts, civic stoas, other public edifices, cult shrines, private shops, commercial buildings, and food stalls. Running diagonally through the agora was the broad Panathenaic Way, named after the celebration that followed its course during Athens' greatest festival, the Panathenaia, immortalized on the Parthenon frieze. Starting by the cemetery and potters' quarter just outside the city gates, the procession ran alongside the *orchêstra* area before rising up to the entrance of the Acropolis itself. In the other direction, the Panathenaic Way joined the Sacred Way, heading down to the sea and the city of Eleusis, the route taken by the initiates to the Eleusinian Mysteries. The market area also housed the famous Altar of the Twelve Gods, where suppliants came for asylum and the spot from which all distances from Athens were calculated. In both a real and a metaphorical sense, the agora was the centre of the *polis*. The fact that the first tragedies were performed there speaks to the importance of

31

the theatre to Athenian self-conception, and its inherently political nature in the democratic city.[2]

Although we have little precise knowledge of the agora's *orchêstra*, that little tells us a good deal about the Athenian sense of what a theatre was. The term *orchêstra* indicates that the area was set aside for dancing, and that accommodating a chorus was its defining criterion. We infer from the sparse literary evidence and from the absence of archaeological remains that there was no permanent theatrical edifice in the agora. Rather than a built-up theatre, the *orchêstra* was a space where people gathered to watch a performance in an area big enough for a chorus to dance. It was out of doors, open to the elements and the light of day, with no preconceived shape or ideal configuration. We do hear of a tall poplar tree that allowed a few agile spectators to see the agora tragedies for free, and there is testimonia that audience members sat on temporary tiered wooden benches (*ikria*). Their collapse one year may have prompted the decision to transfer the dithyrambic and tragic performances from the agora to an area adjacent to the precinct of Dionysus on the other (south) side of the Acropolis.[3]

The move to a location linked specifically to Dionysus seems an obvious step, but we should recall that in the early fifth century comparatively little public activity took place on the south side of the Acropolis. It seems likely that the increasing popularity of the City Dionysia and the ambitious size of its programme necessitated the shift to a larger and less encumbered space. The hillside rising up from the temple and precinct of Dionysus formed a natural *theatron* (literally, 'place to see'), shielding the proceedings from the north wind that blew in early spring and offering more spectators a better vantage than was possible in the agora. Gradually the south slope of the Acropolis was built up, with a covered hall (Odeion) added in the mid-fifth century for music concerts, epic recitations, and the *proagôn* of the City Dionysia, and a new temple to Dionysus erected in the fourth century.[4]

The physical parameters of this early theatre are of great importance for understanding the dramatic instincts of the Greeks and the way in which their tragedies worked in performance. However, the complicated archaeological record frustrates our efforts at reconstruction, since the performance space shifted several times over the 900 years in which the area served as a theatre. The current remains date from the first to the third centuries AD, some 500–700 years after Aeschylus' *Oresteia*. We must think away the stone seats in the cavea, the paved semi-circular orchestra, and the stone stage (*proskênê*, or proscenium) in front of the back façade (*skene*, literally 'tent'). Scattered among the extant ruins are bits of the cement that helped make the orchestra watertight for mock naval battles in the Roman period, traces of the Christian basilica in the eastern *eisodos*, and remnants of the Byzantine fortification wall that ran across the *skênê* (henceforth, simply 'skene'). Remains dating from the original fifth-century theatre are scant and adulterated, leaving room for endless – and often reckless – hypothesizing.

What can we say with a modicum of confidence about the earliest theatre of Dionysus? Starting with the orchestra, there is no substantive evidence that its original shape was circular. Recent examination of the archaeological record, including comparison with other theatres of the fifth century, indicates that there are no theatrical remains from the early period that suggest the original 'dancing area' was circular.[5] As we might expect from the highly practical Greeks, the shape of the orchestra did not differ from the space defined by the seating area in the front, and the terrace wall supporting the orchestra in the back, a retaining wall that kept the packed earth of the dancing floor from eroding down the slope. That is, the early orchestras tended to be of a slightly irregular rectangular form.

The important point is that the fifth-century Greeks acknowledged *no* pre-established template governing the shape of the theatre cavea or orchestra, but instead developed and adapted their theatres according to local topography. They had no visual, theatrical, or ritual commitment to a circle *per se*. No firm evidence substantiates the claim that the circular threshing floor (often adduced in handbooks on Greek theatre) influenced the development or shape of the early theatre orchestra. Perhaps theatre history owes this last idea to the wistfulness of moderns who have lost the feel of the wheat and the chaff; it owes little to recent archaeology, which has unearthed no early circular orchestras. On the contrary, the form of the Greek theatre, including the orchestra, did not become standardized until relatively late, probably under the influence of the theatre at Epidauros (with the first *bona fide* circular dancing place), built in the late fourth/early third century.

Although some stone seating blocks dating from the fifth century have been found in the theatre of Dionysus, we know from Aristophanes that most of the audience sat on wooden benches, and perhaps others used the bare ground, so even in the late fifth century the theatre in Athens had a makeshift quality to it.[6] To put this conclusion in architectural terms, the early theatre was conceived more as a space than as a building. It lacked the inherent controls of programmatic construction and architectural order that defined, for example, the temple and the stoa, the most formally fixed of Greek buildings. Put in dramatic terms, it was not the precise shape of the cavea and orchestra but what happened there that mattered in the fifth century.

Another misconception about the theatre of Dionysus involves the presence of a permanent backdrop rising behind the orchestra, a back wall that could support an elevated stage for the actors. As far as we can tell, the earliest permanent (stone) foundations in the theatre of Dionysus date from the fourth century, radically simplifying our picture of the fifth-century theatre of Aeschylus, Sophocles, and Euripides.[7] We can dismiss the many reconstructions that feature an elaborate stone façade, or projecting areas at the two ends (*paraskênê*), or an inner entrance area (*prothyros*) receding from a long wooden colonnade, and so on. Furthermore, without the secure anchor of a permanent (stone) building for wooden additions, we cannot assume that the fifth-century theatre possessed a playing area defined primarily by an elaborate backdrop. Most surviving tragedies do call for a back façade with central entrance, an innovation that seems to date from the production of the *Oresteia* in 458 BC, but the need seems to have been met by a temporary construction of wood.[8]

We are left, then, with a large, but irregular, orchestra area, backed by a wooden façade with a central door. All extant tragedies can be staged with these basic elements. Some scholars insist that certain comedies of Aristophanes call for more than one door, but their arguments tend to reflect modern concerns for spatial difference and specificity that are not required in Greek drama.[9] Productions of tragedy and comedy would have been compelled to use the same backdrop if the City Dionysia was truncated during the Peloponnesian War. In fact, the two genres probably shared the same temporary façade *throughout* the fifth century. If two or three doors were available for comedy, it seems unlikely that such an experimentalist as Euripides would *not* have used them. However, none of his extant plays call for more than one façade entrance, and his *Suppliant Women* and *Andromeda* (lost) require *no* such door. Greek tragedy exhibits what one critic calls an 'aesthetic of abstinence', and in such a theatre the single door in the skene and the side entrances of the *eisodoi* are both sufficient and aesthetically appropriate.

The backdrop – which could represent a palace, temple, house, tent, even a cave – coincided with the long outside wall of the wooden skene-building. There the actors changed costumes and masks without being seen, and made their entrances through the central door onto the playing area. An interpolated passage in Aristotle's *Poetics* to the effect that Sophocles introduced scene-painting has been used to reconstruct elaborate scenographic systems for the façade, but it is probable that scene-painting played a minimal role (if any at all) in the aesthetics of fifth-century production.[10] The skene structure was strong enough to support actors on its roof, an area that came to be known as the *theologeion* ('place where the gods speak') since stage divinities often appeared there. Access for the actors came by means of a ladder from within the skene-building through the roof, or from behind the structure, or by the *mêchanê* ('machine') from above, giving us the familiar Latin phrase *deus ex machina*, 'god from the machine'. A lever-and-fulcrum apparatus located behind the skene would raise the actor(s) high above the façade to suggest their movement through the air, and then lower them onto the roof of the skene-building.[11]

One of the most vexed questions about the ancient theatre of Dionysus is whether a wooden stage rising above orchestra level stood in front of this temporary backdrop. Since no extant tragedy requires a raised playing area (as opposed, for example, to the *theologeion*), we are better off assuming

*Plate 2* Theatre of Dionysus

there was no such stage. Among the arguments for this structure that betray a basic misunderstanding of the way tragedy works is the claim that the plays demand distinct performing areas for the actors and for the chorus. On the contrary, fifth-century tragedy requires free (and frequent) interaction between chorus and actors, as we shall see in the exemplary plays in Part II. In the second century AD, the theatre historian Pollux wrote that 'the skene belongs to the actors and the orchestra to the chorus'. But he was describing the Neronian theatre in Athens where a raised stage served the demands of a different kind of play, where the chorus was treated as independent of, and tangential to, the action.[12]

The idea that a low raised stage gave an actor visual prominence *vis-à-vis* the chorus fails to grasp the physical relationships and scale involved in the ancient theatre. In a space the size and shape of the theatre of Dionysus, all but a small percentage of the spectators look down on the action, many of them from a great height, as we can see from the photograph in Plate 2. A three-foot raised stage against the back façade – the furthest possible distance from the audience – hardly constitutes a gift to the actor, for visual and oral prominence in such a space is gained by proximity to the audience, not by maximizing the distance from it. Unlike the carefully planned theatre built at Epidauros some two centuries later, the sprawling theatre in Athens had anything but perfect acoustics. In the fifth century, the theatre's back wall was not a large stone façade (which would act as an effective sounding board), but a relatively small wooden construction. Recall the basic principle of acoustics, that sound intensity varies inversely with the square of the distance, which means that if an actor standing ten feet from the audience moves back to a distance of thirty feet, the intensity of his voice will be one-ninth of what it was at the first position.[13]

With the audience spread around the curve of the hillside, the midpoint of the orchestra (however it was shaped) provided the strongest acting area, and we find evidence in the tragedies themselves that the fifth-century playwrights recognized the fact.[14] In play after play the dramatists literally 'orchestrate' key speeches and scenes, setting them up in the middle of the orchestra, the Greek equivalent of downstage centre. Here, for instance, were located various altars required for supplication or asylum as in Aeschylus' *Suppliant Women*, Sophocles' *Oedipus Tyrannus*, and Euripides' *Andromache*. The tomb of Darius in Aeschylus' *Persians*, that of Agamemnon in *Choephori*, and that of Proteus in Euripides' *Helen* also were placed orchestra centre.[15] That the tragedians fully exploited the best acting area in their theatre is hardly surprising – they worked in the theatre and not in the library, and they used the performance space available to them to best advantage.

The central question about any performance space is how it engages the audience. The theatre of Dionysus was irrepressibly three-dimensional, large, out of doors, a far cry from the indoor venues to which modern audiences are accustomed. Epitomized by the frame of the proscenium-arch, the modern theatre supports the central assumption of theatrical realism, namely that the spectator is a hidden observer looking in on a specified location through an invisible fourth wall. The Greek theatre aims at precisely the opposite effect, a sense that the audience has gathered in a public place to be addressed, and confronted, by the play. The empty space of the Greek theatre encourages us to imagine the scene for ourselves, guided by the words and gestures of the performers. Take, for example, the action of *Choephori* that moves from the tomb of Agamemnon to the palace of Clytemnestra and Aegisthus, and there 'shifts' from outside to inside and then back to outside the palace. In the ancient theatre, Aeschylus accomplished these changes without altering the setting or backdrop. In *Eumenides*, the action begins outside the temple of Apollo at Delphi, then goes inside the temple, then moves to the temple of Athena in Athens, and finally ends up in the court of the Areopagos, again with no fundamental alteration in set pieces or background. In his lost *Women of Aetna*, the only tragedy we know was written specifically for production outside of Athens (in Syracuse), Aeschylus changed the location *five times* in the course of the drama. Plays such as Sophocles' *Troilus* (lost) and Euripides' *Children of Heracles* exhibit what we might call 'flexible geography', where the action begins at one place and gradually slides (if we stop to think about it realistically) some geographical distance as the plot unfolds. Collapsible dramatic time is a concomitant of a flexible notion of space, and also poses problems only for the literal-minded. To ask, for example, how the Herald and Agamemnon can arrive from Troy so soon after the beacon fire in *Agamemnon* is to take up the temporal equivalent of 'how many children had Lady Macbeth'.

Later in the century, the *ekkyklêma* or 'roll-out machine' was used to expose interior scenes, such as Eurydice lying dead on the household altar in Sophocles' *Antigone* and Heracles bound to the pillar of the home he has destroyed in Euripides' *Heracles*. Here, too, the playing area remains flexible, for the exposed area gradually shifts from inside the house/palace back to the open air.[16] Unlike realistic drama that demands the strict logic of spatial identity (and with it the convention that a new set is needed to signal a new location), the Greek theatre exploited the possibilities of flexible setting and a transitive notion of indoor and outdoor space. The audience accomplished the necessary adjustments with the strongest of theatrical forces, their own imaginations, sparked by the words and actions of the actors and chorus.

All modes of access to the playing area channelled the performers into the orchestra and out towards the audience. The central door of the façade opened directly onto the orchestra, immediately confronting the actor with the audience. Coming in from either side of the back façade, the two *eisodoi* or 'entrance roads' – also called *parodoi* or 'side roads' – were angled slightly downstage into the orchestra, not upstage towards the backdrop.[17] Since these entrances were aimed in their direction, the audience could see actors and chorus approaching from a distance, and often in some display, for the *eisodoi* were large enough to accommodate the chariot-entrances required by Aeschylus' *Persians* and *Agamemnon*, Sophocles' (lost) *Triptolemus*, and Euripides' *Trojan Women*. Contrast a proscenium stage where entrances from the wings – through side doors of a box-set, or out of 'nowhere' as in ballet – allow the performers to direct their focus across the playing area or even upstage, towards their fellow players and not out to the house. So, too, the vomitoria of a thrust-stage enable actors to enter with their backs to much of the audience, directing their movements and energies upstage towards the theatre wall.

Addressing a speech directly upstage would have been extremely rare in the theatre of Dionysus, due to its size, poor acoustics, and the fact that there was no stone façade to reflect the sound. The vaunted genius of Greek theatrical design did not emerge fully formed at the start, and problems of audibility directly affected the relationship between audience and actor. The distance between mid-orchestra to the topmost seats was roughly 100 feet *further* than in the theatre at Epidauros, although the latter could seat several thousand more spectators. The fifth-century theatre in Athens was not an intimate space, and acting there was of necessity forceful and outward-directed.

The arrangement of entrances, the confrontation with the audience, and the scale of the performance space are aspects of fifth-century production that underline the public nature of their theatre. Neither the plays nor the space in which they were performed support the modern view that individual psychology and character-revelation are the stuff of drama. Many contemporary plays are built around a process of inner burrowing that progressively narrows the focus until it delivers the psychological equivalent of a close-up. Greek tragedy works in a different way, presenting a dynamic exploration of life writ large, where tragic issues and conflicts are aggressively public. Bred as most of us are on a drama of interiors, with the world collapsing to the size of a living room or a television studio, we easily forget that Greek theatre took place in the open air, in the strong, clear light of the Mediterranean sun. At Athens, the natural panorama of southern Attica provided the wider theatrical backdrop – sky, sea, the sun itself, the distant hills and rocky terrain, the river Ilissos, the city walls, the Acropolis looming behind, the very earth on which many of the audience sat – the ever-present, natural correlatives to the actors' words and actions.

The outdoor setting means that the theatre of Dionysus lacked the illusion-making capacities of the modern stage, enclosed by walls and a roof, where performers are confined to a relatively small area and electric lights illuminate the action. Guided only by the actors and the text, the Greek audience themselves created the pre-dawn atmosphere at the opening of *Agamemnon* and *Iphigenia in Aulis* and the pitch-black darkness of *Rhesus*, even as they sat under the bright sun.[18] Drawn together in that common light, the audience saw not only actors and chorus but also each other, made aware of their collective roles in creating the performance. Compare the nature of the response fostered in such an environment with that arising from the darkened room of the modern theatre. Here each spectator is involved (more or less) in a private and relatively remote relationship with the performance, whereas the emotions released in the sunlit theatre of Dionysus were heightened by the simple fact that the 'lights' were focused on performers and audience alike.

The open and public nature of the ancient theatre helps to explain its most basic convention, the masking of actors and chorus. In Greek drama the primary acting tool was the voice, not the face, since the bare human head all but disappeared in a theatre the size of the one in Athens. Far from hindering the actor, the tragic mask projected the persona of his character out to the audience. Since the practice of mask-wearing in Greek theatre seems inextricably linked to the idea of outdoor performance, I propose to analyse the place and function of masks here, rather than postpone discussion to the following chapter that examines other conventions of tragic production.

By focusing on the practical function of masks, I do not mean to underestimate their deep psychological and even metaphysical significance, or to skirt the problems of appearance, identity, and disguise that are relevant to tragic character. Drawing on such considerations, scholars have proposed a number of theories to account for masks in ancient performance. They allow the actor to merge or to lose himself in alternative identities, fitting for a servant of Dionysus, the god of ecstasy (*ek-stasis*), literally 'standing outside' oneself. Masks confront the audience with ambiguities of appearance and change, instantiating the conflicting urge to schematize and to personify. They enable the playwright to present characters in terms of social role and type, rather than as the sum of personal characteristics. Alternatively, masks blur the lines between a group (grasped by recognizing similarities) and separate individuals (identified by isolating differences). They empower the wearer by sympathetic magic and symbolic incarnation, overriding divisions of gender (man/woman), species (human/animal), and ontological category (mortal/god).[19] Much of the anthropological study of mask-wearing focuses on ritual and religious contexts, areas that have significant overlap with Greek tragedy. We discussed in Chapter 2 the place of masks in various Dionysiac cults, and there may be a link between such ritual masking and that used in dramatic performances.

On the other hand, we should emphasize that *all* 'impersonating' performers in the Greek theatre – every actor and chorus member in every tragedy, comedy, and satyr-play – wore masks. If tragedy developed from the dithyramb, then the link with ritual mask-wearing is much weaker than scholars admit, for the dithyrambic chorus members did not wear masks at all. The ancient testimonia on early tragedy further support the idea that masks were adopted *after* the first tragic performances – the legendary Thespis is said to have smeared his actors' faces with wine lees or white lead (the cosmetic of the day), later introducing masks made of linen. A predictable (if not particularly reliable) evolution emerges from the tradition – the tragic playwright Choerilus improves the mask, Phrynichus introduces women's masks (and, so, female characters), Aeschylus uses terrifying and highly coloured masks, and so on.

Whatever the truth about the first tragic masks, the fact that all dramatic performers in the fifth century wore them means that an Athenian would have been as surprised to see an unmasked tragic actor interpreting a role as we would be to see masked performers in *Annie Get Your Gun*. As a scholar observed early this century, 'to wear a mask was to act a part, and the idea that it was ever possible to act a part or to perform a play without wearing a mask was one which never occurred'.[20] Regardless of the psychological, cultural, ritual, and metaphysical significance for the Greeks, masks were above all an accepted theatrical convention. Mask-wearing was not a self-conscious attempt to alienate the audience or to invoke a magical or ritual past, or to contrast the flux of reality with the false notion of fixed character, as it seems to be for modern theorists and the contemporary avant-garde. Modern directors of tragedy looking for meaningful equivalents between our conventions and those of the Greeks would do well to keep this in mind.

It is worth noting that the ancient Greek language identified a human being metonymically with his or her head or eyes, using such expressions as 'dear head' (meaning 'loved one') and the phrase 'eye of [something]', where we might use the term 'heart' or 'inner fire' of a thing. The Greeks employed the same word, *prosôpon*, for 'face', 'mask', and 'dramatic character', literally meaning 'towards the eye'. Sophocles exploits these meanings in *Oedipus Tyrannus*, when the hero returns with a new mask that shows his gouged eye-sockets, an image of his true character, a man who was blind to his own identity. In *Bacchae*, Euripides also develops the connection between mask and character. Possessed by the god Dionysus, Agave holds what she thinks is the head of a lion she has killed, which is in fact the head of her son, represented by the actor's mask. By combining the image of a dramatic character with a self-conscious reference to theatre, Euripides associates dramatic illusion with the destructive power of Dionysus.

In Greek tragedy, both characters and spectators must face what they would rather not, a paradoxical compulsion epitomized by the unflinching stare of the actor's mask. It is hard to imagine a character looking into the terror and instability of tragedy *without* the shield of a mask, for in real life we would instinctively close our eyes. In a manner more powerful than the flash of the naked eye, the mask confronts the audience as well. It is remarkable how frequently head movements are indicated in tragedy, especially with the arrival of a new character, as if to ensure that the actor catches the audience in his full, broad sights. The wide-eyed gaze of the tragic mask does not scatter or divide, but focuses and encompasses, compelling the attention of the entire theatre.

Paradoxically, by forcing its gaze out, the tragic mask draws the audience in, for each spectator projects his or her imagination onto its surface. Observe how the fixed image of a human face seems to reflect the emotions of the situation around it, appearing to alter with description and circumstance. A self-portrait of Van Gogh, for example, possesses its own intrinsic qualities, but when the narrator tells us it is the last he painted before his suicide and the camera zooms in, we begin to see hopelessness, anguish, bitter despair. And yet the same portrait reveals a hard-earned, if tenuous, peace when we hear one of Van Gogh's happier letters read in the background. In similar fashion, a theatre audience revises and reconstrues a mask's physiognomy, when the circumstances, attitudes, and emotions of the character change. One of the great discoveries of Greek drama is that the imagination of the audience is the theatre's greatest resource. The convention of masked acting brings that imagination vitally into play, as the spectators fill out the fixed visage of a tragic character caught in radically changing situations.

Tragic masks and costumes also gave an immediate sense of character-type, gender, age, social status, and economic class, conveying the central tragic conflicts between old and young, men and women, gods and mortals. Comic masks fulfilled the same generalizing and informational ends, but added the possibility of satire. In Aristophanes' *Knights*, for example, the two servants of Demos ('The People') seem to have worn masks resembling the well-known Athenian generals Demosthenes and Nicias; we hear that the mask-makers thought better of fashioning a comparable portrait-mask linking the Paphlagonian servant to the war-mongering politician Cleon (*Knights*, 230–33).[21]

For all their dramatic power and mystery, masks served the practical purpose of allowing a single actor to play multiple roles (including different ages and genders) in the same play. Once established as the convention, masks obviated many of the demands that concern us as heirs to theatrical realism. We are bothered if the mother in Ibsen's *Ghosts* looks younger than her son, or if the family members in Pinter's *The Homecoming* sound as if they came from anywhere other than north London. Because the characters and chorus in Attic tragedy all belonged to the tribe of mask-wearers, questions about the appropriateness of the actor's age, look, and gender did not arise, freeing the audience to concentrate on other matters.

Chief among these other concerns was language. The large, open mouth of the tragic mask emphasized the spoken words, as if they provided the essence of character and the key to action.[22] The performance culture of fifth-century Athens was dominated by rhetoric and oral exchange, and the ancient actor was above all a speaker, as his mask indicates. The enlarged orifice epitomizes the tragic situation, where words and suffering seem co-extensive, where the mouth is always open, always capable of speech, even in the face of the unspeakable. Like a ballet without limbs to dance it, Greek tragedy would cease if the mouth were to close.

Here, the theatre of Dionysus conspired with the tragic mask, for a space where most of the audience sits high above the action demands that performers literally keep their heads up, always projecting forward and outward in order to be seen and heard. Even mute characters wear the possibility of their verbal intervention, silent but never silenced. Consider Pylades in Aeschylus' *Choephori* who says nothing the entire play, only to break his silence for three brief lines, advising Orestes to perform the unthinkable and kill his own mother. In Euripides' *Electra*, produced some forty years after *Choephori*, we expect the mute Pylades to speak at a key moment like his Aeschylean predecessor. But this Pylades *never* speaks, a twist on the tradition that suggests the absence of the gods in the sordid world of Euripides' play.

For all the physical distance between actor and audience in the theatre of Dionysus, both parties found themselves drawn together by natural surroundings in a natural light. Stage conventions that seem exotic to us were practical and effective means to make that common world sustain dramatic life, producing a compelling experience for the audience. To understand more fully how tragic art and artifice combined, we will consider other dramatic conventions in the next chapter. But we should never lose sight of the fact that the Greek theatrical drive was towards reality, a grounding of issues in a public forum where the human world was set in meaningful relationship to nature, a theatre where the world was included rather than shut out.

# 5

# CONVENTIONS OF PRODUCTION

I daresay that audiences in most cultures and historical periods have felt that the dramatic characters in their theatre represented (or were intended to represent) intelligible human beings – whether the form was the American musical, Jacobean tragedy, German *Sturm und Drang*, the Peking opera, Brecht's *Lehrstücke*, medieval Mystery plays, Noh drama, or a Broadway production of *Nicholas Nickleby*. To appreciate the fact that audiences of different cultures and periods viewed their theatre as realistic is to acknowledge the conventional nature of all theatrical representation. A fifth-century Athenian (*mutatis mutandis*) transported to London to see a revival of David Storey's *The Changing Room* would think the production riddled with artifice and convention, presenting a picture far less compelling than, say, Aeschylus' *Seven Against Thebes*. Such an audient might consider the images and language of the locker room too specific to reveal much of value about 'real people', preferring the story of the struggle between two mythical brothers at Thebes for the very reason that it seems closer to the reality of a human situation. Similarly, what strikes *us* as conventional and 'artificial' in a performance of Greek tragedy (or Japanese Kabuki, or Indian Kathakali) would seem to a Greek audience (or their Eastern counterpart) to be perfectly normal and appropriate.

The conventionality of all theatrical performance is worth belabouring, for we cannot hope to understand a given dramatic style or period without grasping the nature of its accepted artifice. To call Greek theatre stylized, conventional, or artificial illuminates little, since the same attributes describe every other drama, even that which strikes a modern audience as perfectly lifelike.[1] Although linguistic metaphors frequently obscure more than they clarify, understanding a given set of theatrical conventions is not unlike learning a foreign language. We realize that our native tongue (with its rules, grammar, syntax, and idioms) is no more or less 'natural' than another, but that any language allows us to represent and operate on the real (non-linguistic) world. As our facility with new languages increases, we come to understand that each tongue has its own strengths and weaknesses, enabling it to work at some tasks better

43

than others, to describe the physical world or to sustain abstractions, with more or less concision, fluidity, power, subtlety, complexity, and specificity.

In similar fashion, if we are to understand and take advantage of the communicative opportunities of a foreign theatrical mode, we must become familiar with the relevant conventions that inform its operations. We then can translate as necessary, using the appropriate conventions from our own theatre. Shakespeare provides an illustrative example. The diction and verse in his plays strike us as highly artificial compared to everyday English, and yet an actor playing Hamlet fails if he sounds like a poetic metronome. On the other hand, if the actor delivers the 'To be, or not to be' soliloquy like a crisis-centre operator, then he ignores the structure, thought, and mode of expression implicit in the metre and the language. We fault the former for failing to make the convention his own, the latter for ignoring the integral connection between theatrical form and content. We fault both for failing to engage the material, since the play demands a living character whose thoughts, emotions, and style of speech are mutually informing.

In this chapter we will examine the major conventions that provide the form and expressive mode of Greek tragic theatre. The term 'convention' is used in a loose sense, a tacit agreement among the various participants in a performance, both on-stage and in the audience, that allows the drama to unfold in a meaningful way. I will concentrate on those conventional aspects of tragic texts and performance that might strike us as odd, recalling that a fifth-century audience would consider them part of the dramatic furniture. Naturally the Greek tragedians could and did use these dramatic givens in innovative and shocking ways, but the conventions *per se* would seem no stranger to a Greek audience than an invisible fourth wall in a proscenium stage seems to us.

We already have examined the constraints and possibilities implicit in a large outdoor theatre where the performers wore masks. Before looking at other conventions, let us begin with the question of dramatic illusion in tragedy, which forces us in turn to consider approaches to characterization and acting style. We then will examine the modes and functions of the chorus, including a brief look at different metrical forms, followed by the conventions of dramatic rhetoric, especially stichomythia (alternating dialogue), messenger speeches, and formal debates or *agôns*. We then will examine costumes, props, and the function of corpses in the plays. To understand how tragedies begin and end, we will look briefly at the prologue and the *deus ex machina*. A conclusion will summarize these conventions in terms of the relationship they establish with the audience, the most important factor to keep in mind when considering appropriate modern equivalents.

44

# IN AND OUT OF THE SCENE –
## DRAMATIC ILLUSION, CHARACTER, AND TRAGIC ACTING

Some critics believe that the actors in Greek tragedy never acknowledged the audience as such, and the audience in turn never was encouraged to view the play as a play, but was caught in a kind of spell where the fiction implicit in the performance went unquestioned. According to this view, the audience watching a tragedy operated in one basic mode, that of belief – or, as is more commonly put, 'a willing suspension of disbelief' – and, as a result, the dramatic illusion of the performance was complete.

This form of presentation might appear to characterize much of the drama on stage, television, and screen today. We understand that the actors represent real people whose lives unfold before us, and we are encouraged to focus our attention on them and *not* on the manner by which their story gets told. Applied to cinema, for example, we remain unconscious of camera angles, changes in perspective, variations in narrative technique (flashbacks, monologues, voice-overs), references to other films, lighting and special effects, all the interventions of the medium itself. We may note in passing the signs of artifice behind the representation, but we are meant to subordinate them *all of the time* to the dramatic events in question.

Brief reflection suggests that this is not how we actually watch a film or a play, for we are (intermittently) made aware of the means, as well as the matter, of production. Greek tragedy operates similarly. The genre was highly conscious of the Homeric tradition that preceded it, alert to the ways in which other playwrights and poets had treated the same stories, alive to the political situation facing the city, and so on. Above all the tragic playwrights were aware of the shifting relationship between the characters on stage and the audience, manipulating with artistry (and an admirable willingness to experiment) the spectators' perspective on, and commitment to, the action. They constructed their tragedies so as to implicate the audience emotionally and intellectually, consciously and unconsciously, not only in the story but in the very processes of the drama.

Although Greek theatre neither maintained nor depended on a seamless dramatic illusion, the argument that it did so is an understandable reaction against the once popular belief that any drama with such strange conventions as masks and chorus could not be interested in representing intelligible people in recognizable situations, or in presenting characters whom an audience could loathe, reject, learn from, laugh at, or sympathize with. The 'dramatic illusionists' also position themselves against the trendy view that theatre is always and only self-referential, endlessly fabricating and unravelling a skein of signifiers that only the naïve would consider to be of any substance.

Once we entertain questions about dramatic illusion and the tragic theatre's relationship to reality, a wide range of issues emerge as problematic, including what we mean by such fundamental concepts as personal identity and agency. In what sense can we think of Sophocles' Oedipus as real, or as a person? Is he a dramatic figure with human capacities, or a fictional construct where we locate our own acts of consciousness? When we introduce the actor, the complexities multiply. What does it – or did it – mean for an actor to 'play' Oedipus? Does he act a part, perform a role, or is there any sense in which he 'becomes' the character? In classical Athens, how did the audience react as they watched this process? Were they conscious of seeing a human being, or a mythical figure, or an actor? The case of Oedipus is difficult enough, but what did the fifth-century audience think when the character who took the stage was a god? Did their response alter fundamentally in such plays as *Eumenides* and *Ion* where one of the deities is Athena, the patron goddess of Athens, the city where the plays were performed? On those occasions did the audience give themselves over to the fiction of the performance? Or was their relationship to the events more like a game of make-believe, with the character Athena serving as a prompt to their imagination? Did they watch in a detached, critical mode, attending to the rhetoric of her speech and enjoying the innovations of the scene? Or, did they hear the goddess's pronouncements as relevant to the city itself, above and beyond their connection to the play?

Simply posing these questions helps us to realize that a lively interplay between belief and incredulity, between emotional proximity and distance, must have operated in the Greek theatre as it does in even the most 'realistic' of dramatic presentations now. After all, unquestioning belief on the audiences' part would convert us from spectators into agents, ready to intervene on behalf of the other characters in the drama. On the other hand, complete distance would turn us into objective observers, emotionally unaffected by the highly charged situations facing the characters. We would react like the hardened paramedic who registers the pulse of every walk-in rather than the friend who cares desperately about the results, or an onlooker who is drawn into sympathy and concern.

If a distanced, scientific, objective response were all that was intended in Greek tragedy, then we would expect a different kind of writing and a different mode of presentation. As Aristotle points out, the great advance that tragedy made over epic was the appearance of characters 'as living and moving before us' (*Poetics*, 1448a.24–25), that is, characters as embodied. The physical presence of the actor defined the earliest drama, and the actor remains the irremovable obstacle in the path of those who view Greek tragedy (or the theatre in general) as a sophisticated playground for mental conundrums, as opposed to a place of live, and lived, human experience. With all due respect for the life of the mind, there is something inhuman about not responding to the humanity of dramatic characters who come to life before us in performance.

The audience of Greek tragedy witnessed recognizable events happening to intelligible human characters (and, occasionally, highly anthropomorphic gods) as they made free choices and discovered the consequences. The responsibilities of the audience included participating with the performers in investing the characters and their dramatic situation with a rich intellectual and emotional life. Yet the form of the plays and the context of their performance also compelled the audience on occasion – and in a manner guided by the production – to view these same characters and circumstances as elements in a consciously constructed drama that pointed to a world beyond the theatre.

Take, for example, the highly poetical and imagistically charged language of Greek tragedy. Given its full weight and complexity, the language takes on a life of its own, appropriate not only to the immediate situation, but also to the overall dramatic project. The brief space of an image can store a powerful emotional experience, enriching the context with each iteration and variation, amplifying the relationship of events and characters towards a more abstract significance. We recognize how fitting it is in *Agamemnon* that the king who threw a net on Troy is netted in the bath, just as Orestes who traps Clytemnestra in *Choephori* is snared metaphorically by the Furies in *Eumenides*. But we also become aware of how the concatenation of images works through the trilogy independently of character and plot, part of the larger case that Aeschylus wishes to make. Through the power of its language, the *Oresteia* expands in scope and texture, alerting us to the wider setting as it deepens the imaginative significance of specific moments. The process is one in which the audience shifts from the immediate dramatic situation to the larger world of the play, and then moves beyond it, constantly negotiating different levels and formulating responses appropriate to them, inspired by (but hardly bound to) the initial commitment to dramatic illusion.

A more obvious sign of the tragedians' interest in keeping the audience alive to the fact of performance involves dramatic irony and humour. Although not a formal convention, the practice of employing ironically charged words and disruptive language alters the audience's relationship to the action. Take, for example, the ubiquitous word-play in Sophocles' *Oedipus Tyrannus* on the name of the hero, *oidipous*, literally 'swollen foot' but also containing the Greek word *oide*, 'he has seen' = 'he knows'. At times the repetition of the name draws us into a horrified sympathy with the protagonist; at other times it distances us from his individual plight until we view the play as an exemplary tale about human ignorance and blindness.

In Euripides the difference between the characters' knowledge and that of the audience can become so involved that we delight in the play of irony for its own sake. In *Helen*, for example, Euripides alters the standard story of the heroine's abduction, presenting a version in which a phantom goes to Troy while the real Helen spends the war years in Egypt. When the Greek Teucer lands there on his way home from Troy, ignorant that the war was fought for a phantom, he meets the real but unrecognized Helen and wishes her the best, then curses Helen of Troy and prays for her death. The ironies are rife, and the audience cannot help but enjoy the play of illusion – that is, until Euripides returns us to the stark reality of the war as Helen laments the suffering inflicted in her name on the women of Troy.

Although not normally associated with tragedy, humorous moments scattered through the plays pull the audience out of the immediate circumstance with a laugh, only to drop them back with a vengeance. In Euripides' *Heracles*, for example, the goddesses Lyssa ('Madness') and Iris arrive unexpectedly in the middle of the play, sent by Hera to drive Heracles mad. Lyssa argues that Heracles has done nothing to warrant such punishment, prompting Iris to respond: 'The wife of Zeus did not send you here to exercise your sanity' (857). Madness appears as the voice of reason and is chided for it, the kind of pointed Euripidean humour that momentarily takes the audience out of the dramatic situation. However, Heracles' ensuing madness is conveyed so vividly that irony and humour are quickly forgotten, and the play shifts from rescue and triumph to slaughter and suffering.

Tragedy also calls attention to itself by referring to (and even parodying) scenes from earlier tragedies, and so introduces a more complex sense of dramatic representation and illusion. Again Euripides is the master, and his parody in *Electra* of the recognition scene between Electra and Orestes in *Choephori* splits the focus of the audience. Part of our interest lies in the earlier treatment by Aeschylus, the other part in the Euripidean version being acted out before us. Distrust of such quirky dramatic practices once led scholars to delete the passage as spurious, but recent critics have recognized that Euripides systematically involves the audience in this kind of dialectical relationship, alternating between their belief in the illusion of the play and their awareness that they are part of the process by which that illusion occurs. The ambiguity that results in *Electra* ultimately serves dramatic ends, for the Old Man insists on the validity of the traditional signs of Orestes' identity against the rationalist arguments of Electra. He proves to be right, confounding Electra's view that Orestes is far too heroic and manly to return home incognito.

Euripides was not alone in exploiting the theatrical conventions available in Greek tragic production. As we shall see in Chapters 6 and 7, Aeschylus and Sophocles also used these basic elements – the messenger speech, the *deus ex machina*, the prologue, stichomythia, the chorus – not only to build their dramatic illusions, but to undermine them as well. In so doing, they forced the audience to confront the material of the play, encouraging them to adopt new perspectives and to reorder their priorities when they left the theatre.

What do these observations regarding dramatic illusion and its violation tell us about the style of acting in Greek tragedy? No handbook on ancient acting has come down to us, and even if it had, we would be suspicious of how representative it was, given what we know of the many conflicting approaches to acting today. We know that acting style changed over the course of the fifth century, judging from the anecdote in Aristotle's *Poetics* (1461b.26–1462a.4). The old actor Mynniscus who had performed for Aeschylus, and lived long enough to win the actor's prize for a Euripidean trilogy in the 420s, criticizes a young actor, Kallipides (who won his first acting prize in 418), for overly naturalistic mimesis, likening Kallipides' efforts to those of a monkey.

Far from there being an unbridgeable gap between ancient theatrical practice and our own, Plato indicates that the way an ancient actor identified with his role(s) was not so alien from what many contemporary performers strive for. In the Platonic dialogue *Ion*, a Homeric rhapsode answers Socrates' questions about his 'process'. He speaks as if he were possessed by the role, that the character was playing him, that he served as a conduit for the poet (or playwright, the difference here is immaterial) and succeeded best when he was least conscious he was acting. This is not the description of acting we would expect from a theatre so frequently characterized as 'stylized' or 'conventional'. Although dating from the first century BC, the description of the tragic actor Aesopus by the Roman Cicero (*De Oratore*, 2.46.193) may capture the feeling of earlier tragic acting:

> What can be more fictitious than poetry, plays, the stage? However, in this genre I myself have often seen the eyes of the actor flashing from behind his mask as he spoke [quoted lines]. . . . And then he would say, lowering his voice to a pitiable tone [quoted lines]. . . . He seemed to be weeping and grieving as he spoke these lines.

There is ample evidence that such close identification between actor and character had a correspondingly strong emotional effect on ancient audiences.[2] Again we are reminded that tragic productions struck the original performers and spectators as realistic, a far cry from the art-pieces to which some modern critics compare them.

This does not mean that tragic acting privileged the idiosyncratic and the personal – the standard rule in psychological realism – over the generic and typical. As we recall from Chapter 4, masked acting in a large outdoor theatre imposed on Greek drama a generic account of human existence. Characters operated more on an ethical than on a psychological level, their status depending on qualities that were socially recognized and sanctioned, not on peculiarities of individual behaviour or consciousness. According to Aristotle, tragedy did not concentrate on presenting individual characters as much as on imitating an 'action'. By action Aristotle meant something like a plot, a poetic structure of events arranged in narrative sequence that tells a story of some gravity and importance, and from which the audience derives pleasure appropriate to the genre.[3] Whatever the original audience's responses to tragedy, it seems unlikely that they arose from watching detailed portraits of highly individualized characters, but rather reflected the overall patterns of the story as informed by the actors who, as we recall, usually played more than one role.

Tragic acting style took its cue from the expansive outdoor theatre, the scale of the dramatic events, and the form the material was given. As a result, acting was big-voiced, front-footed, and fully displayed, not low-key, withdrawn, and inner. Aristotle tells us that the main metre adopted for speeches and dialogue – iambic trimeter (three sets of double-iambic feet, each line scanned ˣ ˉ ˘ ˉ / ˘ ˉ ˘ ˉ / ˘ ˉ ˘ ˣ / where ˉ is long, ˘ is short, and ˣ is either long or short) – was more conversational than epic dactylic hexameter. This fact should warn us against adopting the false analogy between tragedy and musical theatre or opera. Tragic dialogue was neither sung nor accompanied by music, but was deemed to follow the rhythms of common speech, although controlled more formally and expressively than in day-to-day conversation.[4] The actor did most of his work through his voice, and the primary attributes of a would-be performer were the quality and range of his vocal powers.

Ancient actors usually played more than one role, but the task may have been slightly easier than it first appears. There is little indication in the tragic texts (and none in other sources) that the diction of different characters – queen or nurse, king or servant, male or female, Greek or foreigner, god or mortal – was marked in any individualized way. We may contrast, for example, the Professor's speech with that of Waffles in *Uncle Vanya*, or the prose of Roderigo with the verse of the Moor in *Othello*. Unlike Bottom in *A Midsummer Night's Dream* who would 'aggravate' his voice to play Thisbe, we find no indication that Greek tragic actors changed their pitch or delivery in any substantial way when performing different characters within the same drama. Even if they did – if there were, for instance, a characteristic 'vocal quality' for an old woman or a herald – the audience still would recognize the distinctive voice of each of the three actors behind the masks.

The fact of vocal recognition means that doubling roles folded the issues of dramatic character back into the larger patterns of the play, an opportunity that the playwrights fully exploited. For instance, the same actor played both Agamemnon and his rival Aegisthus in *Agamemnon*; both Electra and Clytemnestra, the estranged mother and daughter of *Choephori*; Heracles and Deianeira, the husband and wife who never meet in the course of *Women of Trachis*; Antigone and Haimon, who finally join off-stage in a 'marriage to death' in *Antigone*; Orestes and Clytemnestra, avenging son and murdered mother in Sophocles' *Electra*; Agave and Pentheus, both the mother and the son she kills in *Bacchae*. In Sophocles' *Ajax*, the division of parts broke down along the lines of support or antipathy for the title character – the protagonist played Ajax and Teucer (half-brothers), the second actor, the 'deuteragonist', portrayed Odysseus (sympathetic to Ajax) and Tecmessa (Ajax's wife), and the third actor, 'tritagonist', performed the roles of Athena, Menelaus, and Agamemnon (Ajax's enemies in the play).[5]

Actors performing tragedy in contemporary productions are free of the demands of doubling roles, and from the prodigious vocal projection required in the theatre of Dionysus. Nonetheless, attention to the words and to the ongoing flow of speech and dialogue provides the surest guide for any actor or director who wishes to take full advantage of Greek tragic form. To be avoided is the temptation to convert Greek tragic figures into modern characters by adopting a mode of delivery best suited for domestic/living-room drama – mumbling, using exaggerated breathing as an emotional marker, making inarticulate acknowledgements and prompts, taking long pauses to convey moments of gravity, and employing other irregular patterns of speech and silence. Tragedy demands a different, but no less expressive, discipline, one that subordinates psychological marking via speech/non-speech habits to the 'acoustic mask-wearing' appropriate to its subject and scale.[6] In this kind of acting, character is revealed in the forward movement of speech and dialogue, and the development of a role is in the service of the overall action of the drama and not an end in itself.

Ancient discussions of gesture (*cheironomia*) indicate that physical expression also played an important part in tragic acting. Judging from the plays, the most important gestures involved ritual actions associated with mourning the dead, and we can tell from vase paintings and from the texts themselves something about how they looked. The same is true of gestures connected with pouring libations (liquid offerings), swearing oaths, celebrating a wedding, and making supplication. The last example is particularly important because supplication (placing oneself at the mercy, and protection, of another) provides the organizing principle of several tragedies, giving rise to the sub-genre of the suppliant play, including Aeschylus' and Euripides' *Suppliant Women*, Sophocles' *Oedipus at Colonus*, and several others.[7]

By incorporating patterns of movement and gesture drawn from contemporary ritual and religious practice, the tragedians incorporated important elements of fifth-century life into the world of the mythic/heroic figures who inhabited their stage. In fact, a thoroughgoing anachronism operated in Greek tragedy, making powerful and immediate contact with the lived experience of the original audience. The actors presented the spectators with a vision of the contemporary world writ large, not simply a version of the mythic and heroic world writ small.

## THE GREEK CHORUS

The chorus represent the single aspect of Greek tragedy that is least understood and most rarely honoured, both in productions and in critical writing on the ancient theatre. This situation is unfortunate, since what distinguishes the earliest drama from its later offspring is the presence of the chorus, or more specifically, the coexistence of two contrasting modes of presentation – the rhetoric, or speech of the actor (usually in iambic trimeter, as noted above), and the lyric of the chorus, a combination of dance, music, and verse in a variety of metres.

51

The difference between rhetoric and lyric, between actor and chorus, has been expressed in a variety of ways. The opposition between individuated character and the undifferentiated chorus influenced Nietzsche's vision of the wellsprings of theatre in *The Birth of Tragedy*. In more pragmatic terms, the actor/chorus dialectic did much to energize theatrical group-work and the revival of alternative theatre in the 1960s. The distinction between language as lyric, filled with imagistic and temporal leaps, and language as rhetoric, used for narrative and argumentative purposes, informed the old critical polarities of connotation and denotation, and has found a new critical life in terms of poetic versus public discourse. Considering the non-verbal aspects of choral performance, we may contrast the emotional nature of movement and music/song with the rational, logic-bound control of speech, suggesting the traditional dichotomy of reason and passion, or any number of modern variations, including the distinction between left- and right-brain activity. We also can view the modal differences in terms of the categories of the 'hot' medium of language and the 'cool' medium of the chorus's lyric and dance.[8]

However one construes the differences between the rhetoric of the actor and the lyric of the chorus, the interplay between the two expressive modes sets Greek tragedy apart from other drama. Compare the popular Broadway and West-End fare that consists of people in a room talking, or the contemporary avant-garde 'theatre of images', that provides one stage picture after another with minimal narrative or story-line. At best, each offers but half of the possibilities inherent in Greek tragic form. Some critics argue that opera or musical theatre offers a helpful analogy to Greek tragedy, but the apparent similarities are superficial and misleading. The power of speech is absent or extremely attenuated in opera, with a dearth of argument and case-making, of persuasive rhetoric, of cut-and-thrust dialogue and public debate. Similarly, the opera's use of dance – often balletic interludes or atmospheric pieces of folklore – bears little resemblance to the combination of poetry, song, and movement that constitutes the Greek chorus.

As for the comparison of tragic lyric to popular music theatre, one of the central tenets of the integrated musical is that the song or dance reveals character, or signals a major development in the plot, or (in less well-crafted pieces) offers a 'vehicle' for the star. Think how often in a musical number a character establishes his or her situation, a couple falls in or out of love, an important decision is reached, a discovery made, a deal struck, and so on. As we shall see, the choral lyric of tragedy rarely serves so explicit a function. By providing a different mode from the rhetoric of the actors, the chorus engages the play in an ongoing dialogue with itself. Through the different 'voices' of that dialogue – sometimes complementary, sometimes additive, sometimes opposed one to the other – the tragedy takes shape and comes to dramatic life.

We can get a better handle on how the lyric differs from the surrounding action by looking at the practical demands of choral performance. As far as we can tell, the tragic chorus originally consisted of twelve members, and at some point grew to fifteen, the same performers serving for the entire tetralogy of a given playwright. Perhaps the change to an odd number offered advantages for asymmetrical choreography, or highlighted the role of the chorus-leader, who did most of the speaking when the chorus conversed with the dramatic characters.

The initial arrival of the chorus into the theatre usually took place through one or both of the side entrances called *eisodoi* ('ways in') or *parodoi* ('side roads'), giving the name *parodos* to the first chorus. Frequently the metre for the choral entrance is anapaests – a combination of ˘ ˘ ¯, ¯ ¯, and occasionally ¯ ˘ ˘ in a repeating pattern – often referred to as 'marching anapaests', although tragedies in which the chorus could be said to move into the theatre in military fashion are few and far between (see Chapter 3, p. 27). There are formal processions, as in the opening of Aeschylus' *Choephori* where the slave women bring libations to the tomb of Agamemnon, and in Euripides' lost *Phaethon*, where the chorus enter singing a wedding hymn. In some tragedies the choral entrance is drawn out purposely, as in Aeschylus' *Persians*; in others the chorus arrive with a sense of urgency and dispatch, as in Euripides' *Alcestis* and *Medea*, or with a festive sense of excitement, as in *Ion* and *Electra*. On rare occasions the chorus are discovered in the orchestra when the play begins, moving into place in a 'cancelled entry' that is understood to take place before, and outside of, the dramatic action. Analysed in Chapters 6 and 8, the choruses of Aeschylus' *Eumenides* and Euripides' *Suppliant Women* are pre-set in this fashion.

Once established in the orchestra, the chorus sing and dance a series of odes over the course of the play, usually designated by the general term stasimon or 'standing song'. The name does not imply immobility but simply means that the chorus are already in the orchestra when they perform. Recently the term 'act-dividing song' has been introduced to indicate a more dramatic sense of structure, applied to a choral song that is preceded immediately by an actor's exit and is followed by an actor's entrance.[9]

Although there are odes with no metrical responsion (called astrophic), most choral songs consist of paired stanzas, a *strophê* (meaning 'turn', henceforth strophe) and *antistrophê* ('counter-turn'). In this structure the metrical pattern in one stanza is repeated precisely in the next, then a different metrical pattern is introduced in a new strophe, which is followed precisely in its antistrophe, and so on: a – a'/ b – b'/ c – c'/. Sometimes an independent passage called a mesode ('middle song') is inserted between the two parts of a strophic pair, marking a rhythmical break before the pattern of the strophe repeats in the antistrophe: a – mesode 1 – a'/ b – mesode 2 – b'/ and so on. To close off a chorus, the playwright occasionally employs an epode ('after-song') that does not correspond precisely to any of the preceding strophic pairs. The tragic playwrights worked complex elaborations on the basic schemes, and a graph of the metrical patterns can prove helpful in grasping the overall movement of the lyric. Although we should not mistake the pattern on the page for the experience of an audience during performance, a director of Greek tragedy would do well to remain alert to the interlocking musical patterns, observing the way the lyric brings together different subjects and motifs by virtue of repeated rhythms and movement, or emphasizes tonal shifts by introducing a break in the pattern.

The precise nature of the dance of the chorus has been lost, but we gain some insight from the content and substance of the songs, from representations of dancers on ancient vases and sculpture, and from the lyric metres themselves. It seems likely that the Greek chorus did not eschew mimetic and expressive movements. When they sang of the animal world and the forces of nature, there was a quality in the dance that reflected its power and beauty. When the lyric included threnodic elements and other aspects of mourning rites, or dealt with sacrifice, weddings, athletic contests, or military actions, we may be sure the dance drew on recognizable gestures and movements from those rituals and events. The chorus generally moved and sang in unison, although we may assume that individual dancers could move independently while the group maintained the basic rhythm, and that solo voices emerged when dramatically effective. At times the chorus divided into two half-choruses, allowing one group to move with less restraint while the other carried the song, and vice versa. In modern terms, Greek choral dancing seems closer to synchronized modern dance than to ballet, more in the mould of expressive movement than kinaesthetic abstraction.

There must have been close co-ordination between the dance and the lyric rhythms, but the complexities of Greek metre are formidable, and it is wrong-headed to associate specific metres with a particular set of movements or a single emotional effect. A rough scale of physicality from constrained to wild would put the steady and somewhat repetitive anapaests at one end and dochmiacs at the other. The dochmiac is a syncopated rhythm signalling great tension, anxiety, and even abandonment, with the metrical foot⌣ - ⌣ - in repeated patterns, capable of wide variation including the resolution of all the long syllables into shorts (⌣ ⌣⌣ ⌣⌣ ⌣ ⌣⌣) as at line 1330 of *Oedipus Tyrannus*. In between anapaests and dochmiacs lie a variety of metrical systems, any of which can be adapted to a wide range of emotional and movement possibilities.[10]

English translations rarely aim to capture the lyric variation of the original, a wise course given the limitations of English syntax. As a fully inflected language, ancient Greek uses the endings of words and not their order to signal grammatical function in a sentence. By allowing maximum flexibility in terms of word placement, the Greek language enables remarkably complex metres to be repeated precisely. To identify these lyrical patterns, a commentary on a Greek text is an essential guide, since the editor usually provides a breakdown of the metres of all the choruses. Of course, strict allegiance to the original metrical scheme is neither possible nor desirable in a modern translation or production. But sensitivity to this aspect of choral lyric can help those working on Greek tragedy to a fuller appreciation of the chorus's changing dramatic role, suggesting places where modern theatrical equivalents to metrical responsion can and should be considered.

In approaching Greek lyric, one also should be aware of 'metrical quotations' and references to other genres. As Herington points out, the innovation in tragic lyric did not lie in discovering new metres, but in 'its fusion of the known metrical genres within the compass of a single work'.[11] For example, when dactylic hexametre (the metre of Greek epic poetry) occurs in tragic lyric, the playwright may be suggesting a Homeric and heroic feeling to the passage. Alternatively, hexametres may suggest an oracular tone, since responses from the Delphic oracle also were delivered in that metre. Another genre incorporated in tragic choruses is that of the epinician or 'victory ode' discussed in Chapter 1, invoking the world of athletic competitions and the aristocratic ideal of the 'beautiful and noble' victor. In Euripides' *Electra*, the chorus and Electra welcome Orestes and Pylades back from their murder of Aegisthus with an epinician-influenced lyric, crowning the young men as if they were victors at the Olympic games. The incongruity becomes clear when Orestes presents his sister with the head of Aegisthus, duly reviled by Electra in a long and disturbing speech.

Euripides' *Heracles* illustrates another, related convention in lyric, in which the chorus question the nature of the song they are singing. They compare Heracles' madness to a Bacchic celebration run amok, where the *aulos* accompanies a crazed dance and gives rise to a fatal song (877–79). Of course, the chorus themselves are dancing to an *aulos* in the orchestra, so that their performance comes to signify the inverted Dionysiac ritual they are describing. By transforming the choral dance in the theatre into its own 'negative image', Euripides asks the audience to consider the fabric of song that once praised Heracles as victor and now unravels in disorder and madness. In their final lyric, the chorus express their doubts about what song they should perform: 'What groans/ or dirge or song of death, what dance/ of Hades should I take up?' (1025–27). Euripides answers the question by never having the chorus sing and dance again, with over 350 lines before the end of the play. Perhaps by their collective stillness and silence Euripides suggests that the tragic lyric adequate to the experiences of *Heracles* has yet to be written.

The most famous example of a chorus calling its own activities into question occurs in the second stasimon of *Oedipus Tyrannus*. At this point in the play, Apollo's oracles seem unfulfilled, and the shifting eddies of fortune appear so random that they threaten any sense of human purpose. If such is the state of the cosmos, the chorus wonder, 'Why is it necessary for us to dance?' Their question is self-referential but also tied to the action of the play. Why *should* choruses dance? If events occur only at random, what allegiances are there to the city, the gods, and the notion of a 'cosmos' (the Greek for 'order'), the very things that a tragic chorus gather to explore and celebrate at the festival of Dionysus? By virtue of the chorus's own self-examination, Sophocles raises a fundamental question about the purpose of theatre. How the audience responds to that question is part and parcel of the way *Oedipus Tyrannus* works in performance.

At the end of most Greek tragedies, the chorus leave the orchestra through an *eisodos*. Their exit is often part of the final stage action, as in Aeschylus' *Persians* where the chorus accompany the defeated Xerxes in a dirge back to their homes. Similarly, at the end of Sophocles' *Women of Trachis* the chorus form part of the funeral cortege for Heracles. A dramatically important variation of the convention occurs in *Agamemnon*, where the chorus members do not exit together, but leave in small groups after taunting the tyrant Aegisthus. The fragmentation suggests the unsettled political situation in Argos, the divided *polis* that results from Aegisthus' seizing power. In a more formal acknowledgement of closure, several plays of Euripides end with choral 'tags', short truisms about the unpredictability of events as exemplified in the tragedy, after which the chorus presumably exit in silence. Although we cannot be certain, a few tragedies may have ended without a final exit, substituting a final tableau broken only by the audience's applause and whatever passed for the ancient curtain-call.

In five extant tragedies – Aeschylus' *Eumenides*, Sophocles' *Ajax*, Euripides' *Alcestis*, *Helen* and *Rhesus* – the chorus actually leave the theatre *during* the play, allowing for a second *parodos* when they re-enter the orchestra. In *Eumenides*, for example, the chorus of Furies leave the theatre in pursuit of Orestes, who has fled Delphi for Athens. When Orestes re-enters the now empty orchestra, we have a clear indication that the scene has changed to Athens, and the Furies arrive to track him down again. In their second *parodos*, they physicalize the theme of pursuit and punishment that runs through the trilogy. In *Alcestis*, the chorus's departure sets a very different tone, for they join Admetus in bearing the corpse of Alcestis out of the theatre, a procession modelled on a fifth-century funeral. After an intervening scene between Heracles and a servant (played in the absence of the chorus), the funeral party returns and Admetus compares their desolate homecoming to his arrival with Alcestis years before on their wedding night. By emptying the orchestra, Euripides conveys not only the collective sense of loss brought on by Alcestis' death, but also the transformation that takes place in the figure of Admetus.

Perhaps the most important function of the chorus is to open up the drama to a variety of non-linear influences that a strict narrative can deny or inhibit. Time and again the choral lyric introduces striking images of the natural world, in the manner of the extended epic similes discussed in Chapter 1. In *Agamemnon*, for example, the images of the vultures orphaned of their young, the eagle and the pregnant hare, the lion cub

56

who turns from pet to killer, the nightingale singing of her loss, take on a life of their own. Through the choral lyric, human activities in the *Oresteia* are viewed against the vast backdrop of nature and prove to be both at one and at war with the natural world. Intermingling past, present, and future, the chorus also free tragedy from a strict temporal sequence. By introducing examples from myth, they encourage the audience to view specific dramatic actions within the (relatively) timeless context of mythological paradigms. Space and location also become transmuted in the performance of lyric, as when the chorus of *Heracles* evoke various points at the edge of the known world, or when a chorus sing an 'escape' ode, like the Danaids in Aeschylus' *Suppliant Women*, conjuring a location far from the immediate problems of the play.

By diverging from the strict path of the plot, the chorus enable the audience to view the preceding and subsequent action through a different focusing perspective.[12] For example, the *parodos* of Euripides' *Bacchae* ends with a dynamic image of maenadic worshippers leaping with the natural grace of a deer in the wild. As the chorus finish their dance, two old men dressed in the fawn skins of Dionysiac cult haltingly make their way into the orchestra. The striking juxtaposition is both humorous and instructive, especially when the old men, Cadmus and the blind Teiresias, try to rationalize their 'conversion' to the new religion. Unlike the maenads leaping deer-like in the woods, there proves to be nothing natural or graceful in their worship.

In addition to singing and dancing on their own, the chorus can share the lyric with a dramatic character in a *kommos*, literally 'a beating' of the breasts in mourning. The name indicates that the shared lyric frequently arises at times of grief – the return of Xerxes at the end of *Persians*, after the death of Jocasta and the blinding of Oedipus in *Oedipus Tyrannus*, and during the final appearance of the heroine in *Antigone*, where her wedding hopes end in a funeral procession. On other occasions, characters and chorus can interact in what is called a lyric dialogue, where they maintain their respective modes of rhetoric and lyric. As we will see in Chapter 6, Cassandra and the chorus in *Agamemnon* share such an exchange, but with the roles reversed – Cassandra sings and the chorus speak, until the prophetess draws the group into her dance and together they share a *kommos*.

Actors sometimes perform in lyric metres on their own in what is called a monody, or 'solo song'. The title characters in Euripides' *Ion* and *Electra*, for example, enter the orchestra singing a monody much like a chorus arriving in the *parodos*. After an opening section of anapaests (again, modelled on a choral entry), Ion sings a work song as he sweeps the temple precinct with his broom. The fact that his lyric is divided into a strophe and antistrophe suggests that dance movements accompanied his song. In *Electra* the protagonist returns with a water-jug filled from the well, singing and dancing a lament for her wretched fate. The formal structure reflects her inner turmoil, for each strophe and antistrophe is separated by a short mesode that interrupts the metrical correspondence, underlining Electra's anomalous position as a married virgin and revealing her propensity for self-martyrdom.

Euripides is particularly fond of monodies, and he has two different characters (each played by a different actor) sing significant lyric passages in *Alcestis* (Alcestis and her son Eumelos), *Andromache* (Andromache and Peleus), *Ion* (Ion and Creusa), and *Trojan Women* (Cassandra and Hecuba). Frequently he uses a monody to convey utter isolation at a moment of great emotional intensity, as when Evadne suddenly appears in *Suppliant Women* ready to leap to her death on her husband's pyre, or when Creusa confesses her rape by Apollo in a moving solo in *Ion*. After the lyric monody, the character often presents the material again in a speech or dialogue. For example, Alcestis 'dies' first in a beautiful song and then plays out the death scene again in rhetoric. Cassandra in *Trojan Women* sings a perverse wedding hymn in honour of her union with Agamemnon, afterwards explaining to her mother why the occasion deserves celebrating. The process of 'going through things twice' is highly conventional, for we find no examples where an actor's monody or shared *kommos* is *preceded* by a speech on the same general topic. Since the pattern is conventional, the 'repetition' does not imply inauthentic behaviour or rhetorical posturing, but quite the opposite. The character has undergone an experience of sufficient power and importance to warrant it being presented in two different modes, forcing the audience to grapple with the different perspectives and emotional responses that they elicit.

Just as actors can adopt the medium of the chorus in a *kommos* and a monody, so the chorus occasionally speak. Editors usually assign their dialogue lines to a single *coryphaeus*, or chorus-leader, who takes on the role of group representative, as in the Furies' cross-examination and dialogue in the trial scene of *Eumenides*. At other times, however, we hear various voices from the chorus, as in the exchange after the death of the king in *Agamemnon*, when each member speaks his view on the best course of action. Lines also may have been divided among different speakers in the more conventional utterances of the chorus, such as identifying new arrivals, bidding farewell to departing characters, offering a short break between long speeches, and helping the audience to follow a change in principal speaker (difficult in a large theatre with masked actors) by interjecting a call for moderation between the two contending parties.

It was an established convention that tragic choruses do not 'make speeches', but even here we must allow for the exception. The *coryphaeus* in *Heracles* delivers a twenty-three-line speech, longer than Aegisthus' part in *Choephori*, or Eurydice's in *Antigone*. He focuses on the chorus's impotence to resist the tyrant Lycus, ending with the wish that they might regain their youthful prowess. This unprecedented speech by a chorus member paradoxically emphasizes the group's weakness, further exposing the gap in the action that only the absent Heracles can fill.

This survey of choral function should put to rest the notion that the chorus had a single, consistent character within a play. Some choruses do represent a clearly defined group who operate as such from beginning to end – the elders of the city in Aeschylus' *Persians*, and the Furies in *Eumenides*, for example. But even these groups challenge our assumptions about character consistency in any strong sense. Is raising a ghost the kind of thing Persian elders do? Why should the immortal Furies sing a binding song around Orestes in the manner of a fifth-century Athenian cursing his opponent to render him ineffective at a trial? These questions may seem absurd, but they follow directly from the way some critics and productions have insisted on the continuity and consistency of character in the Greek chorus.

We would do better to approach a chorus with an extremely flexible notion of identity, as exemplified by the group of slave-women in *Choephori*. Literally 'libation-bearers', the chorus are foreign-born servants who, at the command of their mistress Clytemnestra, bring offerings to Agamemnon's grave. However, in the *kommos* the women come to represent the forces of familial memory and outrage that urge Orestes to vengeance. Later they provide the mythological paradigms against which to view Clytemnestra's murder of her husband, only to return to the role of servants loyal now to Orestes and Electra. Acting as key players in the plot, they persuade the Nurse to change her message and help lure Aegisthus to his doom. As the murder of Clytemnestra approaches, however, the chorus shift again to distance themselves from the matricide, and conclude the play as if they were the voice of the house of Atreus, recounting the murders of the past.

Clearly, these libation-bearers are both less and more than their name implies. They are capable of acting as agents in the drama, but equally capable of effacing their identity and participating without any definable character beyond that of a group of performers who bring dramatic pressure to bear as the play requires. We see even greater flexibility in the choruses of Sophocles and Euripides, where the arrival of the group invariably is accounted for as sympathetic friends, elders of the city, visitors, suppliants, and so forth. But this initial identification is forgotten, developed, contradicted, and exploited in various ways as the action unfolds. The appearance of a secondary or 'shadow' chorus is the exception. Here, the playwright introduces a subsidiary chorus to perform a specific function, such as the secondary chorus that escorts the Eumenides at the close of Aeschylus' *Oresteia*.

The dramatic gains from the flexible chorus are enormous. To take but one example, the chorus of women in Euripides' *Helen* sing the following passage in their long-delayed first stasimon:

> Fools! who strive for glory in war,
> in the shock of spear against shield,
> you senselessly try to stop
>            once and for all

the labour of mortal life.
Must contests of blood decide
these things? Then strife will
never leave the cities of men.
You see what these men won – wedding chambers
in the Trojan earth,
                    and they could have
settled it with words, their strife over you.
Ah Helen!

                                   (*Helen*, 1151–60)

This group of captured Spartan women first enter the play announcing that they have left their washing by the river to dry. Nine hundred lines later they sing their first stasimon, a diatribe against war. Euripides has not constructed a set of circumstances, or presented a characterological or psychological profile, that would account for this change in choral sensibility. Nor would the original audience have expected such an undertaking, or found it necessary. The chorus's outburst here is part of a message that the play as a whole develops in several ways, but none of them dependent on the realistic conversion of the chorus from washerwomen to anti-war protesters.

Although looking for character consistency in the chorus is a red herring, maintaining the given gender of the group is not. It is essential to the play that the chorus of Aeschylus' *Seven Against Thebes* and Euripides' *Bacchae* are female. It makes dramatic sense that Medea has an initially sympathetic group of women at hand, and the same can be said for Deianeira in *Women of Trachis* and Creusa in *Ion*. Similarly, the fact that the choruses of *Agamemnon* and *Antigone* are male highlights the essential conflicts and transformations of those plays.

By considering the chorus as a highly malleable but gender-specific entity, we cease to lock the group into a single function or point of view, the tendency of criticism since the eighteenth century. We read variously that the chorus represents the ideal spectator, the city, the common man/woman, the fifth-century world-view opposed to the archaic ethos of the heroic characters, the voice of the poet, and so on. We do better to understand the chorus in theatrical terms, as raw material to be shaped as the mood and plot demand, a group of performers who influence the audience as much as the action, who are not bound to strict determinants of identity or character. Both in what they perform, and in the fact that they usually sing and dance when they perform it, the chorus infuse the play with a different kind of energy from that of the actors, and so change the pulse and temperature of the action. They force the audience to consider elements not strictly related to the plot, and yet not extraneous to the workings of the play. Through their lyric and dance, they cast disturbing shadows back on the scene we have just watched, or throw an interpretive filter over what will transpire.

The chorus are free to support, ignore, question, or reject the actions of the central characters, reorienting our response to the rhetoric as they do. They compel us to experience the drama as an ever-changing dynamic relationship, and not as the unfolding of the inevitable.

## MODES OF TALKING:
## MESSENGER SPEECHES, STICHOMYTHIA, AND FORMAL *AGÔNS*

### Messenger speeches

We have discussed how Greek lyric can canvass time and space, bringing the past and future, the distant and remote, to bear on events in the play. An important convention of the rhetoric of tragedy, the messenger speech also aims at bringing an off-stage world into the theatre, but in a more focused and emotionally charged manner. The theatrical opposite of a large group supported by music, song, and movement, the messenger stands alone, a performer stripped of everything but his capacity to hold the stage while he speaks.

Messengers are rarely named, and in their narrative they subordinate character almost completely to dramatic function. Here, if anywhere in Greek tragedy, the text must speak through the actor. Modern productions rarely grasp the dramatic strength of these remarkable speeches, substituting for hard-edged narration a personally felt, angst-ridden account. Imbued with a sense of '*I* was there', such performances are at odds with the form, for a messenger speech demands that the 'I' should give way almost completely to the 'there'. The audience should focus on the events that are described, *not* on the person giving the description, especially considering the graphic nature of those events – the blinding of Oedipus, the suicide of Antigone and Haimon, the madness of Heracles, the dismemberment of Pentheus. A messenger speech does not benefit from over-interpretation by a performing middle-man, but makes its strongest impact when the actor serves as the medium through which the audience create the off-stage events in their own imaginations.

It is true that the messenger always has a reason for being on the scene – the handmaid of Alcestis describes her mistress's farewell to the house, a servant of Medea describes the death of Glauke and Creon, and so on. However, the point is to present a credible eye-witness who can relate accurately what was said and done, not to lay the groundwork for a fully developed character. The messenger frequently sets up the narration dramatically, as if he or she were a member of an audience either privileged to be there, or forced to observe an event that no one would want to see. In *Heracles*, for example, the Messenger reports how the household gathered as participants in the sacrifice to celebrate Heracles' return and purify the house after the murder of Lycus. But confusion reigns among the servants at the strange behaviour of Heracles: 'Is our master playing, or has he gone insane?' (*Heracles*, 952). The concerned comment of an onlooker anticipates the horrible truth, for Heracles has been struck mad by Hera and proceeds to hunt down his own wife and children.

As this example suggests, a convention of messenger speeches involves the quoting of at least one passage of direct dialogue from someone on the scene. In Euripides' *Bacchae*, the second Messenger reports the words of both mother and son, Agave who is possessed by Bacchic madness and Pentheus who is spying on their mysteries. Agave calls on her fellow Bacchantes to uproot the tree in which her son sits, and the Messenger follows with Pentheus' desperate appeal: 'Mother, it is I, your son,/ Pentheus, whom you bore to Echion./ Mother, please, have mercy on me. I have/ done wrong, but I am your son. Don't kill me' (*Bacchae* 1118–21). Through their own words, crazed mother and doomed son come to life in a moment of tragic clarity, before the Messenger turns to the grisly details of Pentheus' dismemberment: 'One of them bore an arm,/ another a foot still in its boot, and his ribs/ were stripped with their rending. Every hand was red/ with the blood, as they played ball with Pentheus' flesh' (1133–36).

Although there are few passages in drama more gruesome than this, the convention of the Messenger does *not* entail the mistaken notion that all violence in Greek tragedy takes place off-stage. Physical pain, brutality, and even bloodshed do occur within sight of the audience – the hero commits suicide on stage in Sophocles' *Ajax*, the suppurating wound of the title character in *Philoctetes* is constantly before us, the tormented Heracles exposes his pain-wracked body in *Women of Trachis*, and a battered son dies in the arms of his father in Euripides' *Hippolytus*. What distinguishes the convention of the messenger speech is not the compulsion to avoid on-stage violence, but the absolute reliance on the audience's imagination to visualize and re-animate that violence in their minds' eye. We might compare the messenger's report to a modern radio play that depends on the imaginative participation of the audience for its success. Those who have worked in radio drama stress the medium's incomparable visual richness,[13] and the same quality infuses the messenger speeches in tragedy, where language and imagination do the work that modern theatre and film have surrendered too readily to technical wizardry and special effects.

## Stichomythia

Cut-and-thrust dialogue called stichomythia ('story by lines') constitutes another important convention of tragic rhetoric. It can take a variety of forms, normally alternating single lines of dialogue between two characters, but also two lines per speaker (distichs) or only half a line each (hemistichs), not unlike a pentameter line in Shakespeare split between two actors. Although employed in a variety of circumstances, stichomythia usually signals a quickening of tempo and focusing of dramatic energy. In its neutral function, it can mark the transition from the end of one speech to the beginning of the next. For example, the stichomythic exchange initiated by the chorus-leader in *Agamemnon* manoeuvres the Herald from his announcement of the fall of Troy to his account of the disastrous storm that destroyed the Greek fleet. Stichomythia also can be used to identify and welcome a new arrival on-stage, important in a large outdoor theatre where the actors are masked and character identity may not be visually self-evident.

As part of his exploration of tragic form, Euripides experimented boldly with stichomythia. In *Ion*, for example, Creusa's first meeting with her (unrecognized) son generates over *one hundred* lines of stichomythia, by far the longest stretch of such dialogue in tragedy. Here, the rapid exchange of questions, answers, and reactions replaces the series of speeches we would expect to establish the situation early in the play. By using stichomythia to provide the narrative background, Euripides ironically underlines the fact that mother and son, intimately connected by blood and symbolically drawn together in dialogue, continue to be separated by the self-serving secrecy of the god Apollo.

Often plots are laid in stichomythia, as in Euripides' *Electra* where the old Tutor and Orestes map out the murder of Aegisthus. After thirty-five lines alternating between the two, suddenly Electra enters the dialogue, replacing the troubled Orestes as interlocutor and introducing her own chilling plan to kill her mother. Alternatively, the catechistic form of stichomythia can bring a character to an understanding of some larger scheme in which he or she is the victim. In *Heracles*, for example, Amphitryon's dialogue with his son guides Heracles to the realization that he has killed his family in a fit of god-sent madness. In *Bacchae* the stichomythic exchange between Cadmus and his daughter Agave draws her out of her Bacchic frenzy until she sees that the lion's trophy she holds in her arms is really the head of her son Pentheus.

Frequently a character employs stichomythia to persuade another to change his mind. Clytemnestra's dialogue with her husband in *Agamemnon* leads to his walking on the tapestries against his better judgement. In *Philoctetes*, Neoptolemus has a series of stichomythic exchanges with Philoctetes and with Odysseus, highlighting the radically different choices facing the young man. Time and again he repeats the phrase *ti drasô*, 'What shall [should] I do?', perhaps *the* tragic question, whose recurrence reminds us of the strong ethical dimension in Greek drama.[14] By means of stichomythia, characters focus on the issues of choice, decision, and action as determined through engagement and dialogue with others, and not through abstract speculation.

The rapid exchange of alternative points of view also reflects the process by which Athenian juries reached their verdicts. But the lawcourts intermixed cross-examination with prepared speeches, a pattern we observe in such court-influenced tragedies as Sophocles' *Ajax*, where competing arguments for and against the burial of Ajax are presented by Menelaus, Teucer, and Agamemnon. Let us turn to this more elaborate convention of tragic rhetoric, the formal debate between two characters called an *agôn*, or 'contest'.

## The theatrical *agôn*

The political debate in the Assembly and legal judgements in the lawcourts provided the inspiration for comparable scenes on the Greek stage. We find a formal trial scene in Aeschylus' *Eumenides*, a fitting culmination to a trilogy imbued with legal terminology and metaphor, as we shall see in Chapter 6. Scenes of political debate on the relative merits of democracy figure prominently in both Aeschylus' and Euripides' *Suppliant Women* and in Sophocles' *Oedipus at Colonus*. References to specific Athenian political and legal practices occur in many tragedies, reminding us of the thoroughness with which the mythic and heroic characters articulate fifth-century concerns.

A manifestation of the political nature of tragedy is the convention of formal theatrical debate, called an *agôn*, in which a character makes a case as if speaking before a body of jurors or voters. That position is then attacked by the other party in the conflict, responding point by point like a lawyer or political opponent. Although recognizing the conventional aspects of the verbal exchange, the audience is encouraged to come to a judgement, to grapple with the arguments and apply them to the issues raised by the tragedy. Sometimes the play exposes the way that such rhetorical structures are manipulated to serve the ends of power; on other occasions the scene calls into question the efficacy and appropriateness of public debate itself.

The second half of Sophocles' *Ajax* consists primarily of arguments between Teucer and the brothers Menelaus and Agamemnon over the burial of Ajax. In their *agôns*, an ethical principle is challenged and ultimately reaffirmed, for Ajax's erstwhile enemy Odysseus helps to ensure that the burial takes place. The first encounter in *Medea* between Medea and her estranged husband takes the form of a prosecution and defence. By the time the two cases have been argued, Jason has inverted almost everything the audience knows to be true, flouting the very aspects of Greek culture that he claims to have introduced to Medea. He resembles those fifth-century Athenian politicians (and their modern epigones) who clothe personal advantage in terms of justice, making a mockery of the values and institutions they claim to support.

Euripides scrutinizes various argumentative strategies in the *agôns* of other plays. In *Alcestis*, Pheres precipitates a bitter debate with his son Admetus, interrupting the funeral procession for Alcestis who has sacrificed herself for her husband. Ostensibly gathered in her honour, the two men escalate their mutual recriminations until the funeral situation is forgotten. In this *agôn*, played out before Alcestis' corpse, neither party wins and the debate itself is grossly out of place. In *Trojan Women*, Hecuba is confident that a debate will demonstrate the bankruptcy of Helen's sophistry and persuade Menelaus that his unfaithful wife deserves to die. Replete with tonal ambiguities and rhetorical flourishes, the *agôn* between the old woman and young beauty seems at odds with the sombre atmosphere of the play. Hecuba's faith in the efficacy of words is as ill founded as it is touching, for the scene reveals the futility of rational discourse when events have reached such a stage. No matter what is said, Menelaus will welcome Helen back to his marriage bed and Hecuba will continue to suffer.

An even more problematic *agôn* involves the tyrant Lycus and Amphitryon in *Heracles*. Before killing Heracles' family who are suppliants at the altar of Zeus, Lycus unleashes a verbal assault on Heracles for using a bow, the weapon of a coward. In response, Amphitryon does not confront Lycus' treachery, or appeal to the rights of suppliants, or even expose the tyrant's own cowardice. Instead he mounts a point-by-point defence of his son's use of the bow rather than the traditional armour and tactics of the hoplite infantryman. Critics claim that the issue was a topical one in military strategy, and others argue that the bow serves as a problematic image of Heracles' courage. But neither of these explanations accounts for the presence of such extended rhetoric, especially given the dramatic circumstances.

Perhaps Euripides lingers over these speeches to force the audience to consider what lies *behind* the convention itself. Full of contemporary sophistry and 'legalese', the bow debate dramatizes a miss, an *agôn* of ineffectiveness, a failure to engage the important matters of the play. Perhaps the fifth-century audience recognized the misdirected speeches that made up a good portion of public debate during the Peloponnesian War, in full swing at the time of the play's production. If so, then Euripides uses the convention of the formal *agôn* to expose how public rhetoric can skirt or even *displace* crucial issues, as opposed to confronting them directly.

## COSTUMES, PROPS, AND CORPSES

The costumes worn by tragic performers were what we would call 'modern dress' – they resembled contemporary fifth-century clothing and did not aim at reflecting historicist notions of authentic Bronze Age, archaic, or heroic attire. This situation applied not only to the characters' domestic and public costume, but also to military apparel, armour, and hand props (swords, bows, and the like) in plays set during the Trojan War. The contemporary look of the actors, coupled with anachronisms from the civic, political, and military spheres, suggests that the tragedies of the last third of the fifth century set during the heroic wars at Troy or Thebes brought the Peloponnesian War (431–04) immediately to mind.

This is not to imply that an Athenian spectator saw his next-door neighbour on-stage, or mistook tragic action for a slice of life. Nonetheless, the actor playing Agamemnon in *Iphigenia in Aulis*, for example, dressed more or less like a contemporary, and spoke a poetic, but recognizable, version of Athenian speech. His concerns about how to prosecute the war, and what sacrifices it was worth, resonated with contemporary relevance for the Athenians in the theatre. A modern production could do worse than aim for a similar combination of distance and proximity *vis-à-vis* its contemporary audience.

Bridging the gap between the heroic characters and the fifth century, tragic costumes and props often mirrored specific aspects of Athenian ritual life. Evadne appears in her wedding dress in Euripides' *Suppliant Women*, in marked contrast to the chorus who wear the black robes of mourning. So, too, Cassandra in *Trojan Women* perversely celebrates her upcoming wedding with Agamemnon, to the point of carrying her own nuptial torches, normally borne by the mothers of the bride and groom. In *Alcestis*, Admetus dresses in black with his hair cut in mourning to lead the funeral procession of Alcestis. At the end of the play, however, Heracles miraculously hands back the resurrected Alcestis, who is dressed and veiled like a bride, and Admetus accepts the 'stranger' much as a husband does his new wife at an Athenian wedding.

As well as contemporizing ritual activities in tragedy, prop and costume elements could indicate status and character: staffs for old men like the chorus of *Heracles* and for blind prophets like Teiresias in *Antigone*; swords for Aegisthus' guards in *Agamemnon*; special robes to indicate service to a god for the Pythia in *Eumenides* and the priestess Theonoe in *Helen*; wands wound with cotton to identify suppliants in the various suppliant plays; and so on. Costumes could take on a graphically realistic flavour, as in the rags of Euripidean characters that are parodied mercilessly in the comedies of Aristophanes. The shipwrecked Menelaus arrives in tatters in *Helen*, and his change of costume near the end of the play signals a return to the old warrior. In *Electra* the embittered protagonist bemoans her rags and poverty, and makes much of the water-jug she hauls back from the spring. However, she ignores her husband's offer of help with the water-carrying and rejects the chorus's gifts of more festive clothing, revealing herself to be oppressed by wilful self-martyrdom as much as by circumstance.

For all his notoriety, Euripides was not the first to use costume and props to suggest suffering and deprivation. Aeschylus builds the climax of his *Persians* around the return of the defeated commander Xerxes, who is dressed in rags. The Greek word for his apparel, *stolos*, also is used for Persia's naval fleet destroyed at the battle of Salamis. Arrayed in tattered garments and bearing an empty quiver, the young king symbolically wears the defeat of his empire. Sophocles, too, uses distressed costumes to suggest the abject suffering of his hero, from the suppurating wound and wild appearance of the title figure in *Philoctetes* to the tormented Heracles in *Women of Trachis*, borne on a litter and crying in anguish as he uncovers his poison-burnt body.

More common than the representation of physical agony in tragedy is the appearance of corpses or other remains of the dead (usually requiring a corps of mute actors to bring them on- and off-stage). A formal procession escorts the body of Alcestis out for burial, and a similar cortège brings the corpse of Neoptolemus into the theatre in *Andromache*. The bodies of the recovered seven against Thebes are paraded in the orchestra in *Suppliant Women*, and afterwards their orphaned sons return bearing the urns of their ashes. These and other spectacles of the dead recall the importance of burial rites to the Greeks, where preparation of the corpse and funeral rites were performed by the family, not by professionals. In *Antigone* the issue is the catalyst for the tragic action, for Antigone decides to bury Polyneices in spite of Creon's decree outlawing such rites. Although Antigone dies for her actions, it is Creon who must bury the corpses of his loved ones at the end of the play. He returns carrying the body of his son, Haimon, only to learn of his wife's suicide as well. She is revealed on the *ekkyklêma* draped over the household altar, a striking image of the death of Creon's home.

Costume, props, and a corpse often come together at key dramatic moments, a concentrated image of the central action. Sophocles has the tortured heroine in his *Electra* hear the (false) news of her brother's death, and she mourns over his ashes in what she thinks is his funeral urn. Miraculously, the empty container leads Electra to the living Orestes, who reverses the trick at the end of the play. The purported corpse of Orestes lures Aegisthus on-stage, but the covered body is revealed to be that of the murdered Clytemnestra, with Aegisthus soon to join her. In Euripides' *Trojan Women*, the Greeks hurl Astyanax, the young son of Hector and Andromache, from the walls of Troy. His broken body is carried on-stage cradled in the great shield of his father, a chilling symbol of the death of the city's hopes, and the merciless cruelty of the conquerors.

Perhaps the most daring conjunction of costumes, corpse, and dramatic action occurs in Euripides' *Bacchae*. In the famous 'drag scene', Pentheus dresses up in women's clothing to spy on the Bacchic mysteries. We laugh at his cross-dressing ('Is my head cover sitting right?' 'How is the line of my dress?' 930–31, 935–36), but the fact that he is totally under Dionysus' spell gives the laughter a vicious twist. More disturbing for the original audience was the fact that the woman's garment Pentheus puts on reaches to his feet, not normal for Athenian dress but standard for burial raiment. Dionysus dresses Pentheus not only for the Mysteries, but also for his funeral. At the end of the play, Cadmus returns with the dismembered bits of Pentheus' body torn apart by the Theban women in their Dionysiac frenzy, an appropriate closing image for the play's devastating fragmentation.

In some tragedies, stage props provide the locus for choice, a symbol of the dilemma that the tragic hero faces. In Sophocles' *Ajax*, the sword that Ajax received from Hector comes to represent his outmoded heroism and serves as the means of his suicide. In *Philoctetes*, a prophecy states that the hero's bow must be brought to Troy if the Greeks are to take the city. For the wounded and marooned Philoctetes, the weapon is his sole means of survival; for Odysseus, it is the guarantee of victory that he must obtain at all costs; for Neoptolemus the bow comes to represent the ethical choice he faces, resolved when he decides to return the weapon to the wretched hero who entrusted it to him. In the final scene of Euripides' *Heracles*, the protagonist also confronts his bow – the attribute of his heroic labours, but also the instrument of his family's murder. By taking up the weapon, Heracles metaphorically shoulders his tragic past and acknowledges a hostile future, transformed into a new kind of hero as he leaves for Athens.

Less violent props include the letter in *Hippolytus* left by Phaedra after her suicide, although its accusations lead Theseus to utter his fatal curse on his son. More salvific is the letter in *Iphigenia among the Taurians*, which the heroine reads aloud and sets off the recognition between her and Orestes. In *Ion* the tokens that Creusa exposed with her baby act as 'non-verbal' letters, speaking after many years to establish Ion's identity. The pattern of last-minute recognition based on tokens from the past recurs in other plays of Euripides, and in many of his lost works. It became the mainstay of recognition scenes in the New Comedy of Menander, the dramatic genre that became the popular form in the latter part of the fourth century.[15]

## STARTING AND STOPPING THE PLAY: THE PROLOGUE, *DEUS EX MACHINA*, AND THE GOD'S EYE VIEW

Like most plays, Greek tragedies come 'out of nowhere' and adopt some form of closure at the end. Depending on the play, the opening section maps out the dramatic terrain, provides the horizon line against which we are to see the key events, or clarifies the theatrical impulse that shapes the subsequent action. Similarly, the manner in which a tragedy ends can confirm or frustrate our sense of resolution, turning us back to the issues of the play in a thoughtful, chastened, or disillusioned way.

Aeschylus' *Persians*, our earliest surviving tragedy, opens with the entrance of the chorus, appropriate for a play concerned with a people and not an individual protagonist. The gathering of elders in the orchestra is the peaceful counterpart to the great armed convoys they evoke in their song. At the close, their *kommos* with Xerxes marks a fitting end, as the mournful procession out of the theatre reverses their hopeful arrival at the start of the play.

Usually, however, Greek tragedy begins not with the chorus but with a dramatic character delivering a monologue before the chorus enter in the *parodos*. Sometimes the speaker proves to be the protagonist, as with Orestes in *Choephori*, sometimes a less important character, such as Aethra in Euripides' *Suppliant Women*, and on occasion a virtual non-character as in *Ion*, where the god Hermes delivers the prologue and then leaves the play for good.

Often the opening speaker is joined by another, giving a stronger sense of ongoing action as the audience-oriented monologue shifts to an actor-to-actor dialogue. In Euripides' *Medea*, for example, the Nurse welcomes the audience into the play, evoking the legendary journey of Jason and the Argonauts, only to displace the heroic world with one of domestic and marital turmoil. The arrival of the Tutor with Medea's and Jason's children confirms the gap between the epic past and the apparently mundane present. The scene between the Nurse and Tutor is unique in tragedy, consisting of two household servants, a scenario more at home in Greek comedy. Their dialogue establishes a familiar and contemporary tone, important in a play that exposes the destructive nature of the heroic code that leads Medea to slaughter her own children.

The most dramatically charged prologues are those that begin immediately with dialogue, as the scene between Antigone and Ismene at the start of Sophocles' *Antigone*. Here, the conflict evident at the outset prefigures the greater oppositions that emerge in the course of the play. In the opening of *Ajax*, Sophocles goes further, exploiting *three* different perspectives. Speaking from the *theologeion* (the roof of the skene-building), Athena urges Odysseus to revel at the plight of his rival Ajax, whom the goddess has driven mad. From his position below, Odysseus refuses to mock a fellow-mortal, fearful that he could end in the same situation. The *ekkyklēma* rolls out to reveal Ajax surrounded by the carcasses of the sheep that he slaughtered in the delusion that he was killing the treacherous Greeks. Caught between the beasts before him and the goddess above, Ajax embodies the tragic human condition, to which Odysseus finds himself drawn in pity, foreshadowing his role at the end of the play as the champion of Ajax's burial.

Some opening scenes involve two gods, as in Euripides' *Alcestis* where Apollo's monologue is interrupted by the arrival of Thanatos ('Death'), a folkloric bogyman who has come to claim Alcestis. His physical presence establishes that death is a character who can be fought and defeated (at least temporarily), setting up Heracles' miraculous rescue of Alcestis from the grave at the end of the play. The debate between Apollo and Thanatos on their respective plutocratic and egalitarian principles introduces a humorous note that resurfaces several times, supporting age-old doubts about the play's genre. *Alcestis* was the fourth offering in Euripides' tetralogy of 438, meaning that it was performed in place of a satyr-play, even though it lacks a satyr chorus.

Euripides returns to the two-god prologue in *Trojan Women*, where Poseidon describes the situation in Troy after the Greek conquest, pointing out to the audience the prostrate Hecuba who took her position in the orchestra during a cancelled entry. The arrival of Athena transforms the opening from a monologue about the past to a dialogue that predicts the future. Angry over their sacrilege at Troy, Athena persuades Poseidon to destroy the Greek ships on their way home from the war. Although the gods never reappear after the prologue, their opening exchange colours the audience's response to the play. As the Greek brutality escalates, we know that they are blind to the greater forces that will destroy them in turn.

Euripides developed many variations on conventional openings, until his prologues developed into a kind of sub-genre like his messenger speeches, with repeated elements and modifications recurring in play after play. For example, in his innovative version of the story of *Electra*, Euripides gives us *two* prologues. The honest and down-to-earth Farmer emerges from his rustic cottage to deliver the opening monologue, explaining that he was given Electra in marriage, but he has respected her desires and not slept with her. His speech deftly establishes the innate difference between his honest and direct nature and the self-martyring tendencies of his wife. After the stage empties, we expect the chorus to enter in the *parodos*, but instead Euripides gives us a second prologue as Orestes returns incognito from exile, fearful of being recognized but not afraid to talk. Significantly, it is only after the Farmer leaves for good (431) that the play turns its attention to vengeance, as if murder could not be countenanced in the presence of someone like him.

Turning to the end of tragedies, the most difficult convention to understand is also the most familiar, the so-called *deus ex machina* or 'god from the machine'. The machine was a kind of crane used to suggest movement through the air; at other times gods and goddesses appeared on the roof of the skene-building, known as the *theologeion*. Taking their cue from Aristotle's judgement that the *deus*-ending in *Medea* is inadequate, Renaissance critics associated the appearance of a god at the end of a play with an artificial, last-minute resolution to an inept plot.[16] This description fits few, if any, Greek tragedies; when it does seem to apply, a closer look reveals a lively dramatic tension at work between the body of the play and its dénouement.

The appearance of a divinity near the end of a tragedy interrupts the action, surprising the dramatic characters and the audience alike. Although the device became increasingly popular later in the fifth century, not every tragedy employs a *deus ex machina* and there is no way of predicting on the basis of earlier action if a god will appear at the end. The *deus*-figure usually provides an explanation of what has transpired, predicts what lies ahead, and offers an aetiology for the foundation of a cult connected with the tragic events. The combination of summary and prophecy carries the material of the play into the fifth century, in that the cult practices described by the *deus* usually were well known to the audience. But even with a link to the present, the sense of closure provided by a *deus ex machina* varies enormously from play to play. Irony, iconoclasm, and camouflage can operate no less than the sense that expectations have been fulfilled and the rough edges rounded off.

It would be wrong to confuse the utterances of a highly theatrical stage divinity with divinely sanctioned truths from Olympus, or to conclude that the god provides the key to the play's meaning, or serves as the mouthpiece for the poet. Take, for example, the *ex machina* appearance of the Dioskouroi, Castor and Pollux, at the end of Euripides' *Electra*. Although the twin gods are connected to the action as the brothers of Clytemnestra and Helen, their entrance is neither required by the plot nor expected by the characters on-stage. Pollux remains silent, following the convention of a dramatic mute such as Pylades earlier in the play, but Castor has come to talk. He insists that Apollo bears the responsibility for the murder of Clytemnestra, a proposition that receives little support from the body of the play. Castor then reveals that the Trojan War was fought over a phantom Helen, part of Zeus' plan to unleash strife among mortals. Turning to the future, the god arranges for Electra to marry Pylades, who will set up her erstwhile husband, the Farmer, in business. Orestes will be absolved of his crime in a trial at Athens, where a cult of the Furies will be established, while he travels north to found an eponymous city in Arcadia.

The *deus* speech in *Electra* gains little purchase on the play as experienced by the characters or the audience. Euripides has revealed the all-too-human motivations for murder, and the claim that it was all Apollo's fault convinces only the gullible. The god's assurance that happiness awaits brother and sister has little effect on Orestes and Electra, who stand drenched in their mother's blood. After an initial question, they barely acknowledge the voice from on high. For all the excuses, revelations, and promises uttered *ex machina*, Castor cannot break through to the mortal sphere, where guilt and regret, finally acknowledged, are not so easily dismissed. It is as if Castor were trying to rewrite the ending at the last minute, like a political spin-doctor in the US presidential debates, convincing the audience that something contrary to their experience has, in fact, taken place.

The *deus* convention allows the playwright to probe the relationship between humans and their gods. At the end of Euripides' *Hippolytus*, Artemis leaves the *theologeion* because Hippolytus is dying – being immortal, she wants nothing to do with death. Abandoned by the goddess he has served, Hippolytus forgives his father whose curse has killed him, affirming purely human values in an inhuman universe.[17] At the opposite end of the spectrum is the realization that the god from the machine can be too much *like* a human. At the end of Euripides' *Bacchae*, Dionysus manifests his divinity after striking Agave mad and causing her to kill her own son Pentheus. Confronted with the horror of Pentheus' dismemberment, Agave's father

Cadmus cries out to the deity who has destroyed him: 'Gods should not be like men in their anger' (1348).

On other occasions, the *deus* resolution is so improbable that it forces the audience to reconsider the situation that *almost* transpired, in the manner of Gay's *Beggar's Opera* and Brecht's *Threepenny Opera*. The clearest example is Euripides' *Orestes*, where a triple-levelled dénouement aggravates the horror of the play by virtue of its very incongruity. After killing Helen and setting fire to Menelaus' palace, Orestes stands on the *theologeion* representing the palace roof, holding a sword at the throat of Menelaus' daughter, Hermione. Menelaus himself looks on helplessly at the orchestra level, locked out of his burning home. Suddenly Apollo appears from the machine to halt the proceedings, announcing that Helen was spirited away before her death and now dwells as an immortal among the stars. Apollo then directs Orestes to put down the sword and take Hermione as his wife, a marriage union that Menelaus accepts without protest. Not to leave anyone out, the god arranges for Electra to marry Pylades, and a tragedy of blood-crazed madness arrives at its 'happy ending'.

*Deus* endings are associated particularly with Euripides, as over half his extant tragedies conclude with a god or goddess appearing on high. But Sophocles, too, utilized divine appearances, and we know that in his lost *Niobe* Apollo and Artemis suddenly appear on the roof in the middle of the play. While her brother Apollo speaks, Artemis, armed with her bow, picks off one by one the daughters of Niobe, who stand in the palace courtyard behind the façade.[18] Sophocles also ends his *Philoctetes* with the totally unexpected appearance of Heracles on the *theologeion*. Loath to think Sophocles could be as theatrically daring as Euripides, critics continue to argue that Heracles' command that Philoctetes go to Troy is a perfectly natural, rather than a disturbingly ironic, close to the drama. Similar problems posed by the *deus ex machina* endings arise in Euripides' *Suppliant Women* and *Ion*, discussed in Chapters 8 and 9.

A variation on the convention of the *deus ex machina* is those occasions when a mortal character arrives in godlike fashion to effect a sudden change. In Euripides' *Heracles*, the goddesses Lyssa and Iris appear unexpectedly in the middle of the play to strike Heracles mad. They are 'replaced' at the end by the equally unexpected arrival of the Athenian hero Theseus, who tries to redeem on a human level what the gods have destroyed from above. His efforts to convince Heracles to persevere and make his life in Athens raise questions about human society, friendship, heroism, and the kind of gods who are worth worshipping.

If the *deus*-like Theseus brings comfort and encouragement, the appearance from the machine of the protagonist in Euripides' *Medea* does just the opposite. Jason rushes on-stage ready to break down the palace door and save his sons, and we expect the *ekkyklêma* to roll out revealing their dead bodies. Nothing prepares us for Medea's appearance on high in a chariot of the sun, her children's corpses draped over the railings. Invested with all the properties and functions of a stage divinity, she stands above her estranged husband, predicting the future, and providing the aetiology of a cult in Corinth that will expiate the murders. There is no mistaking that Medea triumphs absolutely in this *coup de théâtre*, and yet triumph implies a victor. The Medea we see has been destroyed, emptied of all maternal love and compassion. As her vile exchange with Jason suggests, she occupies the position of a stage goddess only to emphasize the dehumanizing effect of what she has done, removed from Jason and cut off from the sympathy that once tied her to the audience. The fact that Medea will make her way to Athens, the city of the original performance, indicates that Euripides locates the issues of the play very much in his contemporary world, using the convention of the *deus ex machina* to bring those problems home to his audience with special force.

## THE *AGÔN* IN THE AUDIENCE

Many tragic conventions appear self-evident, in that we might expect something similar in any attempt to represent intelligible characters through a dramatic medium. But even in such standard conventions as costume, speech, and gesture, Greek tragedy built a far more immediate relationship with its audience than we often are led to believe. The costumes were contemporary, the specialized gestures reflected the world of ritual activity familiar to the audience, and the dialogue, although poetic, adopted a rhythmical form closer to everyday speech than its epic predecessor. Even the complex lyric of the chorus contains elements from other genres well known in the fifth century, including cult hymns, epinician odes, wedding songs, funeral laments, and so on.

More elaborate conventions involving rhetoric and formal debates point to the world of the Athenian Assembly, the lawcourts, the agora, the day-to-day arguments and decision-making that played an important role in democratic public life. Even the appearance of stage divinities reveals a tendency towards incorporating the local and familiar. Zeus, the father and *primus inter pares* of the Olympian gods, seems never to have appeared on the Attic stage, although he often is addressed and prayed to. On the other hand, Athena, the patron goddess of Athens – whose image adorned public buildings, free-standing sculpture, and the coins of the city – appears several times. In the setting of the action or the destination of the protagonist at the end, several tragedies forge an especially strong link with the city of Athens. The implication is not that she offers a refuge from tragic conflict, but quite the opposite, that the city of the audience is where the tragic tensions meet and must be confronted.

The conventions of tragedy return us to our starting point, the performance culture of Athens where a participatory democracy played out its political and ethical concerns in an aggressively public and performative fashion. In terms of tragic theatre, the conventions of representation allowed a variety of contemporary elements to be drawn into, and indeed to inform, the dramatizations of the myths and legends of the past. Empowered by such conventions, and the willingness to experiment with them, the tragic playwrights brought their stories home to the audience with such urgency and power that, paradoxically, they transcend their local origins and speak across the centuries.

# Part II

# EXEMPLARY PLAYS

# 6

# AESCHYLUS' *ORESTEIA* TRILOGY

At the City Dionysia of 458 BC, two years before his death, Aeschylus presented his dramatization of the myth of the house of Atreus. Later known as the *Oresteia* ('the story of Orestes'), Aeschylus' version takes the form of a connected trilogy that unfolds in chronological sequence, with continuity of subject-matter, imagery, characters, and story-line. *Agamemnon* tells of the title figure's return after conquering Troy, and his murder (along with his Trojan concubine Cassandra) at the hands of his wife Clytemnestra, who seizes power with her lover Aegisthus. Her exiled son Orestes returns to avenge his father's death, murdering Clytemnestra and Aegisthus with the help of Electra and the slave-women of the house, who give the second play its name, *Choephori* or *Libation Bearers*. After the matricide, Orestes is pursued by the Furies, spirits who take vengeance on those who shed kindred blood, tracking him first to Delphi and then to Athens. There Athena establishes a court to try cases of homicide, and the goddess herself breaks the jury's deadlock by voting to free Orestes. She calms the Furies' anger, persuading them to reside in Athens as spirits of marriage and fertility, transforming them into 'the kindly ones' or *Eumenides*, the title of the third play. Following the trilogy a satyr-play, *Proteus* (now lost), told the escapades of Menelaus, Agamemnon's brother and husband of Helen, when he was shipwrecked in Egypt on his way home from Troy.

To understand how the trilogy works requires a double focus. First, we must remain alert to the theatrical unity of the piece and the various ways in which Aeschylus achieves it, combining an incomparably rich poetic text with a strong sense of dramatic momentum. But we also must attend to the differences that operate from play to play, for the triadic structure means that each tragedy establishes its own relationship to the audience. With this double focus we engage the moment-to-moment unfolding of events, even as we place them in the larger pattern of history and chronology that the trilogy compasses.

In *Agamemnon* the action plays itself out in a murky light. Ambiguity and *double entendre*, dark prophecy and deceptive hopes create an atmosphere of anxious uncertainty. Events and emotions keep turning into their opposites

77

– affirmation leads to denial, good news presages disaster, victory breeds defeat, beauty gives rise to destruction – as the triumphant return of the king proves but a prelude to his murder. In contrast to *Agamemnon*, the action of *Choephori* is tightly focused, unfolding with precision and clarity, almost claustrophobic in its effect. Aeschylus radically alters the relationship between stage and auditorium by drawing the spectators into the murder plot as co-conspirators, committed to the plan and its success. The audience's relationship to the dramatic events shifts again in *Eumenides*, where the mythical Orestes moves out of his own story and into that of Athens, playing a crucial role in the foundation of Athenian civic, ritual, and legal customs. Here the fifth-century audience approximated the jurors at Orestes' trial, arriving at a judgement and yet aware of how the case (and the drama itself) was subsumed in the virtual history of their own city.

The trilogy works via a progressive movement towards the audience – from obscurity to clarity, from past to present, from monarchy to tyranny to democracy, from retributive to collective justice, from ancient Argos to near-contemporary Athens. The theatrical embodiment of the process lies in the transformation of verbal imagery into dramatic action, the realization of the world implicit in the word, as language literally 'takes the stage'. Pivotal images and figures of speech assume a visual and physical life, until the institutions of the city where the play was performed are 'founded' before the audience's eyes, and with their help.

# AGAMEMNON

The *Oresteia* begins with one of the great opening monologues in the history of drama (1–39). An unassuming Watchman lies on the roof of the house, waiting for the beacon fire that will bring news of Troy's fall. With his first word 'Gods!', he begs the higher powers to release him from the pain of a year's watch. He speaks of the great cycle of stars, doubtful that in such a panoply a single torchlight could appear, but still he obeys 'the command/ of a woman who thinks like a man' (10–11). The sudden appearance of the beacon turns his fear for the house to joy, the fire-signal gleaming like the dawn of a new day. As the Watchman leaves to wake Clytemnestra and 'start the dance' (31), he recovers some of his early guardedness, refusing to divulge what he knows, but calling on the house to tell its own story.

Like all well-written dramatic characters, the Watchman has something specific to do – stay awake, keep watch, spread the news when a single torch ignites the story of Agamemnon's return. His monologue has a natural ring to it, as if he were welcoming the audience into the play. But the prologue also presents a tightly wrapped bundle of proleptic themes and images that will be played out over the next three and a half hours in the theatre – the gods, sickness and pain, night and day, sleeping and wakefulness, women and men, good news and conquest, speech and silence.

The Watchman's desire to 'start the dance' anticipates the entrance of the chorus, old men of the city left behind when the army sailed for Troy. The *parodos* opens with an anapaestic prelude (40–82) that moves back ten years earlier, when the brothers Agamemnon and Menelaus first 'brought suit against Priam' (41) in the form of the Trojan War. Priam's son Paris had abducted Helen, the wife of his Greek host Menelaus and sister of Agamemnon's wife Clytemnestra. In so doing, Paris violated the Greek code of hospitality, *xenia*, guaranteed by the god Zeus, who sends the two sons of Atreus and a thousand ships to win Helen back. The chorus call the war-dead 'a first offering' (literally, a 'preliminary sacrifice', 65), the word referring to the sacrifice before a wedding, presumably that of Paris and Helen. The perversion of a marriage ceremony is the first of many such maimed rituals in the trilogy, linking weddings with death.

The chorus themselves emphasize their age ('fallen leaves that crumble', 79–80) and powerlessness ('we wander, a dream through the daylight', 82). And yet they suddenly grow animated by the sacrifices that burn through the city. Addressing the absent queen Clytemnestra, they wonder if the burnt offerings mean that good news has come from Troy. The very thought of Clytemnestra and the prospects of victory overcome their impotence and energize their reflections, serving as the catalyst for the chorus's shift from anapaests into full lyric.

Characteristic of the play, the same impulse that drives the action forward takes us back in time, back to the scene at Aulis before the Greek army sailed for Troy. In the complex lyric that follows, a series of narrative vignettes – what we might call 'choral events' – stands out. The chorus recall the eagles that appeared as portents of success, until 'swooping down on a pregnant hare big with young,/ they tore and feasted' (118–20). The chorus try to reverse the pattern of good omens turning bad by sounding a refrain they will repeat two more times in the course of the *parodos*: 'Sing sorrow, sorrow, but may good win out in the end' (121).

The chorus re-enact the prophet Calchas' interpretation of the oracle, with a single chorus member delivering Calchas' lines, a technique that operates later in the ode when Agamemnon sacrifices his daughter. The prophet predicts triumph, but prays that no god 'darken the bit/ you forge on Troy' (131–33), leading the chorus to repeat their refrain of sorrow that hopes for victory. The group then turn their thoughts to the ships penned in at Aulis by contrary winds, a delay in the war that leads to a more ominous sacrifice than that of the pregnant hare, and to strife that (literally) 'lies in wait, terrible, ready to break out again,/ keeping house with deceit, a child-avenging wrath that never forgets' (154–55). The piling-up of adjectives gives some sense of the complexity of Aeschylean lyric. The two lines evoke the sacrifice of Iphigenia at Aulis and of Agamemnon at Argos, and the feast of Thyestes in the previous generation, but the references are muted and jumbled, waiting for the play to elucidate them.

As if voicing the audience's desire for clarity, the chorus sing for the last time their refrain that sorrow might achieve some ultimate good. They then utter a desperate prayer to Zeus, the god 'who sets men on the path/ to learn by suffering' (176–78). Acknowledging that divine wisdom comes violently, against men's will, the chorus consider the Greek army at Aulis as an example of this cosmic lesson. Angry at the eagles' feast of the pregnant hare, the goddess Artemis sends contrary winds to keep the ships from sailing. While the soldiers grow restless, Agamemnon as commander-in-chief must either sacrifice his daughter to assuage the goddess or abandon the expedition. A single chorus member takes on the role of the tortured king, debating with himself (still in lyric) as he realizes there is no way without evil. The group describes how Agamemnon 'put on the yoke of necessity' (218), a paradox that emphasizes both his individual choice and the way that fate necessitates it. To rephrase the decision, we might say that Agamemnon freely chooses to do what he in fact has to, a situation re-enacted later in the play when he walks on the red tapestries.

The climax to this extraordinary *parodos* is the re-creation of the sacrifice of Iphigenia, an innocent girl whose blood is shed so that more blood can flow. Through the vivid language and choral movement, we see her pray to her father for mercy while the soldiers shout for war. Bound and gagged, lifted like a goat over the altar, Iphigenia strikes each of her killers with eyes that cause pity, like a picture straining to speak. The images are striking, unforgettable – a twisted sacrifice, the perversion of paternal love in the face of the cry for war, the death of innocence, the waste of a young life. On the verge of the fatal blow, the chorus stop short and refuse to say what happened. Their sudden reticence reminds us of the Watchman at the end of the prologue, who also refuses to divulge all that he knows.

Suddenly the chorus-leader shifts into iambic trimeters and greets Clytemnestra, who enters from the palace. Her first words cap the opening movement of the play: 'Good news! as the saying goes,/ when dawn is born from her mother night./ Joy beyond your greatest hopes – / the Greeks have seized Troy' (264–67). The confirmation of triumph coincides with the appearance of Clytemnestra, who will dominate the play both rhetorically and dramatically from now on.

In her famous Fire speech, Clytemnestra describes the beacon signals that announce Agamemnon's victory with a series of stunning similes – torches like a relay race, bonfires that rise up like the sun and then break through the clouds like a full moon, flames racing like ships across the water and dancing in the clear mirror of the sea. Even as the language dazzles, it draws the worlds of Argos and Troy together, bound by a chain of fire. The news that arrives at the house of Atreus is a blaze descended from the holocaust of Troy.

Clytemnestra further explores the relationship between the Greek victors and their Trojan victims in her next speech, imagining the chaos of a fallen city. Psychically attuned to the victims, she creates the pathetic scene of Trojans falling on the bodies of their dead, of women weeping for their husbands, of children clutching at the legs of the old men. The Greek conquerors, on the other hand, roam the city freely and sleep 'like happy men,/a night when no guard stands watch' (336–37). Implying their defences have fallen too quickly, Clytemnestra fears that the Greek army may be 'conquered by what they have won' (342). They still must return home, where 'the anger of the slaughtered may wake,/ and evil break out again' (346–47).

With these two extraordinary speeches, Clytemnestra forces us to see that the fate of Troy and that of Argos are bound inextricably together. With her poetic and rhetorical power, she takes control of the play, and as she returns to the palace we know that she is the force to be reckoned with.

Left alone in the orchestra, the chorus celebrate the victory in their first stasimon, returning to their view that Zeus guarantees the rights of *xenia*, punishing mortals who 'trample untouchable things' (371). They move from the general idea of human excess to the specific example of Paris, who came as a guest to Menelaus' home and stole his wife. The chorus also consider Helen, who brought to Troy a 'dowry of death' (406–08), and then they cross the waters back to Menelaus and Sparta. The household laments the royal bed and the fading print of Helen's body, and Menelaus finds no respite in sleep, for the dreams of his lost wife slip through his arms.

The chorus leap quite naturally across space and time, just as they did when alternating between human victory and its divine underpinnings at the opening of the stasimon. Changing focus again, they leave the royal palaces for the hearth of an average Greek home, where a lone woman confronts the deadly commerce of war:

> War is a money-changer of bodies;
> his balance rests on the point of a spear.
> From the fires of Troy, he sends dust that weighs heavy –
> packed in the hold
> > urns swollen with powder
> to take the place of a man.
>
> (*Ag.*, 437–44)

The blow of Zeus, so clearly marked in the fate of Paris and the fall of Troy, also operates on the Greeks who conquered the city. Popular anger swells against Agamemnon and Menelaus, and the stasimon ends in a mood far different from the jubilation with which it began. A great victory has turned into a series of defeats, and collective celebration at the sack of a city gives way to individual grief. The shift is so complete that the chorus begin to doubt the news of the victory itself, wondering if the beacon-story was simply Clytemnestra's dream, a woman's rumour, swift to spread and swift to die (486–87).

A bedraggled figure enters the orchestra through one of the *eisodoi*, no spectacular return of a victorious army but the arrival of a solitary soldier. The chorus leave the lyric mode to welcome him in regular iambic trimeter, a human voice that will confirm or deny the wordless message of the beacon.[1] Instead of news of victory, however, the Herald expresses his amazement that he has come back at all, 'with all my hopes shattered except one – / that I might . . ./ die here, and be buried in my home soil' (505–07). After enumerating the simple pleasures of survival – the earth, the sunlight, the sight of home, the presence of protecting divinities – the Herald celebrates a victory that eradicates those very blessings:

> Digging up the soil of Troy,
> he [Agamemnon] worked it with the pick-axe of Zeus –
> altars smashed, temples rubble,
> the seed of the land destroyed.
>
> (525–28)

Agamemnon has 'yoked' Troy, paying Paris back for the rape of Helen that 'harvested' only death for his country (529–36). The reversals are complete – the natural world is uprooted and the places of the gods obliterated. Clytemnestra's warning that the Greeks let 'no passion make them ravage what they should not' (341–42) has gone unheeded.

A strange stichomythic exchange follows, the first real dialogue in the play, and yet one that brings very little to light. The chorus-leader adumbrates that those at home also suffered during the army's absence, but he refuses to elaborate, using silence as a 'long-practised remedy from harm' (548). For the third time in the play, the dark side of the past is exposed only to be covered up with silence. As the Herald tries to understand the veiled hints, he finds himself drawn back to the war – the blazing sun on the decks of the ships, the dank heat and sweat of their berths, the worm-eaten rations, the fear of camping near the walls of the enemy, the steady drizzle, the slow rot of their clothes, the teeming lice, and the winter cold that slaughtered birds, sweeping down from Mt Ida. After his graphic account of the realities of war, the Herald desperately tries to resurrect the joy of conquest:

> But why count the dead?
> Have we lived only to think of them?
> Must their wounds break out again?
> No! I say good-bye to disaster./. . ./
> It is good to boast in the light of the sun,
> my words soaring over all land and sea,
> Troy has fallen! . . .
>
> (570–77)

But the shift to the triumphant mode seems forced, as if the horrors at Troy have spoiled any simple sense of victory.

Suddenly Clytemnestra appears at the threshold of the palace, upstaging the Herald and the chorus in the orchestra. In control of the entrance to the house, she tells the Herald to return to her husband and urge him to hurry back 'like a lover to his city'. For a woman, 'no light shines brighter than her man/ when she opens wide the gates and welcomes him home' (601–05). The language is daring, an erotic voice in the midst of the war-talk of the Herald, and no less dangerous. Clytemnestra returns to the palace after another dynamic appearance in which she reasserts her dominance.

With the queen's departure, the chorus turn their attention to Menelaus and learn that his ship was lost from sight. The Herald's secret is out – a storm at sea destroyed the fleet on its return.[2] In a *tour de force*, the Herald recreates the catastrophe – fire and water (lightning and sea) joined forces against the Greek ships, like a crazed shepherd driving his flock to doom. After the storm, 'when the shining light of the sun rose up,/ we saw the Aegean flower with corpses' (658–59). As elsewhere in the play, the rising sun with its promise of renewal dawns on desolation. The oxymoron 'flower with corpses' has a similar effect, a symbol of beauty and growth that turns into its opposite. The poetic imagery reflects the dynamic structure of the scene, for the report of victory that the Herald has brought becomes, in the telling, news of disaster.

The Herald exits, having brought the war and its aftermath wrenchingly to life, one of the great secondary roles in Greek tragedy. In a mood markedly different from that which started their previous stasimon, the chorus burst into lyric by attacking Helen, the paragon of beauty who spread only ruin: 'Helen – hell for ships, hell for men, hell for cities' (688–90). Aeschylus puns on the word *hele*, a form of the verb 'to destroy', as if Helen's name encapsulates her fate and provides the frame for her dramatic character. Developing the idea that she and Paris have made a marriage to death, the chorus describe her as 'a spear-bride fought over by both sides' who abandoned the 'gentle veils' of Sparta, perhaps suggesting the bridal veil worn at a Greek wedding. The 'wedding hymn' that the Trojans sing when Helen arrives turns into a funeral dirge, and the marriage-bed becomes a 'bed of death' (705–14). The arrival of Helen at Troy accomplishes 'bitter rites of marriage' that reveal her as 'the bridal-weeping Fury' (739–49), the noun 'Fury' ringing out as the final word of the strophe. The conflation of weddings and funerals brings home to the audience the depths of the violence unleashed at Troy, and also serves to link Helen and her sister Clytemnestra, who fatally undermines the sanctity of her own marriage as well.

In this stasimon Aeschylus exploits the freedom of lyric to incorporate material unbounded by strict logical and psychological constraints. In the story of the lion cub, for example (716–36), the chorus introduce a dramatic image so vivid that it assumes a life of its own. Raised in the home, the cuddly animal grows from pet to killer as time reveals its true nature. The specific relevance to Helen (or Clytemnestra, or Agamemnon) is left open, since there is no simile at work. Rather, the lyric suggests correspondences by image, metre, and juxtaposition, as when the chorus move abruptly from the havoc wreaked by the lion to the day of 'windless calm' that brought Helen to Troy. The peaceful arrival seems far removed from the violence and bloodshed of the beast grown wild, until we learn that the new bride herself proves to be a Fury who unleashes untold death.

At the end of the stasimon, the chorus shift to anapaests to welcome Agamemnon, their formal address capturing the paradox of the returning hero: 'King, who ravaged Troy,/ offspring of Atreus ...' (783–84). As the leader who destroyed a city, Agamemnon bears responsibility for his actions; as the child of Atreus, an heir to a past over which he has no control, Agamemnon is guiltless. The double edgedness of human circumstance, so briefly but tellingly marked here, emerges time and again in the trilogy and provides much of its vitalizing tension.

Driving his chariot into the orchestra, Agamemnon symbolically brings the Trojan War with him. Standing at his side, unnamed but visible to the audience, is Agamemnon's war-prize, the Trojan princess and prophetess Cassandra. The chariot with a standing man and woman reflects fifth-century wedding iconography, for we know that an Athenian husband would drive his bride to her new home in a cart, frequently heroicized in vase-painting as a chariot. The confusion of weddings with war in the previous stasimon (through the marriage of Paris and Helen) now takes concrete visual form with the arrival of Agamemnon and his 'war-bride'.

Speaking from the chariot, Agamemnon greets his city and describes the gods who helped him to victory, but his account of the moment of triumph is disturbing:

> Shield-bearing young of a wooden horse
> timed their birth to the setting stars.
> A lion leapt the walls
> and gorged itself on a frightened city,
> lapping up the blood of kings.
> (825–28)

We hear echoes of the omen at Aulis, where eagles devoured the young of the pregnant hare, but here the new-born animals do the feasting. The army is a lion – like the cub in the second stasimon that grows to destroy the house that raised it – feeding on the blood of a great city. Given the poetic richness of the *Oresteia*, choice of language can implicate a character in a way he or she does not intend, and here Agamemnon's description triggers a complex set of responses that take the audience back to events preceding the war, particularly those leading to the sacrifice of Iphigenia.

When Clytemnestra appears at the threshold, the situation turns electric. She delivers a riveting speech that merges public with private, intimacy with boldness, culminating in the play's famous dramatic action, the spreading of the dark-red tapestries to welcome Agamemnon home. However, she begins by addressing the chorus, not Agamemnon, a *gestus* for the alienation she felt while her husband was at Troy. In a domestic version of the Herald's speech on the hardship of war, Clytemnestra describes her loneliness at home when rumour broke around her like a plague. Fear was her sole companion, as she heard reports of Agamemnon being wounded and even killed, driving her to thoughts of suicide. At this rhetorical high-point, Clytemnestra shifts gears and addresses her husband obliquely: 'So your child is not here, as should be the case,/ the living proof of our love for each other,/ Orestes' (877–79). By holding off the name, Clytemnestra leaves open the possibility that she has Iphigenia in mind, and the effect in the theatre is palpable.

Having spent many wakeful nights waiting for the beacon, and having endured the nightmares that followed when sleep did come, Clytemnestra at last can welcome her husband home:

> I call on my husband –
> sheepdog of the flock
> mainstay and mast of a warship
> central pillar of a great hall
> a father's only son
> land to the sailor lost at sea
> calm after a night of storm
> spring water to the parched traveller.
> (896–901)

The hyperbole generates its gestural counterpart, as the queen orders her slaves to spread the tapestries before Agamemnon, so that 'justice may lead him to the home/ he never hoped to see' (911).

For a long moment the talking stops, as the servants lay out the lush red tapestries in the orchestra for Agamemnon to walk on. Do they flow out of the palace to suggest the bloodshed that lies ahead, and the past violence that has stained the house of Atreus? Or are the tapestries spread out from Agamemnon's chariot leading up to the palace entrance, as if the blood spilt at Aulis and Troy symbolically swamps the orchestra? Or are they strewn from both ends, linking the fates of Troy and Argos, binding the past to the present? However the scene is staged, the tapestries cut the orchestra with a dark-red path, a striking visual field that draws together the various images of bloodshed in the play.

Agamemnon contemptuously rejects the oriental excess and obsequiousness of his wife's welcome, fearing that by trampling such wealth he might inspire envy from the gods. Now Clytemnestra raises the dramatic stakes, initiating a rapid stichomythic exchange with her husband, and after a dialogue of only fourteen lines, Agamemnon yields to her request. Critics have tried to glean the rational basis for his change of heart, but in performance the crucial shift is less a question of argument and deliberation than of rhythm – Agamemnon is swept up by Clytemnestra's verbal pace and energy. Put in psychological terms, tragic stichomythia respects the mystery of decision without attempting to explain it away, acknowledging that men and women often pretend to rational choice while really making a stab in the dark.

Before stepping down from the chariot, Agamemnon introduces Cassandra and orders his wife to welcome her as a new slave into the house. But Cassandra quickly is forgotten once Agamemnon tramples down the dark-red path. His conduct is not sacrilegious (the cloth is not sacred); rather it symbolizes Agamemnon's destruction of the wealth of the house. Clytemnestra enforces that sense as she coaxes her husband inside, vowing to drain the sea for the dyes needed to colour miles of such fabric, willing 'to lay out all the bounty of the house to be trampled,/ .../ weaving the strands that bring this life home' (963–65). Her verbal excess matches the boldness of the action, and when her husband reaches the palace, she utters a final prayer that seems to signal his imminent death: 'Zeus, Zeus, harvester! Ripen my prayers./ Turn your mind to the harvest at hand' (973–74). She follows Agamemnon inside, the carpets are removed, and the chorus are left to consider what has happened, and what lies ahead.

In a quick-paced, agitated ode, they admit that the king has returned safely, but they cannot silence their premonitions, a 'dirge of the Furies' that sings within (900–02). Try as they may, the chorus cannot find words for their fears, for the 'fire that burns in the mind' (1034). We expect the off-stage death-cries of Agamemnon to resolve their uncertainties, but suddenly Clytemnestra emerges from the palace. Both she and the chorus have forgotten Cassandra.

Clytemnestra alternately encourages and cajoles the Trojan prophetess to follow her inside, to stand by the sacrifice she has prepared to welcome Agamemnon home. But Cassandra refuses to respond, and her silence could not be more eloquent or effective. For the first and only time in the play, Clytemnestra and her verbal pyrotechnics do not control the action. When her last strident threat fails, the queen beats a sullen retreat back into the palace, and all eyes turn to Cassandra, the solitary figure still standing in the chariot. What will she say?

On-stage and mute for some 250 lines (the last thirty-one of which focus directly on her *refusal* to speak), Cassandra breaks her silence not by speaking at all, but by singing. She lets out a heart-rending cry, followed by the name of her destroyer, the god Apollo. After each of her lyric utterances, the chorus respond with two lines of spoken dialogue, inverting the normal pattern in which the chorus use lyric metres and the actor speaks. The transference gives this lyric dialogue exceptional power, and Aeschylus fully exploits its dramatic possibilities, for eventually the chorus adopt *Cassandra's* lyric mode, swept up in the events that the prophetess conjures in her song and dance.

Raped by Apollo, Cassandra denied the god children, so he cursed her with the gift of prophetic insight that no one would believe (1202–12). A victim of male force in its many manifestations, Cassandra finds herself bound to Agamemnon, the commander of the army that destroyed her family and razed her city, and she foresees her death at the hands of Clytemnestra, a woman too much like a man.[3] Powerless in a world she can predict but cannot control, Cassandra sees other victims of bloodshed in the house, the children of Thyestes who were served in a feast to their father (1095–97). The fate of the slaughtered children suggests the sacrifice of another youthful innocent, Iphigenia, whose death forges an important link in the chain that now binds Cassandra to her new home.

Turning from the past to the immediate present, Cassandra reveals Clytemnestra's plan to kill 'the husband who shares her bed' (1108), the very events taking place off-stage. At the precise moment that Cassandra envisions the netting of Agamemnon in the bath, the chorus leave the rhythms of speech and move into the dance, shifting from iambic trimeters to lyric dochmiacs (1121). They exclaim that Cassandra's 'prophecy does not make us happy', a phrase that literally means 'your word does not wash me clean'. Unconsciously the chorus echo Cassandra's description of Clytemnestra 'washing her husband clean in the bath' (1109), caught up in her images and mode of expression. Metaphorically netted in a *kommos*, the chorus now alternate with Cassandra in lyric as she evokes Agamemnon's off-stage murder, the fate of Troy, and her own 'sacrifice' at the side of the king.

We should linger a moment over the importance of the bath as the place of Agamemnon's death. Commentaries on the play emphasize the Homeric practice of a wife bathing her husband (an anachronism in fifth-century Athens), but they fail to appreciate the contemporary relevance of a wife dutifully (if ironically) washing her husband's body before his burial, one of the responsibilities of women in the Greek funeral ritual.[4] There is a hint of nuptial bathing as well – Clytemnestra is Agamemnon's 'bedmate' (1116), suggesting a twisted version of the ritual bathing that took place as part of the Athenian wedding. We already have seen how the play masterfully confuses weddings and funerals – the 'preliminary offering' of the corpses of Greek and Trojan soldiers at the wedding of Paris and Helen (65); the wedding song that turns into a dirge when Helen arrives at Troy (705–16); Cassandra driven to her new home like a bride in a chariot, only to 'die together' (1139) with Agamemnon.

Cassandra's lament reminds the chorus of the nightingale's song (1142–46), referring to the myth of Procne and Philomela in which Procne's husband Tereus raped her sister Philomela, and then cut out her tongue.[5] When Philomela communicates the deed in her weaving, the two sisters take their revenge by killing Tereus' son, Itys. Transformed into a nightingale, Procne forever sings for her dead child; turned into a swallow, the speechless

Philomela sings a garbled, inarticulate melody, which the ancients associated with the swallow. Comparing Cassandra to Procne is apt, for she is raped by Apollo, forced to 'marry' Agamemnon, and finally sings a lament for the loss of her family and city. But Cassandra also takes on the other voice of the myth, for earlier Clytemnestra likens her to a swallow who sings incomprehensibly (1050–51), the Philomela figure in the story. Aeschylus exploits both aspects of Cassandra's persona, the lyrical and the inarticulate, finding an appropriate mythical paradigm to elicit the audience's double sympathy.

These connections between myth, ritual, and dramatic character should not be dismissed as recondite or irrelevant to the stage. A modern production of the *Oresteia* could costume Cassandra to suggest a twisted wedding, and the actress could use the bridal imagery as a way to grapple with the character's inner visions. The movement and the music accompanying her song could suggest, alternately, a marriage hymn and a funeral dirge, perhaps echoing the recreation of Helen's arrival at Troy in the second stasimon. The bird imagery – from the eagles in the *parodos* to the swallow and nightingale associated with Cassandra – could be linked by dance and gesture to signal both the innocence and the ultimate power of nature. These theatrical ideas are encoded in Aeschylus' language and should be given their due if a modern production (or contemporary reader) wishes to tap into the trilogy's full imaginative life.

After this unprecedented exchange, Cassandra moves into speech to 'talk through' what she and the chorus have just experienced. She delineates the strands in the web of past, present, and future, but only after she has swept the chorus and the audience up in them. Her first words in dialogue metre clarify the nuptial motifs scattered through the lyric: 'No more like a newly-wedded bride/ will my prophecies peek out from under veils' (1178–79). Fifth-century art often represents bridal veiling and unveiling, an important aspect of the Greek wedding that occurs at crucial moments in other tragedies. In Euripides' *Alcestis*, for example, the climactic return of Admetus' wife takes the form of a bride unveiling before her husband. Earlier in *Agamemnon* Helen left the 'delicate veils' of her marriage-bed in Sparta for a disastrous wedding at Troy (690–92), and now Cassandra throws off her metaphorical veils before she enters the palace at Argos.

With her visionary insight, Cassandra sees a chorus of Furies who never leave the house, a band of revellers who 'sing their hymn as they besiege the chambers' (1186–91). The fifth-century audience may have envisaged the group of Furies as symposiasts at a drinking party, or as the celebrants who accompany the nuptial procession and sing outside the newlyweds' chamber. Instead of praising the bride and groom, however, their hymn denounces the betrayal of a wedding, 'a brother's bed and the man who trampled it' (1193). The reference is to Thyestes' fatal seduction of Atreus' wife that prompted Atreus to arrange a feast of Thyestes' own children. The 'trampled' bed also carries undertones of the twisted marriage of Paris, who abducted Menelaus' wife Helen and so 'trampled untouchable things' (372), and it suggests the adultery of Helen's sister Clytemnestra, whose unnatural liaison with Aegisthus links her to Thyestes' only surviving child. Finally the image of trampling recalls Agamemnon's exit down the dark-red tapestries. He 'tramples' the cloth (957, 963), just as Cassandra will 'trample' her way into the palace (1298).

The chorus are amazed at Cassandra's resolution, walking to her death like 'a god-driven bull to the altar' (1297–98). The sacrificial imagery links Cassandra to Iphigenia, whose sacrifice features so prominently in the *parodos*. The young girl's death at Aulis served as a 'preliminary offering' for the ships (*proteleia*, 227), the same word used for the first casualties at Troy, offered for the wedding of Paris and Helen (60–67). Cassandra views her own death as a sacrifice, but not for a marriage – her warm blood will sanctify the funeral of Agamemnon (1278). Iphigenia once sang paeans at her father's table (242–46), only to provide a silent offering when she is gagged like an animal wearing a bit (234–46). Clytemnestra berates Cassandra for *refusing* to wear the bit (1066), and the prophetess sings inauspicious lamentations to Apollo rather than the customary paeans to the god (1074–75, 1078–79). Through poetic image and situation, the death of Cassandra reduplicates the sacrifice of Iphigenia, the blood of innocent women fertilizing the ground for new acts of bloodshed.

Unlike Agamemnon who blindly walks the red tapestries to his death, Cassandra sees clearly what lies in store for her, and her last words reveal a tragic nobility in the face of the known and inescapable. She proclaims that life is at best a shadow, and, at worst, as ephemeral as a picture erased by a wet sponge. In language that echoes the unveiling image with which she began her speech, Cassandra prays 'that the blow is sure . . . and I close my eyes at last' (1294). Only with the fall of the sacrificial blade will this unveiled bride escape the horrors that her prophetic visions force her to see.

After her long scene with the chorus, Cassandra finally enters the palace, and we expect to hear the off-stage death-cries, just as we did after Agamemnon's exit. Once again our expectations appear to be frustrated, for the chorus begin to chant in anapaests (1331–42), the steady rhythm that introduced the *parodos* (40–103) and the first stasimon (355–66). The metre leads us to expect that a full choral ode is gathering steam, when suddenly the blood-curdling cry of Agamemnon is heard from behind the façade. Thanks to Aeschylus' manipulation of lyric metres, the long anticipated murder of Agamemnon now comes as a shock.

At the king's outcry, the chorus fracture into twelve voices (1348–71), their tone varying from the impassioned to the ludicrously timid. Some call for immediate intervention in the palace – 'I cast my vote/ for action' and 'Better to die than live under tyrants.' Others advise caution – 'From the evidence of cries alone/ are we to prophesy that he is dead?' 'It is one thing to guess, another to know.' The last speaker adopts the wait-and-see attitude

– 'I add my vote for that opinion' – meaning that the chorus split down the middle, six for delay, six for action. Although no one in the audience is counting, the division of the chorus seems to be the same as that of the jury in *Eumenides*. The stage-picture in the orchestra – a chorus divided over Agamemnon's murder – may have been mirrored in the final play, when the jury's vote is split over Orestes' guilt.

The appearance of Clytemnestra with the corpses of her two victims dispels any doubts.[6] In an extraordinary speech, Clytemnestra recounts the murder of her husband, shifting to the present tense when she describes the death-blows. Classicists write somewhat dismissively of the 'historical' present tense without appreciating the powerful clue it gives to the actor. It is as if Clytemnestra's emotional memory works so strongly that she actually relives the crucial moments. She revels in Agamemnon's blood as if it were a seminal rain that falls on the crops in the spring, infusing the seeds with life (1389–92).

Not only does she confuse death blood with life-giving rain, but Clytemnestra assaults the ritual order of the city as well. She speaks of Agamemnon's blood as the third offering that honours 'Zeus below the earth, the saviour (*sôter*) of corpses' (1387), conflating the ritual offerings to the dead with those poured at a banquet, where the third libation traditionally went to Zeus *Sôtêr*. Clytemnestra also appropriates Agamemnon's funeral rites to herself, denying the chorus the right to lament the corpse, supervise the interment, and speak at the grave (1551–54). With grisly irony, Clytemnestra already has given her husband his funeral bath, and now he lies in public view, a perverse laying-out of the body wrapped in its net-cum-funeral shroud. The ritual inversion spoke directly to the original audience, who saw before them a powerful image of their world gone awry.

Responding in dochmiacs, the chorus alternately attack the queen's brazenness and mourn the dead king. Clytemnestra defends her actions by pointing to Agamemnon's sacrifice of their daughter, Iphigenia. We have observed the close ties between Iphigenia and Cassandra, and now Clytemnestra implicitly brings them home, for she speaks of Agamemnon's sacrificial victim while standing over the corpse of her own. Drawn together by imagery and circumstance, the two innocent females personify the destruction caused by Agamemnon and Clytemnestra. The king had to die, in no small part because of the sacrifice of his daughter Iphigenia, and Clytemnestra's murder of Cassandra, perhaps more than the slaying of her husband, distances her from the audience and makes her death seem dramatically right.

As Cassandra predicts (1326–29), the chorus bewail Agamemnon without mentioning her, but Clytemnestra cannot get the Trojan prophetess out of her mind. After alluding to her own adulterous liaison with Aegisthus, Clytemnestra desecrates the dead Cassandra as the whore of the Greek army, boasting that her death 'brings an added relish [side-dish] to my bed'

(1447). So distorted is Clytemnestra's view of her victim that the audience realize she is no less blind than her husband was to the events in train. She has slaughtered an innocent woman, a second Iphigenia, but one whose loss the audience feels personally, by virtue of Cassandra's long and moving scene before her death.

The chorus answer each speech of Clytemnestra with a lyric outburst, mainly in dochmiacs, increasing their pressure until the queen finally leaves the metres of speech and meets the chorus halfway in anapaests. The dramatic effect is that of two opposed parties battering their way towards a precarious cease-fire. In the process, major themes and characters reappear with striking vividness – Helen, Clytemnestra's crazed sister who brought death to so many at Troy; the blood-thirsty curse, an avenging force that works in the house; the role of Zeus, both cause and fulfiller; the wounds of the past that break out again; the king Agamemnon, who is caught in the web of a spider; his sacrifice, and the sacrifice of Iphigenia; Thyestes' feast on his own murdered children; the *lex talionis* that blow must answer blow, and who acts must suffer. At the end of the exchange, a provisional resolution seems within reach – an emotionally drained Clytemnestra prays that a pact might be made with the demon in the race to leave things as they are, if only the madness and bloodshed would depart.

Suddenly Aegisthus appears from the palace and shatters the mood in the theatre:

> Light of dawn, break on this day of justice.
> The gods bring vengeance,
> they look down on the sins of men.
> I know when I see this man at my feet,
> tangled in the robes of the Furies.
> It brings me joy . . .
>
> (1577–82)

It is as if Aegisthus enters in the wrong mode, with the wrong energy, into the wrong play. Coming after the lyric exchange between the chorus and Clytemnestra, his speech upsets the precarious balance that has been achieved, renewing the drive towards vengeance and propelling us into the next play of the trilogy.

Aegisthus recounts the story of his father Thyestes, who ruled Argos with his brother Atreus until rivalries led to Thyestes' banishment. Atreus later welcomed his brother home with a banquet made of the cooked flesh of his own children, and in horror Thyestes cursed the house. The sole surviving son of Thyestes, Aegisthus boasts that the curse still lives, for now he stands over the corpse of Atreus' son, Agamemnon. The gruesome banquet, referred to earlier by Cassandra and the chorus, lies behind the other images of slaughter and eating in the play – the eagles devouring the pregnant hare, the lion cub that grows to feed on the household flock, the Greek army

91

that drinks Trojan blood like a ravenous lion. By clarifying the archetype of perverted feasting in the last scene of the play, Aeschylus prepares for the re-emergence of the motif in *Choephori* and *Eumenides*, where Clytemnestra dreams of a snake that drinks her blood and the Furies hope to feed on the living Orestes.

The chorus treat Aegisthus with open hostility, berating his cowardice and decrying his seizure of political power in Argos. When they raise the spectre of Orestes' return from exile to take vengeance and claim the throne, Aegisthus calls out his armed bodyguards, whose arrival confirms that a tyrant rules the city. The play began with the distant war at Troy, and now chaos has come home to Greece in the form of political repression and potential civil strife.

Silent since her anapaests with the chorus, Clytemnestra intervenes firmly and decisively. She reminds her new husband of the bitter harvest they have reaped already and the blood they have shed, and she urges the chorus to disperse to their homes. Instead of leaving *en masse*, which is usual at the end of a tragedy, the chorus break into small groups and each has a final, shrill exchange with Aegisthus before exiting from the theatre. The fragmented, vitriolic departure of the chorus gives the visual and verbal lie to Clytemnestra's wish for herself and Aegisthus: 'You and I shall rule/ and make the house well again' (1672–73). The final scene of *Agamemnon* makes it clear that more bloodshed and a new cycle of violence must be unleashed before there is any hope of cure.

## CHOEPHORI

*Agamemnon* begins with waiting; *Choephori* opens with an arrival. Two young men enter the empty orchestra, and we learn that Orestes has returned from exile with his friend Pylades. He offers belated funeral rites for his father, cutting off a lock of hair and putting it on the grave, a ritual act that establishes the place and dramatic circumstance. We need not imagine a grave-mound hastily erected between plays, for Orestes' words and actions 'create' the tomb in the centre of the orchestra. As well as establishing his filial piety, the ritual gesture signals Orestes' new maturity, for Athenian youths dedicated locks of hair on reaching manhood. The activities at the grave cease with the sudden arrival of the chorus of women, causing Orestes and Pylades to withdraw and observe these new visitors to the tomb.

In this brief prologue, Aeschylus differentiates *Choephori* from *Agamemnon* in several essential respects. The protagonist (Orestes) appears at the outset, moving the story into a new generation. He shifts the focus from the palace-façade at the back to the tomb of Agamemnon in the centre of the orchestra, meaning that the palace must be 'thought away' by characters and audience alike until Orestes arrives there at line 652 to begin the revenge plot. Put in more dynamic terms, the action moves out towards the audience for the first half of the play and then pulls back to the façade for the murders. The fact that Orestes and Pylades withdraw to observe the new arrivals presents the audience with a mirror-image of our own relationship to the play. Like Orestes, we are onlookers and we share his perspective, especially when Electra discovers the offerings he made at the grave – we know who left them and we know he is watching. As the plot unfolds, our position as spectators shifts from fellow-observers to 'accessories before the fact', accomplices who watch with full knowledge the entrapment and murder of Aegisthus and Clytemnestra. Contrast our relationship to *Agamemnon*, where we know that something untoward is happening, but the details are not divulged until the Cassandra scene, and then from the point of view of the victim and not the perpetrator.

Dressed in black, singing threnodies, and bearing libations to the grave, the chorus (accompanied by the silent Electra) continue the funeral motifs begun by Orestes. After a terrifying nightmare, Clytemnestra has sent her slave-women to calm the spirit of her dead husband with offerings. The chorus know their libations provide no remedy, since 'no stream can wash away/ blood that stains the hand'. The earth is so clotted with gore that 'no liquids can flow' (66–75). In a play that focuses on murder, the revulsion of nature at human bloodshed is emphasized from the start. After the *parodos*, Electra asks the chorus for help as she pours Clytemnestra's offerings. In a short dialogue, the women convince her to alter the designated prayer and call instead for the death of Aegisthus and Clytemnestra, demanding murder for murder. As Electra prays for vengeance, the chorus crown their libations with a lamentation that draws the play's first movement to a close.

Aeschylus has set the stage beautifully for the emergence of Orestes from hiding. Electra spies a lock of hair at the tomb and concludes that her brother has returned, only to reject the thought as impossible. Like the chorus in *Agamemnon* unsure of the beacon fire, Electra needs a human voice to answer her doubts. The sight of footprints adds to her mental anguish, and the appearance of Orestes in person compounds it. In a quick stichomythic exchange, she asks the stranger 'Why do you wind me in this net?' and Orestes responds, 'It traps me as well' (220–21). The reunion of brother and sister takes the form of mutual entrapment, the alternating lines of dialogue articulating the strands of the net. The imagery reveals that the world of *Agamemnon* – the net thrown on Troy, the snare that traps the returning king – is still alive in the next generation.

The recognition scene also develops the idea of germination, the small and insignificant generating the large and momentous. We see Orestes plant the dramatic seed by leaving a lock of hair, and we watch it burst into life when Electra seizes on it. Knowing that a 'vast trunk can grow from the smallest seed' (204), Electra welcomes her brother as a 'seed of hope, watered by tears' (236). However, we recall from the first play that Agamemnon uprooted the city of Troy, only to have his own blood fall like spring rain on the newly planted seeds (*Ag.*, 1388–92). Now the renewing acts of homecoming and recognition take place at his tomb, where the metaphors of birth and growth are harnessed to death, generating fresh plans for bloodshed.

Orestes describes the forces that drive him to vengeance, chief among them Apollo's oracle prophesying what he would suffer if he failed to avenge his father and regain his patrimony. The principle of retributive justice provides the impulse for the long lyric *kommos* that follows, lying at the heart of the trilogy. The chorus, Orestes, and Electra steel themselves to the task ahead, invoking support from the spirit of Agamemnon and various deities above and below the earth. Critics have argued long and hard over the dramatic purpose of this complex interchange, the longest lyric passage in extant tragedy. Does the *kommos* convert Orestes from a hesitant to a single-minded avenger? Or is the energy directed primarily at the spirit of Agamemnon? Or does it focus on the audience, a gathering of dramatic forces (both seen and unseen) that convert the theatre itself into a place of vengeance?

Beginning in anapaests, the chorus call Orestes and Electra to the inexorable demands of the *lex talionis*. In the lyric sections that follow – strophic pairs with intermezzi, alternating Orestes–chorus–Electra–chorus – the siblings lament their father's fate while the group keeps up the refrain that blood must pay for blood. The pattern of speakers, metre, and responsion shifts when the chorus and Electra recount the aftermath of Agamemnon's murder, driving Orestes to deliver his strongest cry for vengeance. All three parties invoke Agamemnon's spirit to rise and join them, completing the transformation of the offerings sent by Clytemnestra to calm Agamemnon's anger in the *parodos*. Just as Electra changed her prayer when pouring the libations over the grave, now she and Orestes follow the chorus's lead in rousing Agamemnon's spirit to action.

As Cassandra does in *Agamemnon*, so Orestes and Electra 'talk through' the events of the lyric in regular speech, a formal reiteration of the essential issues of the *kommos*. In the brief exchange with Orestes that follows, the chorus recount Clytemnestra's nightmare that led her to send libations to Agamemnon's tomb. Although editors commonly attribute these lines to the chorus-leader, they may have been divided among the individual members of the group. The voices coming from around the orchestra would give the sense that Orestes was surrounded and trapped by the very dream that terrified his mother – he is the snake born to Clytemnestra that feeds at her breast and drains her lifeblood along with the milk.

With the attention now focused on him alone, Orestes outlines his plan for revenge. Disguised as travellers, he and Pylades will approach the palace, ask for hospitality, and, once inside, kill Aegisthus – Orestes makes no mention of Clytemnestra. He advises the chorus to be silent when appropriate, and to speak when the time is ripe, setting up their intervention with the Nurse later in the play. Electra exits through one *eisodos* (and out of the play, for she never returns), Pylades and Orestes depart via the other, and the chorus are left alone for the first time.

Functioning as a true 'act-dividing song', the lyric snaps the moorings of locale and setting, as the chorus sing of strange beasts from the earth and sea, of celestial terrors made of air (hurricanes) and fire (thunderbolts), all four elements of early Greek cosmology. However, these natural prodigies prove no match for the human monster, illustrated by three myths and epitomized by Clytemnestra's murder of her husband.[7] The last image in the stasimon is of a *new* murder returning home as the child of former murders, and the final word is 'Furies'. Orestes appears from an *eisodos* and demands entry at the palace, fulfilling in the flesh the chorus's description. A young Fury has come home to perpetrate a crime that is the offspring of prior bloodshed in the race.

The return of Orestes and Pylades introduces the play's second act, and the first scene could be called 'getting inside'. Orestes knocks at the palace door and calls impatiently for a servant, an odd set of actions for a tragic hero but a scenario quite at home in Greek comedy where getting a servant to open the door is a stock routine. Orestes announces that he brings news to the rulers of the house, more fitting for a man to hear than a woman. We are surprised, therefore, when Clytemnestra appears at the doorway instead of Aegisthus. She promises the strangers all due hospitality, including 'a warm bath and soft bed to soothe you' (670). Given the welcome to her husband in *Agamemnon*, Clytemnestra's offer of a bath is almost grotesque. However, the irony here operates totally at her expense, and its edge sharpens when the unrecognized young man claims that he brings news of Orestes' death, adding disingenuously 'But perhaps I am speaking to those who are not concerned. I do think his father should be told' (690).[8]

Why does Aeschylus throw such strange shadows over the action – the comedic door-knocking, Clytemnestra's unwitting *double entendre*, and Orestes' conscious irony delivered from the safe distance of disguise? The answer may lie in the relationship that these elements help to forge with the audience. The incongruous tone binds us even faster to the revenge plot, for the prior knowledge that allows us to laugh to ourselves also fortifies our complicity in, and commitment to, the impending deed. The audience are 'in' on the joke, just as we are 'in' on the plans for murder.

Clytemnestra reacts to the news with a cry of grief, prompting some critics to conclude that she is capable of manufacturing any and all emotions at the drop of a word. A more effective approach to her character is to take these moments of strong feeling at face value. It is far more powerful, and theatrically more disturbing, if Clytemnestra wants her husband home when she says she does in *Agamemnon*, if she considers him worthy of the praise she bestows, in a fifth-century form of wish-fulfilment. Now she cries out instinctively when she learns that another child of hers has been taken: 'Stripped of my loved ones, and now Orestes./ He did well to keep his

distance/ and not step near this morass of death' (695–97). The play-actor
here is not Clytemnestra, but Orestes himself, who stands before his mother
biding his time before he adds her blood to the swamp. Orestes asks that his
hosts not stint their welcome because of the news he brings, an appeal to the
guest–host relationship that resonates uneasily, for we know that Orestes
will violate its sanctity just as Paris did with Menelaus. But the ploy works,
and Orestes accomplishes the task set for the scene in the space of only sixty
lines, as Clytemnestra welcomes him and Pylades inside.

Again alone in the orchestra, the chorus call on various powers to join
the battle and guide Orestes' sword. They repeat the word 'now!' on three
occasions, giving the impression that the murder of Clytemnestra is at
hand. Suddenly the chorus-leader spots the figure of the Nurse, Cilissa,
bustling from the palace, sent by Clytemnestra to fetch Aegisthus. Even
more surprising than her appearance is the speech she delivers, a disarming
account of her sorrow at the news of Orestes' death. She relates in unabashed
terms what her life was like as the wet-nurse for the baby Orestes – waking
in the middle of the night, nursing 'the little beast' (753), trying to guess his
needs, and ending up washing nappies:

> Young insides are a law unto themselves;
> you just have to guess. Like a prophet I was,
> but many's the time I guessed wrong . . .
> Washwoman and child nurse, they're one and the same.
>
> (757–60)

The Nurse's speech intensifies the tragedy, for we imagine Orestes as an
infant, connected like everyone at that age to the most basic bodily functions.
*This* is the man who now waits in the palace to commit murder, and we
wonder again at the complex weave of events that could lead from the
instinctual cries of a baby to the deceit of a matricide. In some respects
the Nurse is a counter to Clytemnestra – her manner of expression and
conscious self-irony ('like a prophet I was') contrast with the rhetoric of the
queen, and her commitment to the baby Orestes puts in relief Clytemnestra's
claims to feel a mother's concern. In the final analysis, however, we enjoy the
Nurse's account because we know that the object of her care and love is still
very much alive.

With typical tragic economy, Aeschylus now makes the unknowing Cilissa
a linchpin in the plot. The chorus convince her to alter the message she brings
to Aegisthus, so that he will come without his customary bodyguards, the
thugs introduced at the end of *Agamemnon*. The intervention of the women
here demonstrates the inadequacy of the oft-repeated rubric that the tragic
chorus never materially affect the action. Sensing that better news might lie
ahead, the Nurse leaves to do as her fellow-slaves suggest.

With the stage empty, the chorus embark on their second act-dividing song,
three strophic pairs with a mesode between each strophe and antistrophe

(a – mesode 1 – a'/ b – mesode 2 – b'/ c – mesode 3 – c'). The tripartite structure – itself built on triads – links the divine world to that of the human characters, foreshadowing the ultimate resolution of the trilogy where gods and humans stand together in common purpose. Praying for Orestes' victory, the chorus appeal to Zeus, the household divinities (perhaps implying the Furies who live in the race), Apollo at Delphi, and Hermes who leads souls to the underworld. In the final triad they turn to the mortal agents, imagining Orestes in the palace face to face with Clytemnestra: 'When she cries, "Son!"/ say to her "My father's!"/ and drive death home' (828–30).

Given the chorus's emphasis on the fatal meeting between mother and son, the audience once again expect a death-cry from the palace. Instead, Aegisthus enters briskly down an *eisodos*, barely concealing his delight at the news from the Nurse. The chorus play their part to perfection, flattering the tyrant's vanity by urging him to find out the truth for himself, inside, man to man. Eager to cross-examine the Messenger, Aegisthus exits into the palace with self-assurance bordering on the ludicrous, proclaiming with his last words that the stranger 'cannot trick a man whose eyes are open' (854). Appearing for the first and only time in *Choephori*, Aegisthus is so incongruous and his dispatch so rapid (the entire scene takes twenty lines) that he makes an almost comic impact. His arrogant confidence that his 'eyes are open' as he walks into the trap brings to mind his rival Agamemnon, who also walked blindly to his death through the same door.

The pace accelerates as the chorus shift to lyric anapaests, again praying for Orestes' victory. As soon as they hear Aegisthus' death-cries, however, they pull back from the murder: 'Stand back till the verdict is in/ and we will seem guiltless' (872–73). The women who transformed Electra's opening libation into an offering for vengeance, who urged Orestes to bloodshed in the *kommos*, who intercepted the Nurse and changed her message, and who guided Aegisthus to his doom – these very women now distance themselves from the outcome. At the same time, the pace of exits and entrances accelerates. A servant rushes from the palace crying that Aegisthus has been slain, the queen enters to ask the reason for the alarm, and she learns that 'He who is dead has killed the living' (886). The servant then exits after an on-stage life of only twelve lines, followed almost immediately by the appearance of Orestes and Pylades at the palace doors. The confrontation between mother and son finally comes to pass.

This flurry of entrances and exits has led theatre historians to conclude that the skene had more than one door, since handling the comings and goings from a single entranceway would be awkward. But that is precisely the point. In *Agamemnon* Clytemnestra guards the threshold, overseeing access to the house, and controlling the events that take place within. The situation changes radically in *Choephori*, for the tomb of Agamemnon in the orchestra provides the scenic focus for the first 600 lines of the play, during which the façade is ignored. The palace emerges as a locus only when the incognito Orestes arrives there, inaugurating a series of increasingly short scenes, each involving at least one 'transgression' of the central door. At the homecoming, Clytemnestra enters from the palace, and she, Orestes, and Pylades exit back into the house. In the next scene the Nurse enters through the same door, and departs down an *eisodos* fifty lines later. The third encounter takes less than twenty lines, as Aegisthus meets the chorus in the orchestra and exits into the palace. The fourth scene begins with the servant entering through the same palace door, followed by Clytemnestra ten lines later. In another five lines Orestes and Pylades also enter from the palace, and after the great confrontation of forty-five lines, all three return through the same door, mirroring their first exit.

This spate of entrances and exits, unprecedented in tragedy, shatters Clytemnestra's control of the threshold. The effect would be lost if there were another entrance into the palace. There must be only one, a single passageway that Orestes penetrates. The irony is that his initial success in doing so unleashes a scurry of comings and goings, all leading to the deed that drives Orestes *away* from his home even as he reclaims his rightful place in it.

In the crucial scene between mother and son, Clytemnestra reminds Orestes that by killing her he will be stabbing the mother's breast that nurtured him. For a moment the thought chills Orestes, and he turns to Pylades, asking his friend what has been called the central tragic question, *ti drasô*, 'What shall I do?' (899). In a three-line response, his only words in the play, Pylades tells Orestes to follow the oracle of Apollo, incurring the enmity of mortals rather than the anger of the gods. The dramatic situation could not be etched more clearly. A heretofore silent character, one who has loomed in the background as a symbol of Orestes' exile and alienation from his natal family, steps forward and speaks for the matricide. Short of a *deus ex machina*, Aeschylus could not introduce a more compelling voice than that of Pylades, emanating both inside and outside the action, and Orestes 'judges' (903) in his friend's favour.

Clytemnestra initiates a stichomythic exchange that propels the scene to its climax. Pleading for her life, she threatens Orestes with 'the bloodhounds of a mother's curse', a vivid periphrasis for the Furies. She finds her son no more approachable than a tomb, and in a flash of insight Clytemnestra realizes that he is the snake she bore in her dream. Orestes drags his mother off-stage to kill her over the corpse of Aegisthus: 'You killed whom you should not, now suffer what should not be' (930).

While that paradox still echoes in the theatre, the chorus-leader introduces the third and final stasimon with a four-line speech, noteworthy for the sympathy it shows Orestes' victims. The ode proper constitutes the victory song the chorus referred to earlier, the form similar to that of the previous stasimon, with a mesode intervening between each strophe and antistrophe. However, the note of triumph is tempered by the predominance of dochmiacs, the agitated metre associated with the Furies at several points in the trilogy. The tension between the drive to resolution (the repeated phrase 'it has come'), and the unsettling rhythm with which it is expressed, underlines the horrible ambiguity of Orestes' action.

Orestes returns from the palace with the bodies of Clytemnestra and Aegisthus, and the stage-picture recalls the scene in *Agamemnon* where Clytemnestra exults over the corpses of her husband and *his* lover.[9] In both plays, the victims lie wedded to death, while the killer conjures images of the adultery that helped motivate the murder. For all the dramatic differences between *Agamemnon* and *Choephori*, the two plays confirm that the cycle of violence will continue – bloodshed engenders future bloodshed as inexorably as one generation follows the next.

Along with the two bodies, Orestes displays the robes that trapped Agamemnon in the bath, and he struggles to find the right name for them – chains, shackles, bath-curtains, a snare, a trap. Returning to the funereal mode with which the play began, he delivers a eulogy for his father and then shifts almost immediately to mourn 'the act, the suffering, the whole race,/ since I win no glory but wear the stain of victory' (1016–17). Like Agamemnon before him, Orestes has returned a conqueror, but unlike his father he realizes how compromised his conquest is.

Sensing that he is losing the reins, Orestes takes hold of an olive bough garlanded with cotton, the traditional sign of a suppliant. Facing exile for killing his mother, Orestes will return to Delphi in supplication, as Apollo advised. The chorus reassure him that by 'killing the vipers you freed the land of Argos' (1046–47), but the young man cries out in terror – the vipers he sees are not lying at his feet but writhing in the hair of women who approach him, clad in black, dripping blood from their eyes, 'the bloodhounds of a mother's curse' (1054). Orestes describes his visions in a stichomythic dialogue with the chorus, the strict form encapsulating the madness even as it underlines the growing chasm between the hero and the group. With the associative power of a nightmare, it is as if the black-clad chorus women have metamorphosed into Furies, the snakes in their hair recalling the viper of Clytemnestra's dream that has grown up to be Orestes himself.

Isolated by his encroaching madness, Orestes flees from the theatre, armed only with his suppliant bough. The fact that he cannot withdraw inside the palace makes it clear that the cycle of bloodshed must be stopped elsewhere, in a new dramatic world. Alone in the orchestra for the last time, the chorus shift to anapaests to describe the generational storms that have struck the house: first, the feast of slaughtered children, referring to Thyestes' horrific banquet; second, the death of a husband, king, and commander-in-chief, killed by his wife in the bath; third, Orestes' murder of Clytemnestra, an act that may restore the house or bring on its doom. It is fitting that the chorus close the play with a question: 'Where will it end?/When will it sleep, this force of ruin?' (1075–76). The destructive energies that have

99

worked their way through *Agamemnon* and *Choephori* remain to be dealt with in the final play.

## EUMENIDES

The last act of the trilogy opens at Apollo's temple in Delphi, the most important oracular site in the Greek world. At the centre of the orchestra, where the tomb of Agamemnon was located in *Choephori*, stands the *omphalos* or navel stone of the earth, marking the inner sanctum of Apollo's shrine. In a cancelled entry, Orestes takes his suppliant's position at the *omphalos*, and the chorus of Furies (perhaps covering their masks with their cloaks so to hide them from the audience) scatter on the orchestra floor, asleep. To begin the action, the priestess of Apollo delivers her prologue back by the façade, unaware of what lies at the centre of the orchestra, which represents the 'interior' of the temple.[10]

The Pythia's speech outlines the devolution of prophetic power at Delphi, moving peacefully through a series of female deities until control of the shrine is conferred on the god Apollo. The priestess prays in orderly fashion to a string of deities, articulating a careful hierarchy that culminates with Zeus, the 'Fulfiller' or 'Harvester' (28). Because the audience can see what the Pythia cannot – namely that the monstrous Furies surround the bloodstained Orestes at the *omphalos* – we maintain an ironic distance from her opening genealogies and formulaic prayers. The audience's 'split' vision infuses the Pythia's prologue with the tension it otherwise lacks, when compared to the inherently dramatic situations facing the Watchman in *Agamemnon* and Orestes in *Choephori*.

At the conclusion of her prayer, the priestess 'enters' the temple by walking into the orchestra. At the unexpected sight of Orestes and the Furies, however, she scrambles out in terror on her hands and knees. The Pythia describes in vivid terms Orestes at the altar and the Furies surrounding him, a tableau still present before the audience but as yet unanimated. She portrays the Furies much as Orestes imagines them at the end of *Choephori*, first as women, then as gorgons, then harpies without wings, dressed in black, defiling the temple, noses dripping, eyes oozing a horrible liquid. The precision of the Pythia's verbal picture fills in what most of the audience could make out only vaguely, given the size of the theatre of Dionysus. Once again, it is the words working on the audience's imagination, as much as graphic physical details, that create the sleeping Furies and their prey in the orchestra.

Leaving the problem of the temple's pollution to Apollo, the Pythia exits out one *eisodos*, even as the god himself enters down the other. The overlapping entrance and exit give the impression that events have reached a stage where divine interference is required. Promising his suppliant release from the Furies, Apollo advises Orestes to flee to Athens and take refuge at

Athena's cult-statue. There the goddess will find 'judges for your case,/and words that cast a calming spell, the means/to rid you forever from this pain' (81–83). Apollo calls on Hermes to protect the traveller, and the god's role as intermediary between the earth and the underworld suggests that Orestes' flight to Athens is like a journey back into life. Hermes' physical presence is not necessary, although the god (played by a mute) may have entered with Apollo and led Orestes off at the end of the scene.

As Apollo and Orestes exit out one *eisodos*, the ghost of Clytemnestra (yet unnamed) enters down the other.[11] This second 'flowing' exit and entrance reinforce the rhythm of flight and pursuit, introducing the very force that Orestes would elude, the murder victim who demands vengeance from the living. Moving among the sleeping Furies, she rouses them to pursue Orestes who, like a fawn, has escaped their net. The physical manifestation of the Furies – sleeping, waking, dancing, hunting, tracking – strengthens the sense that they represent a natural force, that their outrage at kindred bloodshed demands a primordial respect that cannot be gainsaid, even by Apollo. In perhaps the strangest dialogue in tragedy, each of Clytemnestra's exhortations is followed by a groan or whimper from the chorus, one of the few ancient stage directions that has survived. The Furies 'chase the prey in a dream,/ like howling dogs that never leave the track' (131–32). Goaded by Clytemnestra, they finally wake to vengeance and pursuit, rising from the orchestra floor to begin the *parodos* as the ghost disappears.

The stage picture of Clytemnestra waking the Furies recalls the *kommos* of *Choephori*, in which Orestes, Electra, and the chorus wake the spirit of Agamemnon. If Agamemnon's tomb and the *omphalos* at Delphi both are located orchestra-centre, then Clytemnestra's effort to rouse the forces of vengeance mirrors the *kommos* in subject and staging. At the end of *Eumenides*, Athena will 'replace' Clytemnestra's ghost in the centre of the orchestra (both parts were played by the same actor), reversing the energy unleashed here by putting the anger of the Furies to sleep and converting them to beneficent spirits.

The *parodos* proper begins with the chorus already in the orchestra, where they perform three strophic pairs in a mixture of iambic and dochmiac metres, an agitated rhythm that fits their anger that the prey has 'slipped from the snare' (147). In the last four lines of the second strophe and antistrophe, the metrical correspondence is more than exact – word-breaks occur at precisely the same place, and several phonetic and syntactic echoes are heard. The effect is to bind together the Furies' drive for vengeance with the stain that Orestes has spread over the navel of the earth. Accusing Apollo of polluting his own temple, the chorus vow to track Orestes down even if he flees to the underworld.

As if hearing his cue, Apollo bursts back into the orchestra to drive the Furies out of his temple. In a clash of irreconcilable opposites, the beautiful, gold-clad Olympian assaults the blood-dripping, subterranean daughters of

Night. He associates them solely with torture and mutilation, rejecting their ancient office of bringing to justice those killers who shed kindred blood. Apollo argues that the bond between husband and wife surpasses ties of birth and kinship, and so, by not pursuing Clytemnestra when she killed her husband, the Furies have dishonoured the sanctity of marriage. The chorus respond instinctively, vowing they will never let Orestes go, and they leave the orchestra 'driven by a mother's blood/ to track and hunt him down. We go for Justice' (230–31).

As Apollo follows them out through an *eisodos* vowing to help Orestes, Orestes himself arrives down the other *eisodos* to take refuge at the altar of Athena. This last 'flowing' exit and entrance effect the transition from Delphi to Athens. Orestes establishes that the orchestra represents the temple interior by addressing the cult-statue of Athena at the centre-point (235–43). Given the flexibility of the Greek stage and the power of language to create location, it is likely that the marker used earlier for the *omphalos* at Apollo's temple now represents the ancient, aniconic image of the goddess.[12] Situated in the strongest acting position in the ancient theatre, Orestes makes his appeal to Athena at the same place he called on Apollo for help, and where he and his sister prayed to their murdered father in *Choephori*.

His prayers are answered not by Olympian intervention but by the arrival of the Furies, one of the most powerful entrances on the Greek stage. Performing a second *parodos*, the chorus fill the large open space of the orchestra with images of the hunt, moving like dogs tracking a wounded fawn or cowering hare (244–53). The simile recalls the pregnant hare in the *parodos* of *Agamemnon*, killed by eagles who feasted on her unborn children. That act of bloodshed led to the sacrifice of Orestes' sister, Iphigenia, and now Orestes himself must give the Furies his blood to drink as payment for killing his mother.

Surrounded by these manifestations of the forces of vengeance, Orestes clings to the goddess's image and cries out again for Athena to save him. Here Aeschylus subtly shifts away from the strange and bizarre towards the recognizable world of fifth-century Athens. Orestes calls on Athena in Libya, where Athens recently had sent a large expedition to support a local revolt against Persian rule. Orestes also refers to a treaty between Argos and Athens, concluded only a few years before the production of the *Oresteia* in 458.[13] As *Eumenides* unfolds, Aeschylus relates the situation of the play more and more directly to the audience and the city where the action now takes place. Although the specific Athenian references mean nothing to us, they do point the way for a modern production that wishes to explore and establish comparable equivalents for a contemporary audience.

Once again, the only response to Orestes' appeal to Athena comes from the Furies. Binding Orestes 'in the chains of their song' (306), they too move towards the recognizably contemporary, casting a spell on their victim that mimics the Athenian practice of depositing curse tablets before a trial, pre-emptory magic aimed at silencing an adversary when he comes to testify. The Furies modulate from speech to anapaests and then into lyric proper – three strophic pairs interspersed with mesodes in an intricate structure, followed by a final strophe and antistrophe with no mesodic interruption. The changing rhythms and interlocking patterns mark a progression from outrage to assertive clarity. The third mesode contains particularly violent dance-rhythms, reinforcing the way the Furies spring and bring down their human victims, but the cadences grow calmer in the closing stanzas, as the chorus assert that their rights were spun out by the Fates and are part of the make-up of the universe.

At last Athena appears, probably at orchestra level, since her strategy throughout is to insist on parity and work towards inclusion. Although surprised to see the Furies in her temple, she treats them and the suppliant Orestes with equal consideration. In a stichomythic dialogue, Athena questions the Furies and gains a major concession when they grant her authority to judge the issue by trial. She next questions Orestes, who responds with his longest speech in the play, recapitulating the action of *Agamemnon* and *Choephori*. The slower pace allows Athena and the audience to realize the full dilemma before them – how to choose between a suppliant who brings no harm to the city and the Furies whose ancient offices must be honoured. If they leave without victory, the goddess predicts 'the poison in them will seep/ over this land, an endless plague' (478–79). To resolve the crisis, Athena establishes a court to try the case, and she leaves to gather the jury, 'the best people of my city' (487).

In the stasimon that follows, the Furies consider the larger context in which Orestes is but an example. If Athena's court overturns the *lex talionis* by letting Orestes go free, then the human urge to commit crimes will run unchecked. The imperative verbs and second person pronouns (at 526–28, 538, 542) suggest that the Furies are addressing the audience and appealing to the Athenian sense of justice, presenting themselves as the guarantors of social order conceived in terms of fifth-century popular morality. Euripides uses a similar strategy in his *Bacchae*, produced some fifty years after the *Oresteia*, where the chorus of Bacchantes – who represent wild and foreign forces at the outset of the play – uphold the middle ground of conventional Athenian morality in the second stasimon. The change in *Bacchae* is temporary, since the horrific violence unleashed later in the play undermines any claim for Dionysiac moderation. The shift in *Eumenides*, however, serves a more integrative function, for the Furies embody complex forces that demand both fear and respect. They remind us of the fragility of the human family and the restraint needed to keep anarchic tendencies from bursting the bonds of community.

The merging of play and spectator gathers momentum when Athena returns with a herald, a trumpeter, and twelve Athenian jurors, a kind of surrogate audience brought on-stage. Athena directs the Herald to call the trial to order, and he uses the audience in the theatre as the crowd he must quiet.[14] The trumpeter sounds his call, the only time in an extant tragedy that the instrument was heard. According to ancient sources, a trumpet blast signalled the start of dramatic performances at the City Dionysia, serving as the cue to begin a new play. By using the sound here to open the trial, Aeschylus links the dramatic action to the theatrical festival in which it is a part, further inviting the audience to see themselves as an integral part of the play.

Athena promises to teach the city her new ordinances, but Apollo enters unexpectedly and interrupts her 'founder's speech'. Normally a new arrival in Greek tragedy is announced by someone on-stage, or the character makes the identification when he or she first appears. Aeschylus observes neither convention here, indicating the anomaly of the god's arrival. Surprised by his appearance, Athena asks Apollo what business he has in the case and then postpones her speech on the future of the court, declaring the trial open.

Although the physical set-up is uncertain, an appropriate staging would leave Orestes in the centre of the orchestra, Apollo on one side, the Furies on the other, and Athena standing upstage-centre between the two voting urns brought on by the jurors, who take their seats near (or perhaps even in) the audience. This arrangement allows the prosecution and defence to avoid upstaging themselves when they make their arguments, and encourages the audience to view themselves as the extension of the jury come to judge the case. In rapid-fire stichomythia, the Furies cross-examine Orestes, who justifies the matricide as revenge for the death of his father and Clytemnestra's husband. Since the Furies privilege the murder of a mother, related by blood, over that of a husband, Orestes' plea makes little impact on them. Taking up Orestes' defence, Apollo points to his oracle commanding Orestes to avenge his father's murder, and then advances the specious argument that no blood tie exists between a mother and her offspring anyway. According to Apollo, the mother of a child is not really a parent at all, and therefore the Furies have no business pursuing Orestes.

This notorious speech (657–73) deserves comment, for it often is quoted as evidence of Aeschylean misogyny and proof that the *Oresteia* encodes and legitimizes the repression of women. The politics of gender in the trilogy (and the society that produced it) is more complex than often is admitted, and the assumption that Apollo acts as the mouthpiece for the poet should be rejected as naïve and simplistic. Among other things, such an interpretation neglects the dramatic context in which the god appears in the trilogy. Recall the strong negative associations of Apollo in the Cassandra scene in *Agamemnon*, and the god's dismissive arrogance towards the Furies at the opening of *Eumenides*. The contrast with Athena, who protects the suppliant Orestes without driving the Furies away, could not be more pronounced, and the goddess herself reinforces the difference by reminding Apollo that he may do what he likes in Delphi but not in Athens.

This background strongly colours the audience's response to Apollo's speech, where he argues in sophistic fashion that the father is the mother of the child. The god offers as proof the strange birth of Athena, who sprang fully formed from the head of Zeus. According to Apollo, women are not really parents, but merely the nurturers of the seed that the father generates. Therefore Orestes' murder of his mother is not as unnatural as it appears, since there is no real blood connection between a mother and her child.

Of course the position that women were not really parents was anything but the popular or the legal view in the fifth century. The Periclean citizenship law of 451 limited Athenian citizenship to individuals both of whose parents were Athenian, and we know that the marriage of *homometric* siblings was forbidden as incestuous, while a man could marry a sister by the same father as long as they had different mothers. Besides the counter-intuitive nature of Apollo's argument, the most telling reason for the audience to reject it derives from their experience of the trilogy in the theatre. If a mother is not a parent, then why does Aeschylus highlight the image of the pregnant hare devoured with her unborn children, or use it as a means of foreshadowing the destruction of the Trojan War in *Agamemnon*, where the 'shield-bearing young of a wooden horse/ time their birth to the setting stars' (825–26)? If Apollo is right, then Orestes' murder of Clytemnestra raises no serious questions about blood ties, pollution, and matricide; the Furies have no business haunting Orestes, nor has Orestes any reason to feel haunted; and the dramatic heart of the trilogy – the *Choephori* – suffers cardiac arrest.

Apollo further compromises his position by offering a bribe to Athena and her city (667–73), something against which Athena specifically warns her people (693–95, 704). Aeschylus also suggests the shady side of Apollo by failing to give the god a clear exit when he slips off-stage at some point after the jury casts its vote. Apollo neither speaks nor is spoken to, an anomaly in the ancient theatre, as if his argument had little significance in a court where mortal agents make the difficult decisions. Viewed in the full dramatic context, Apollo's speech denying that women are parents of their own children radiates with something less than the pure white light of Aeschylean approval.

Athena follows Apollo's defence with a plea that her city continue to honour the homicide court down through the ages. Three times in her charter speech she addresses the Athenians of the future, as if to remind her citizens in the audience that the trial scene acts out their own, ongoing history. At her instruction, the jury rise from their seats to vote, moving to the urns (probably large and free-standing), placing a hand into each, but dropping a white pebble in only one. In *Agamemnon* the conquering king describes the fall of Troy in similar terms:

> Hearing no pleas for justice
> the gods made their verdict clear.
> An urn of blood filled with votes
> for manslaughter and the death of Troy.
> At the other urn, the shadow
> of hope, her hand wavered . . .
> now smoke holds that city.
>
> (*Ag.*, 814–19)

That imaginative vision of the gods' destruction is redeemed by the actual process of voting. Human jurors decide the murder trial, moving between Apollo and the Furies who remain in their fixed positions on opposite sides of Orestes. As they file across the orchestra, the Athenian jury symbolize the freedom and responsibility of democratic justice.

After the last juror returns to his seat, Athena steps forward to speak, perhaps taking her stand between the two urns.[15] She announces that, if the votes are equal, she will cast the tie-breaker for Orestes. Born without a mother, Athena champions the male principle in all things and so refuses to honour the death of a woman more than a man. It seems at first that the goddess simply parrots Apollo, but she complicates her position (and vote) by adding that her respect for the masculine does not extend to marriage.[16] The ballots are counted and found to be equal, an image of deadlock that – thanks to Athena's intervention – allows Orestes to go free. In a long speech of gratitude, Orestes promises that Argos (the home city to which he returns) will join in a non-aggression pact with Athens, an alliance he vows to guarantee even from the grave. In *Choephori*, the tomb of Agamemnon was the locus for vengeance; the tomb of his son, Orestes, will be the source of a different kind of energy, uniting cities and honouring the role of Athens in establishing a new mode of justice.

As Orestes exits via the *eisodos*, Aeschylus' story of the house of Atreus draws to a close. But the play does not, for *Eumenides* continues another three hundred lines, almost a third of its length. The Furies and Athena still remain in the orchestra, two female forces locked in the most important conflict of the trilogy. Their confrontation shapes up as a battle between two contending modes of expression – lyric and rhetoric – that proved so important in *Agamemnon*. Enraged at Athena's verdict, the Furies explode into lyric, threatening to release a plague on Athens and her people. Each of their lyric outbursts is matched by a speech from Athena, who tries to persuade them that their defeat is, in fact, a victory. After four such lyric eruptions from the chorus and spoken responses from the goddess (778–891), the Furies finally agree to 'put the black wave of bitter anger to sleep' (832), leaving the dance and joining Athena in regular speech.

Describing their conversion as 'falling under a spell' (900), the Furies accept the position of honour and authority in the city that Athena offers. The scene ends with the chorus lying on the orchestra floor and Athena standing over them, recounting the blessings they are to sing for their new home.

The metamorphosis to Eumenides ('kindly spirits') reverses the transformation at the start of the play, when the ghost of Clytemnestra rouses the sleeping Furies to vengeance and pursuit. Instead of waking them to anger, Athena calms their rage, moving among them in a mirror-image of that earlier scene, enhanced by the fact that the same actor played both Athena and Clytemnestra. The visual parallels take us back to the *kommos* of *Choephori*, where the chorus, Orestes, and Electra wake the spirit of the dead Agamemnon to help them exact vengeance. But the seeds of these enactments of sleeping and waking are planted in *Agamemnon*, when the Watchman struggles to stay awake, afraid to close his eyes, and the chorus sing of Zeus leaving the memory of pain in place of sleep (*Ag.*, 179–80). Clytemnestra imagines the victorious Greeks at Troy, sleeping with no guard on watch and unaware that the anger of the slaughtered may wake against them. The Herald describes the sea dozing in the heat of summer, and the terrors of sleeping beneath an enemy's wall. The chorus tell Cassandra to put her prophecies to sleep (1247), and they protest after Agamemnon's cry that the murderers' hands are wide awake (1357). From its poetic genesis in the first play, the actions of sleeping and waking culminate in the final transformation of the Furies who 'awaken' from their vengeful anger and rise from the orchestra floor to bless the city of Athens.

By persuading the Furies to remain, Athena redeems another pattern central to the trilogy, that of homecoming. The opening play dramatizes the return of Agamemnon and his fatal entrance into the palace. *Choephori* also features a homecoming, one not fatal to the returning party (Orestes) but to the rulers of the house. However, the son comes back from exile only to flee again, haunted by his crime of matricide. *Eumenides* continues the pattern, opening with the flight of the Pythia from her temple, followed by Orestes' departure for Athens, pursued by the chorus of Furies. After his acquittal, Orestes returns to his patrimony in Argos, while Athena persuades the Furies *not* to leave, but to make their home in Athens. When the chorus do exit from the orchestra at the end of the play, it is to take up residence in their new city as honoured and permanent guests.

The crowning action of *Eumenides*, the Furies' 'departure to remain' fulfils the theatrical possibilities suggested earlier in the trilogy. After the spell of persuasion cast by Athena, the chorus wake to bless the city and her people, and the goddess joins their song half way, moving into lyric anapaests. A similar metrical scheme operates after the murder of Agamemnon, when the chorus confront Clytemnestra in lyric and she responds in regular speech, a pattern that repeats until she finally shifts to anapaests. At the end of the trilogy, however, Athena moves into the mode of the chorus to reflect a basic harmony with them, although there are intriguing contrapuntal motifs. While the chorus abandon their retributive tones for the blessings of Eumenides, Athena sounds increasingly like the Furies earlier in the play, emphasizing the need for the old laws and respect for ties of blood.

A subsidiary chorus of women, the attendants of Athena's temple, enter to escort the Eumenides to their new homes. The women bring torches, sacrificial animals, and purple robes that the chorus put on, and they sing a final song in praise of the new residents of their city. The entire company including Athena parades out of the theatre, mirroring two great processions of Athens – the Panathenaic festival, which celebrated Athena as patron goddess of the city, and the City Dionysia, in which the performance of the *Oresteia* itself was a part.[17]

But we needn't look outside the play for the relevance of the costumes and visual detail, since the chorus's dark-red robes re-introduce the colour of the tapestries on which Agamemnon walked. Once a symbol of bloodshed, the colour now celebrates the peaceful inclusion of the Furies into the city. The torch-led procession takes the audience back to the opening scene of the trilogy, where a lone watchman struggled to see a single beacon under the panoply of the stars. The fiery message of conquest broke out like the sun at dawn, only to rise over a scene of destruction. Now, the torchlights signal a different kind of victory, one in which the city truly wins and the defeated party not only shares in the triumph, but is essential to it.

The exit of the Furies from the theatre is not a departure but a homecoming, marked by blessings of fertility, health, prosperity, and hope. Transformed into spirits of birth and regeneration, the Eumenides reunite the animating forces of nature with life-producing marriage, a synthesis that seemed hopelessly shattered in *Agamemnon*. However, the promise of civil concord, of men and women finding their way together, remains only a promise. No secure solution could follow the acts of bloodshed in *Agamemnon* and *Choephori* without trivializing the plays and ignoring the complex network that made the murders necessary. Looking at the Furies, Athena proclaims 'from their terrible faces/ I see great gain for my people' (990–91). Although their bodies are covered in robes of respectability, the horrifying masks remain. The visual dialectic is essential to the *Oresteia*, where good news turns to defeat, homecoming leads to death, and the forces of vengeance and justice are inextricably linked. As the dramatic workings of the *Oresteia* make clear, Aeschylus' trilogy offers at best a provisional resolution, one that must be fought for again and again in the theatre and in the society that produces it.

# 7

# SOPHOCLES' *OEDIPUS TYRANNUS*

Long considered the 'classic' Greek tragedy, Sophocles' *Oedipus Tyrannus* holds a special place in the history of Western theatre. In some respects the notoriety of the play helps it work on the contemporary stage, since most audiences know the outline of the story. Compare the lack of familiarity with Aeschylus' *Seven Against Thebes*, or Euripides' *Ion*, or Sophocles' own *Philoctetes*. However, exposure to the Oedipus myth has its drawbacks as well, for much of the modern fascination with the play derives from Freud's use of the story as the paradigm for his psychoanalytic theory of male infantile desire. There is no denying the importance of the Oedipal complex as a psychological and interpretive model, but it sheds little light on the play Sophocles wrote and, when applied to a production, leads the audience down a theatrical blind-alley.

So, too, does the application of psychological realism to the play, epitomized by questions like 'Why did Oedipus marry someone old enough to be his mother?' *Oedipus Tyrannus* is not a cautionary tale of crime and punishment, where the audience are meant to think that Oedipus and Jocasta should have known better. The issue held no dramatic interest for Sophocles since it never is hinted at in the text.

A more insidious form of theatrical reductionism arises from the mistaken belief that the characters in the play are simply puppets in the hands of the gods. Although Oedipus is born to doom, everything he does on-stage he freely chooses. Even while matching his life to the terrible fate inscribed for him, Oedipus continues to act autonomously, following the best information available. Thinking he is the son of Polybus and Merope, he strives to avoid the pollution of parricide and incest by fleeing Corinth; as political leader of Thebes, he struggles to rid his city of the plague by tracking down the killer of Laius; and, when the opportunity arises, he applies his energies relentlessly to untangle the riddle of his own identity.[1]

This last effort, the most compelling in the play, returns Oedipus to the riddle of the Sphinx on which his earlier fame rests. The answer to the question 'What creature goes on two, three, and four feet?' is man. Oedipus himself personifies the enigma, a tragic figure who is more than one (terrible) thing at a time. It is important to note that in his confusion Oedipus manifests no moral failing or 'tragic flaw', a (mis)translation of Aristotle's term *hamartia*, which implies an archer 'missing the mark', not hitting a bull's-eye. Oedipus errs through simple ignorance of the material facts of his own birth. Out of that situation Sophocles crafts a play that is both keenly particular (Oedipus is like no man) and broadly universal. Do any of us know who we really are, what we are doing, the full consequence of our actions?

The audience's familiarity with the story operates to best advantage in the play's ubiquitous ironies. As Oedipus drives towards the truth, he unwittingly participates in a remarkable series of puns, perhaps nowhere more striking than on his own name. Meaning 'swollen-footed', a reference to the pierced ankles he suffered when exposed as a child, 'Oedipus' contains the Greek word *oide* meaning 'I know', literally, 'I have seen'. The prophet Teiresias taunts Oedipus with 'not knowing who lives with you' (337–38), prompting the retort 'but I/the one who knows nothing, Oedipus, I stopped the Sphinx' (396–97). The verbal play, more prominent in the Greek than in most English translations, suggests that Oedipus' name signals his destiny. A man of intellect, whose rational gaze saw through the riddle of the Sphinx, gradually comes to realize how flawed his vision and understanding have been. His self-blinding adds further irony to his name, 'Oedipus – the one who has seen'. He stabs his eye-sockets (Greek *arthra*, 1270), the same word for ankle-joints (*arthra*, 718) that were pierced as a child. And as he stumbles forth in his blindness, Oedipus' troubled feet and failed vision bring the ironies of his life to their physical fulfilment.

The audience in the theatre resemble the gods who foresee Oedipus' destination but are ignorant of its precise course. That is, we know in general terms where the play is going, and we watch galvanized with horror as Oedipus leads himself (and us) to recognize what always has been present. Critics from Aristotle onwards have marvelled at the working of the plot, unwinding with the precision of a perfectly balanced watchspring. But formalist criteria cannot account for the fact that Oedipus' struggle draws us into the emotional turmoil of his situation, gradually undermining our god-like position as ironic observers until, by the end of the play, we are less sure of the future than Oedipus is.

That Oedipus will lead us through the drama is manifest in the opening scene. Before any dialogue takes place, a group of suppliants gathers at the orchestra altar – small children, young adults ('the unmarried youth'), and older men (probably the chorus itself), the entire assembly led by an old Priest.[2] If the three age-groups represent the three ages of man from the riddle of the Sphinx, as some critics think, then the stage-picture suggests Oedipus' past success as well as his present challenge, the task of saving the city again. Emerging from the palace, Oedipus addresses the suppliants as 'children' (the first word in the play), establishing his paternal responsibilities as ruler and hinting at the underlying cause of the plague that ravages the city – the child who killed his own father and then fathered children by his own mother.

The Priest describes the wasted earth of Thebes, the dying flocks, the stillborn cries of women, the teeming house of death, the city like a storm-tossed ship whose prow is swamped in blood. Looking to Oedipus for guidance, the Priest does not consider him 'equal to the gods' (31), but first among men, and Oedipus accepts the challenge, declaring to the crowd that 'no one/ among you can make his sickness equal to my own' (60–61). Metaphors of 'making equal', of number, sum, and balance, recur throughout the play, suggesting the equilibrium that Thebes has lost and the hidden truth that Oedipus is 'equal to himself' in truly horrifying ways. Slowly the numbers turn on him, until the notorious place where three roads meet will show him to be equal to his father's killer.

These figures of speech, and the verbal play on ones, twos, and threes, find their theatrical correlative in the organization of actors in successive scenes. Sophocles masterfully exploits symmetry and imbalance in each dramatic encounter, shifting from one-, two-, and three-actor scenes as the play drives towards its climax. At the outset, for example, Oedipus' entrance balances the Priest and suppliants who have gathered in silence, until the arrival of the third actor, playing Creon, tips the action in a new direction. Apparently symmetrical scenes, such as that between Oedipus and the prophet Teiresias, end in discord, and the play's masterfully written triangular scenes – each involving the protagonist and two other characters – eventually reveal Oedipus as the perpetrator of the very deeds he has tried to avoid. He stands alone as the paradoxical still-point where the imbalances of the play – the plague, the murder, the oracles, the three roads – all come together.

When the Priest begs him to help with the plague, Oedipus announces that he already has sent Creon to consult Apollo's oracle at Delphi. As if on cue, Creon returns with the prophetic response, one of many juxtapositions that keep the play moving at speed. Learning that the plague arises from the unsolved murder of Laius, Oedipus vows to find the criminal and 'drive off the pollution/ for no absent loved ones, but for my own sake, and self' (137–38). He means that he will make his rule more secure by finding the killer of the previous king, but the audience hears the unintended irony that twists Oedipus' proclamation back on himself.

In their *parodos*, the chorus graphically evoke the plague that sweeps the city. At one point (190–94) they link the sickness to Ares, the god of war, not the normal Greek divinity associated with disease. It appears that Sophocles intended the epidemic ruining Thebes to call to mind the great plague that ravaged Athens in the early years of the Peloponnesian War (429 and again in 427–26), around the time of *Oedipus'* first production.[3] The predominant dactylic metre, with several lines in full hexametre, points to Apollo's oracle, since prophetic responses from Delphi took that metrical form. The chorus's pleas for divine help also give parts of the ode the feeling of a fifth-century cult hymn. Clearly the horrific description of the plague and the desperate search for some remedy carried specific contemporary relevance for the audience.

After the *parodos*, Oedipus returns to the stage and vows to track down the killer of Laius 'as if this man were my father' (264). Standing alone before the chorus and the audience, Oedipus curses the murderer and brands him a pariah. The next time Oedipus stands as the sole actor on-stage will be after his self-blinding, when he is caught in the curse that he now, unknowingly, pronounces on himself. The chorus suggest that Oedipus consult Apollo's prophet Teiresias, only to find that Oedipus has sent for him already. As with Creon's return from Delphi, Teiresias arrives almost as soon as he is mentioned, adding to the feeling of irrepressible momentum. Holding a staff for support, the blind prophet is led into the orchestra by a child, a memorable image that foreshadows the appearance of Oedipus at the end of the play, holding onto his children and clutching a blind-man's stick.

Oedipus begs Teiresias to save the city that lies in supplication before him (326–27). Unlike the suppliant scene at the opening of the play, however, this appeal to community and civic responsibility falls on deaf ears. A far cry from the gentle English vicar that classicists once imagined, Teiresias is a dark, uncompromising character, shrill, unpleasant, inaccessible, but one who happens to know the truth and prefers not to share it. Teiresias' intransigence in the face of such desperate public need strikes Oedipus as treasonous, and he suspects collusion between Apollo's prophet and Creon who brought word from Apollo's oracle. The accusation of treachery leads Teiresias to denounce Oedipus himself as the city's pollution, the very murderer he seeks to find. The claim seems so outlandish, and the dramatic pitch rises so quickly, that Oedipus hears nothing but mockery and abuse, and the scene degenerates into one of invective and diatribe. Oedipus taunts Teiresias with blindness and failure to solve the riddle of the Sphinx, and the prophet counters by predicting the blinding insight that awaits Oedipus, the revelations that will 'make you equal to your own children' (425).

The paired speeches give way to a short stichomythic exchange, allowing a real question to surface out of the virulent recriminations. Provoked by a comment about his background, Oedipus asks Teiresias about his parents, and again the prophet answers enigmatically: 'This day will give you birth, and ruin' (438). Oedipus counters that his personal fate is of little consequence 'so long as I save the city' (443), but Teiresias is unmoved and calls his young attendant to lead him off. The prophet's final speech comes somewhat unexpectedly, and it may well be that he delivers it out to the audience while Oedipus stands behind him, back by the palace door. The words ring out with terrible clarity, but not to the man for whom they are intended:

> That man [Laius' murderer] is here, present: a foreigner by name,
> but he will show himself born a Theban,
> a great occasion, but it will not make him happy.
> A blind man after seeing, a beggar after being king,
> he will feel the ground before him with a stick
> as he makes his way. And he will show himself
> to be both father and brother to his own children;
> to the woman who bore him, both son and husband;
> a fellow-sower with his father, and his blood-letter.
>
> (451–60)

This daring summation of the truth, revealed so early in the play, reminds us that Sophocles has not written a detective story or murder mystery. Rather, his dramatic technique involves the projection of an overriding pattern, guaranteed by the oracle and grounded in the myth, but one that his protagonist cannot see. Acting on his own best instincts, Oedipus must uncover the truth on his own, and the audience watches riveted as he comes upon what has always been there.

After Teiresias and Oedipus exit, the chorus perform their first stasimon. They imagine the killer of Laius roaming the wilds, breaking through the timbers like a mountain bull hunted down by the prophetic voice from Delphi. For the audience, the description of the desperate fugitive applies to Oedipus, his plight all the more pitiable given that he plays the role of hunter as well as the hunted. Twice the chorus call the charges levelled by Teiresias *deina*, an untranslatable word that occurs throughout the play, meaning 'terrible', 'strange', 'clever', 'awful', and 'wonderful' – in the sense of awe-inspiring and full of wonder – something that surpasses, or violates, the norm.[4] The chorus distinguish between the gods who are beyond question and their human interpreters such as Teiresias who are not. They reassert the civic priorities with which the play began, refusing to believe that the prophet's accusations convict the man who once saved the city from the Sphinx.

Creon enters from an *eisodos* to answer the charges against him, charges that he, too, labels *deina*. He reminds the chorus that his life is bound up with theirs, that he considers nothing worse than to be called evil by the city he loves. Time and again Creon describes Oedipus as not thinking or seeing straight, the figure of speech suggesting the underlying twistings of the truth that prompted the charge of treason in the first place. Oedipus confirms how off the mark he is when he bursts onto the stage, accusing his brother-in-law of suborning the prophet and plotting against the throne. Creon mounts a strong defence in a speech that became a *locus classicus* for the disadvantages of holding power, explaining that he prefers the status and sway of second-in-command to the responsibilities of rule. Reasonable, cautious, well intentioned, sober, Creon reveals the gulf that separates him from Oedipus, who is excessive and impulsive, driven by duty and circumstance to press beyond where a reasonable man would go.

Creon points out that Oedipus rules in Thebes with 'power equal to Jocasta' (Creon's sister and Oedipus' wife), and that he himself is 'equal with a third share' (579, 581), possessing the advantages of kingship without the worries. The image of Oedipus as first among three equals takes theatrical shape when Jocasta enters from the palace as the third party, diffusing the tension between the other two. She shames the men for 'stirring up/ private quarrels when the country is diseased' (635–36). Although she frames her commands as questions, Jocasta effectively takes charge, telling her husband to go inside and ordering her brother home. The only female in the play, Jocasta restores temporary sanity to the proceedings, and the chorus help by initiating a *kommos* with Oedipus, persuading him to let Creon live. After his departure, Jocasta joins the chorus and Oedipus in the *kommos* as she tries to find out what led to this confrontation. The lyric ends with an image of order restored, the ship of state with Oedipus at the helm guiding the city through the present storm.

Jocasta's forceful entrance, coupled with the *kommos* that follows, marks the key transition in the play. The first half of the lyric ushers Creon out of the action, and the second half recalls the situation facing the city and Oedipus' role in leading her to safety. When the lyric dies away, we are in a different dramatic world. Gone are the public pronouncements to the city, and gone too are the heated encounters between Oedipus and the men he suspects of treason. In their place, Sophocles presents an intimate, even confessional scene between husband and wife.

Jocasta calms Oedipus' fears of conspiracy linked with the Delphic oracle by disclosing a long-buried story from her past. An oracle came to her husband Laius that he would die at the hand of his own child, but the king was killed by brigands where the three roads meet. As for the child, mother and father pierced his ankles and left him to die on Mt Kithairon. On the basis of personal experience, Jocasta concludes that the gods can make the future clear, but their human intermediaries – prophets, oracles, and seers – should not be trusted.

One of several accounts of the murder of Laius in the play, Jocasta's story reveals a single detail so surprising to Oedipus that he fails to hear anything else she says. Deaf to her account of the exposed child, he zeros in on the fact that the murder took place where three roads meet. Oedipus begins to cross-examine Jocasta in stichomythia, driven to fit together the pieces of his past. The intensity is palpable, a kind of white heat that takes the play to a deeper dramatic level. Matching Jocasta's confessional tones, Oedipus then tells his wife of his youth in Corinth, the insult at a banquet that led him to wonder if he was a bastard, his trip to Delphi where he heard an oracle that he would kill his father and sleep with his mother, and – most critically for the moment – his fatal encounter with an old man at a place where three roads meet.

Oedipus relives that meeting in vivid detail, a masterful description of spare, etched moments that culminate in a brief flurry of violence – the party tries to drive him off the road, he protests, the old man strikes him like a beast, he kills them all. If that man was Laius, then Oedipus stands self-cursed, condemned to exile from Thebes. Even in the face of so terrible a prospect, Oedipus fears a worse eventuality. No matter what happens to him at Thebes, he vows never to return to Corinth where he would risk killing his father Polybus and marrying his mother Merope, as the oracle foretold. The implicit reminder to the audience that worse discoveries lie ahead for Oedipus confirms the truth of his observation – 'Someone who judged that these things came against me from a raw, savage god,/ would he not speak in a straight line?' (828–29).

There remains a slim hope that the shepherd who survived the attack will confirm the initial report that several brigands and not a single agent committed the murder. Oedipus sends for the old man: 'If he still says/ that *they* killed him, the same number, then I didn't./ No, it's not possible for *one* to equal *many*' (843–45). Again, Oedipus finds himself in a numbers game where incommensurates come out equal. Jocasta insists that no matter what the shepherd says, the oracle did not come true, for Laius was not killed by his own son. In the cruel world of the play, she takes comfort from the fact that her baby, 'that poor, wretched thing' (855), died long before. Oedipus and Jocasta withdraw together into the palace, a wounded couple striving to make the best of their broken past. The audience see how ragged their hopes are, since their very union is the knotted curse they cannot escape.

Against this dramatic backdrop, the chorus dance out their sense of the sacred, the divine laws that order the world: 'No/ mortal nature, no man/ gave them birth, never will forgetting lull them to sleep./ A god is great in them, does not grow old' (868–71). The chorus then contrast the human drive towards excess that ultimately proves self-destructive, moving out from the killer of Laius to any mortal who acts irreverently and 'touches untouchable things' (an echo of Aeschylus' *Agamemnon*). If these men prosper and their actions are honoured, the chorus wonder, 'Why should we perform the dance?' (896). The question is self-reflexive in the extreme, challenging the *raison d'être* of the tragic chorus, and asking the audience to examine their own presence in the theatre. If no divine force supports the world, if it is 'best to live at random as best one can' as Jocasta will claim later (979), then why bother to participate in dramatic festivals and attend the theatre? Why gather to watch the story of Oedipus being acted out?

Before we dismiss the question as too much for any play to ask of itself, recall that fifth-century tragedy was no mere entertainment or celebration of individual expression, but rather a means of engaging the city in a process of self-questioning, self-correction, and self-definition. If someone literally gets away with murder, as the killer of Laius seems to have done, if one can toy with the world, profit from injustice, trample the sacred with impunity, then on what meaningful basis can the theatre exist? Sophocles' answer seems to be radically simple and humanly complex – tragedy can neither justify nor sustain itself if the world is as random as it appears to the chorus at this moment in the play. This does not mean that the order behind the apparent chaos is pleasant or comforting, for the truth that the play reveals is uncompromising and cruel. Nonetheless, it takes on meaning and significance in the very process by which a character like Oedipus exposes it, and then finds the strength to stare it in the face.

For all its broad implications, the question is grounded in the dramatic situation, the chorus's considered response to the turmoil of the play. The cross-currents batter them as well as the main characters, and in the final antistrophe they threaten to abandon Delphi and the other sacred shrines 'unless these things fit together,/ pointing the way for all men' (901–02). Recalling Jocasta's view that oracles need not be heeded, the chorus fear that 'the things of the gods have passed away' (910). It is as if the physical anguish caused by the plague, vividly present in the prologue and *parodos*, has metamorphosed into a more fundamental, existential fear. The process of that fear is suggested by the last lines of each strophe and antistrophe, moving from faith to disbelief: 'A god is great in them [the sacred laws] and does not grow old' (872); 'Always the god is champion' (882); 'Why should we perform the dance?' (896); 'The things of the gods have passed away' (910). Until Oedipus is found out, the gods and their oracles *must* seem false. Until the murderer is discovered, the civic and religious institutions that make up the *polis* are under attack.

The very moment the chorus proclaim that worship of the gods has left the city, Jocasta enters from the palace and makes her way to the altar of Apollo, bearing a suppliant's wand and offerings to the god. Jocasta's striking about-face underlines the radical insecurity that affects her and everyone else in the play. The queen prays to Apollo to 'untie the knot and make us clean' (921), desperate for her husband who now fears he is Laius' murderer and still is haunted by the oracle that he will kill his father and sleep with his mother. As if answering her prayer, a messenger from Corinth arrives unexpectedly, bearing the news that Polybus has died and Oedipus has been proclaimed the new king. The juxtaposition is remarkable, and Jocasta calls her husband from the palace, overjoyed that the part of the prophecy involving parricide now lies in the grave.

Normally a father's death would be met with grief and lamentation, but the world into which Oedipus and Jocasta have been thrown reverses such natural reactions, and they rejoice at the news. Learning that Oedipus still fears he will sleep with his mother, the Corinthian Messenger happily lifts the burden by informing him that neither Polybus nor Merope was his natural parent. Oedipus learns that he was found as a baby on Mt Kithairon and handed over to the very man now speaking, who pulled the pins out of his ankle-sockets and named him Oedipus, 'swollen foot'. The Corinthian received the baby from an old shepherd, the same man Oedipus sent for at the close of the previous scene as the sole surviving witness to Laius' murder.

Throughout the stichomythia between the two men, Jocasta says nothing, but the audience knows that her worst nightmare is coming true. Sophocles exploits the potential of the three-handed scene with keen precision, as the spotlight turns inexorably back on the figure who had dropped out of the dialogue. Jocasta finds herself caught by the very forces of chance she hoped would free her husband from divine prediction. The principle of living at random reveals the world (and the oracles) making brutal, all-too-coherent sense, and she begs Oedipus to stop: 'If you have any care for, any love of your own life,/ don't track this down. My disease is enough' (1060–61). The plague that afflicts Thebes now finds its source in Jocasta, who sees the truth, and in Oedipus, who does not. But he knows that he is on its trail, and he will not be side-tracked by anyone, even his wife. Jocasta races into the palace keeping the horrible knowledge to herself, behaviour that strikes Oedipus as the vanity of a woman who fears she married beneath her. Ironically, Oedipus now adopts Jocasta's principle, valorizing the randomness of his own birth: 'I consider myself a child of Chance [or 'Fortune']/ ... / ... Such is my nature/ and I would never wish to be otherwise' (1080, 1084–85).

Oedipus and the Corinthian Messenger remain on-stage during the lyric celebration of the chorus, who praise Mt Kithairon as the mother, nurse, and native land of Oedipus, a child of Fortune. Did some god beget him – Pan dallying on the slopes? or Apollo lying with a nymph? or Hermes? or Dionysus cavorting in the meadows? Given the ominous departure of Jocasta, this outburst in honour of Oedipus and his mountain-mother is shockingly out of place. The audience may compare this surge of lyric eroticism and fertility to the opening plague chorus, describing the stillborn labours of the Theban women. In the previous stasimon the chorus had asked 'Why should we perform the dance?' and now they seem to answer the question with a dance for Mt Kithairon. Something is terribly wrong. Whatever 'chance' and 'fortune' are, whatever Mt Kithairon symbolizes, they do not represent the order on which the life and health of the city rest. The radical shift in choral mood underlines the instability at the heart of the play, as the dramatic pendulum swings back and forth with increasing violence.

Into the imaginary world of Mt Kithairon, this sexual playground for gods and mortals, enters a real dweller of the place, the mountain Shepherd who was summoned earlier as a witness to Laius' murder. His arrival begins the final three-handed scene, drawing together the separate strands of Thebes, Corinth, and Kithairon. As before, Sophocles couples the speakers in different combinations – Oedipus interviews the Shepherd; the Messenger takes up the questioning, pressing the old man about the child he handed over years before; and when the old Shepherd grows reticent, Oedipus resumes the interrogation, threatening him ruthlessly to get at the truth. At this point neither Oedipus nor the play can tolerate delay:

> *Shepherd*: Ahhh! I am on the verge of it, of saying it – *deina*.
> *Oedipus*:  And I on the verge of hearing it. It must be heard.
>
> (1169–70)

The child was Laius' son, whom the Shepherd took from Jocasta with orders to kill it because of a fearful prophecy. Feeling pity, the Shepherd disobeyed and gave the baby to the Corinthian to raise far from Thebes. Now, years later, the same three parties stand together, reunited, confronting what that original meeting has led to.

With ruthless honesty, Sophocles shows that the noble intentions and simple instincts of men and women have wreaked havoc on Oedipus. The Shepherd responded with pity and saved the baby Oedipus; the Corinthian felt sympathy and took the infant to Corinth; the childless king Polybus and queen Merope adopted the orphan as their own, lovingly raising him to be heir to the throne; the Corinthian as Messenger brought the good news that Oedipus was king of Corinth, and then removed his fear regarding his Corinthian 'parents'. As for Oedipus, he strove to avoid the parricide and incest he was warned of at Delphi, only to bring about the very predictions he tried so hard to escape.

The three parties who originally came together on the mountain years before now go their separate ways – the Shepherd and the Corinthian leave via the two *eisodoi*, and Oedipus returns to the palace. For the first and only time in the play, all three passages are used simultaneously, a powerful visual image of the various triads that have led Oedipus to self-knowledge, in particular the three roads that brought him, blindly, face to face with his destiny.

Left alone in the orchestra, where the three theatrical paths converge, the chorus sing a moving tribute to their king. They recount the mutability of all human fortune, where joy and accomplishment vanish like a dream, where success and honour turn to agony and shame. From general observations that mankind is 'numbered equal to nothing' (1188), the chorus turn to the paradigm of Oedipus himself, who surpassed all men, defeated the Sphinx, saved the city single-handedly. In the second strophe they consider his fall 'into the marriage-bed of both son and father' (1209–10), the mark of Oedipus' undying infamy. Time, the agent that brings all things to light, judged Oedipus' and Jocasta's marriage to be no marriage at all, revealing breeder and child to be one and the same. At the close the chorus shift into a more personal mode, wishing they had never seen Oedipus, and yet mourning his fate as if lamenting the dead: 'I shut my eyes in a sleep of death' (1222).

The images of light, darkness, revelation, and sleeping eyes anticipate the news that the Messenger brings from the palace. He tells the audience they have been spared much of the horror, since they did not have to view it with their own eyes. This incessant concentration on eyesight and seeing is more than an ironic foreshadowing of Oedipus' self-blinding. Via the chorus and the Messenger, Sophocles seems to be encouraging the audience to adopt Oedipus' new mode of perception, to 'close our eyes and see', creating from the Messenger's words the dreadful events that have taken place off-stage, out of sight.

We hear first of Jocasta's suicide, and because it is her response, it cannot be Oedipus'.[5] As he earlier dismissed Jocasta's pleas to stop his search, he rejects her answer to what that search unravelled. Instead of ending his life, Oedipus chooses to make literal what was figuratively true about him, and he blinds himself. The Messenger's vivid description of the self-blinding suggests that Oedipus begins the first in a series of confrontations with his past. We hear how he smashes through the bolted bedroom doors, cuts down Jocasta who has hung herself over the bed, and then repeats an action he had performed for so many years. He undresses his wife, taking out the pins that hold her dress, but now he uses them against himself:

> . . . again and again, not just once
> he stabbed and spitted his eyes. Each time the gore
> from the sockets soaked down his cheeks,
> not spurting out drop by drop, but in a gush
> like a black cloud of hail, till the blood softened his face.
>
> (1275–79)

With the specificity of a sexual nightmare, the final meeting of Oedipus and Jocasta, of son and mother, becomes a telling re-enactment of the physical relationship they enjoyed as man and wife. Gouging out his eyes in the bedroom beside Jocasta's corpse, Oedipus confronts the person with whom he has been most intimate and most ruinously unaware. With that encounter behind him, Oedipus is prepared to return on-stage and face the public.

The palace doors open to reveal the blind hero, and the chorus find the sight *deina* (1297), most *deina* (1298), a judgement they repeat later (1312, 1327) in the *kommos* they share with Oedipus. Drawing on the heightened intensity of the lyric, Oedipus expresses an almost Beckettian amazement that even a disembodied trace of his life remains: 'My voice/ why does it fly/ why does it carry?' (1309–10). He knows the world around him only by sound: 'though all is shadow, I recognize your voice' (1326). Wishing he had died on Mt Kithairon, Oedipus curses the Theban Shepherd for saving his life, and the chorus take his comments to their logical conclusion. Leaving the lyric for regular speech, they suggest that Oedipus would have done better to kill himself rather than to live blind.

Their pronouncement has an immediate effect – Oedipus follows the chorus into iambic trimetres, delivering a speech that begins unequivocally, 'What I did was done for the best./ Don't instruct or advise me' (1369–70). He vehemently defends his action as the harsher and more fitting punishment. By living blind, Oedipus has cut himself off from all society, fulfilling the curse he pronounced on the killer of Laius early in the play. Moreover, blindness will free him from gazing upon the father he killed when they meet in the underworld, and he will never have to look his incestuous children in the eye.

The competing tensions within Oedipus give the speech its exceptional power, and the actor playing the part must convey the desire both to close off the past and to remember it; to terminate experience and to prolong it; to give up and to fight on. The specificity of the details etched in Oedipus' memory provide their own paradoxical rationale for continuing the struggle: 'Three roads and a hidden glen,/ the oaks closing in where the three ways join – / you drank my father's blood, and my own, shed by these/ hands of mine – do you still remember me?' (1398–1401). The turn of the last question is remarkable, revealing something of the depth of Oedipus' character, a man who earlier wanted to 'wall off the ears/ and dam up the flowing stream of sound, close it all off . . . and dwell outside all reminders of evil' (1386–90). But Oedipus cannot help but remember, to the point of wondering if the signal places in his life remember him.

Oedipus' need to resurrect and reiterate the past reflects what one critic has called a 'definitional fondling of the truth'.[6] By confronting his prior life so forcefully, Oedipus emerges from the chorus and takes the stage on his own. In the final step of his orchestrated return to full strength, he now steels himself for a scene with another actor, facing again the drama of dialogue and conflict. As Creon enters, Oedipus recalls their earlier encounter when he wrongly accused his brother-in-law of plotting to seize power. The reversals of the play are such that Creon, who had no desire for the throne, now stands as the new ruler, and Oedipus is at his mercy.

Sophocles wastes no time in making the audience aware of how different their experience in the theatre would have been if the play were *Creon Tyrannus*. Although he brought word from the Delphic oracle himself that the murderer of Laius should be exiled, Creon now decides to send someone back to Delphi to make sure. Oedipus instinctively knows that his exile is best for the city (1449–58), and the audience too feels that the blind man's rightful place is the slopes of Mt Kithairon, a prophetic voice at home in the wilderness. But the new king insists on the cautious path, slowing down the momentum and refusing to allow the play the closure it has earned.

Deprived of his political and physical powers, Oedipus nonetheless asks the questions, makes the demands, and drives the action forward. Sophocles gives us a verbal *gestus* of the situation when Oedipus launches a long speech with the forceful words, 'And you [Creon], I command you – and I beg you . . .' (1446). The break mid-sentence reflects Oedipus' awareness of his weak position, and yet it admits to no diminished authority.[7] Although there are moments of abject self-pity, the basic tone of Oedipus' speech remains one of natural dominance, so much so that the very last lines Creon speaks confront the blind man with his true situation: 'Don't think you can rule always./ You have survived, but not your power' (1522–23).

Nowhere is Oedipus' indomitable spirit more evident than in the meeting with his two young daughters, whom he begs to hold one last time. That these previously unseen and unnamed children make the final entrance of the play is a daring piece of dramaturgy. The image of a polluted father embracing his daughters/half-sisters would have seemed monstrous and indecorous to the original audience, something to be kept out of sight. Perhaps for this very reason, their brief scene of reunion achieves a kind of redemption. For the first time since he came to self-knowledge, Oedipus does not focus on himself but on others. His kingdom has shrunk from the great city of Thebes – whom he addressed as his children in the opening scene – to two small, incestuous daughters. Yet he is still *their* leader, predicting the harsh future that awaits them and imploring Creon to help soften it: 'Do not make them equal to my own evil' (1507). Earlier Oedipus asserted that the sight of his children would bring him no pleasure, that he wished he had died on Mt Kithairon, that he would like to cut off all sensory experience. Now he clings to his daughters and acknowledges in their embrace the tangled web of his own life:

> Children, if you were old enough, if you had understanding,
> the things I would tell you . . . But now, I pray only
> that you may live where occasion allows, that you find a life
> better than that of the father who brought you into it.
>
> (1511–14)

Thinking back over the play's long dénouement, we realize that Sophocles has recapitulated Oedipus' life, presenting a series of encounters between the protagonist and the major players in his past – Jocasta (as reported by the Messenger), the chorus (in the *kommos*), Creon (in their scene together), and his own daughters. Although there is no literal second meeting with Teiresias, Oedipus himself evokes the seer's presence. Groping for his daughters, he resembles the blind prophet led on and off the stage by a small child. Oedipus adopts a prophetic voice, predicting what lies in store for his children and prophesying his own future: 'I know this much – no disease/ no natural cause will kill me, nothing. For I never/ would have been saved from death if it were not for something strange [*deina*] and terrible' (1455–57). But for all their similarities, Oedipus remains essentially different from Teiresias. Oedipus vowed to save the city no matter what the personal cost, but when he and Thebes looked to Teiresias, the prophet turned away. Now, as he huddles with his wretched family in the orchestra, Oedipus again manifests the commitment to human society that separates him from the self-contained prophet of Apollo.

For the first three-quarters of the play the audience knows what lies in store for Oedipus, and yet we marvel at the way the inevitable falls into place. The precise dovetailing of the plot, the collusion of fate and mortal choice, the dynamics of language and action draw us into the experience of the protagonist as he goes from ignorance to knowledge. After the blinding, however, Sophocles has Oedipus lead us in another direction, where the boundaries are not marked so clearly. With no riddle to solve, no blinding flash of insight to signal the climax, a humbled mortal struggles to live with the truth, and then slowly recovers his strength of purpose and need for human contact. There is no softening here, no sentimental concessions or surrender to heart-warming fellow-feeling. For the play ends with Creon separating Oedipus from his children and forcing him off-stage.[8] And yet the audience has rediscovered the Oedipus who was always there before them – accursed, wilful, inquisitive, courageous, inspiring. Ultimately, Sophocles' play appeals to the theatrical imagination not because of Freud, or fate, or human folly, but because it presents a compelling and fully tragic drama, one in which man is not destroyed, but found.

# 8

# EURIPIDES' *SUPPLIANT WOMEN*

If there is something forlorn about an unperformed play, as Jonathan Miller puts it, then Euripides' *Suppliant Women* cries out with a particularly theatrical eloquence to be reclaimed by the living stage. Set at Eleusis, home of the famous Eleusinian Mysteries, the action juxtaposes the promise of spiritual rebirth with the basic human drive to bury the dead. Not one, but two choruses – the suppliant women of the title and a secondary group of their grandsons – occupy the stage before the action even begins. Later in the play, a long funeral cortège fills the orchestra, only to be followed by a *second* procession bearing the cremated ashes. In between these spectacles of the dead, a distraught wife enters unexpectedly and, from high above the orchestra, leaps into the funeral pyre of her husband. With unrivalled theatrical daring, Euripides explores the compulsions to violence and the costs of war in this neglected masterpiece.

The play opens with Aethra, the mother of the Athenian leader Theseus, making offerings before the temple of Demeter and Persephone at Eleusis. The rite she performs, the Proerosia, was intended to guarantee fertile sowing and bountiful harvests for Attica, sharing with the Mysteries a focus on rebirth and regeneration as reflected in the agricultural season. Aethra takes her position in a cancelled entry, surrounded by suppliant women from Argos, who 'bind her' to the altar with suppliant wands (32). They have come to plead that Athens intervene on their behalf and procure the corpses of their sons, the famous Seven against Thebes, who have been denied burial by the Thebans. In addition to the cluster of women around the altar, the Argive leader Adrastus lies prostrate before the entrance to the temple, and near him stands a secondary boys' chorus representing the sons of the Seven.

Through the long opening scene the Eleusinian setting is never forgotten. The altar where Aethra stands (33–34, 291) is 'the holy hearth of the twin goddesses, Demeter and Kore' (as Persephone is called). The chorus admit that their request is inappropriate to Eleusis, given that the Mysteries represent a symbolic conquest over death, for they have come to consign corpses eternally to the underworld, to 'bury the dead' (173–74). That

123

phrase rings out like a leitmotiv throughout the play, and the word 'corpse' is sounded as the first or last word of the trimetre line *eighteen times*. In a tragedy overwhelmed with the dead, the contrast with the Mysteries and the Proerosia is striking – a cycle of violence and death set against the rites of rebirth and regeneration.

The opening tableau makes a clear distinction between two groups – the women around the altar closer to the audience; and the old man and young boys back near the façade – and the focus alternates between them. The play begins with Aethra's prologue followed by the lyric of the Argive mothers, literally the *parodos* although the chorus are already in the orchestra (1–86). After Theseus' entrance, the action shifts to an exchange between the men, as Theseus interrogates Adrastus and finally rejects the Argive supplication (110–262). The women regain the initiative with the second lyric section and Aethra's long speech urging her son to change his mind (263–333). The scene closes with Theseus' acquiescence, his decision to seek Athenian support on the suppliant's behalf, and the freeing of his mother from the altar (334–64).

The shift between male and female points of view is mirrored in – and supported by – the patterns of stage movement, and it is helpful to work out what Euripides' actual blocking might have looked like. Theseus makes the first proper entrance in the play at line 87 via one of the *eisodoi*, setting the pattern for *all* subsequent entrances and exits (except Evadne and Athena who appear on the *theologeion*), for the temple façade is never used. After an introductory five lines to cover his arrival, Theseus notices his mother surrounded at the altar and continues downstage while speaking to her, stopping on the same axis to one side of the altar. At line 104, the groaning of Adrastus directs Theseus' (and the audience's) attention away from Aethra, and Theseus crosses upstage to the old man who lies near the façade. He persuades Adrastus to uncover his veiled head and stand (110–12), and from that position the two men play out a scene of some 150 lines.

Setting the Theseus–Adrastus exchange in the stage area behind the orchestra maintains the thematic blocking that separates men from women. At the outset of the play, a silent group of males (Adrastus and the boys' chorus) observes the activity of Aethra and the suppliant women; now a silent group of women watches as two male representatives make their respective cases regarding the suppliants. Since the altar is sufficiently downstage of the backdrop, the audience views the Adrastus–Theseus dialogue through the filter of the women. Even though they take no part in the actual debate, Aethra and the Argive mothers occupy the visual foreground, an arrangement that anticipates their ultimate importance in Theseus' decision. As almost all seats in the theatre of Dionysus are above the performance level, the group at the orchestra altar does not obstruct the scene taking place back near the façade. Most likely the chorus sit or kneel on the ground (as they are said to at 10, 44, 271–72), and Aethra sits at the altar as she did earlier (93).

At the conclusion of their debate, Theseus rejects Adrastus' request that Athens intervene to recover the corpses, and the Argive leader instructs the chorus to leave their suppliant wands and depart. Instead of exiting from the theatre, the women take their appeal directly to Theseus, first in iambics (263–70) and then in dactylic hexametres (271–85). They divide into two half-choruses, allowing the non-singing contingent of each section to perform the movements demanded by the text while the other group sings. Taking Theseus by his knees, chin, and hand, the women re-enact the supplication of the opening tableau but move it upstage, leaving Aethra alone at the altar for the first time. The stage-picture is as follows: the supplementary boys' chorus stand with Adrastus close to the backdrop; Theseus stands in the upstage part of the orchestra surrounded by the Argive women on their knees; and Aethra remains at the altar in the centre of the orchestra.

From this position, Theseus and Aethra are on the same vertical axis running from the orchestra altar back to the façade; this alignment allows Theseus suddenly 'to see' his mother again, having neither spoken nor referred to her since line 108. Instead of responding to the chorus after their emotional appeal (they have literally fallen at his feet), Theseus addresses Aethra: 'Mother, why are you weeping, covering your eyes/with your robe?' (286–87). In a striking visual echo, Aethra's veiling and collapse at the altar (286–90) recall the gesture and posture of Adrastus earlier (110–12), who also covered his head in shame and lay on the ground. Urging his mother to raise her head and throw off her veil, Theseus crosses back to her at the altar, reversing the upstage move he made to Adrastus when he encouraged the old man to stand and speak.

If this reconstructed blocking is correct, then Euripides has carefully brought together mother and son for what proves to be the crucial exchange of the opening section. By having the chorus leave the orchestra altar to bring their supplication to Theseus, Euripides frees the strongest acting area in the theatre, allowing the two Athenian principals to stand together 'downstage centre'. The stage is set for the colloquy that Aethra passed up earlier when she deferred to Adrastus, and mother and son are now the focus of the theatre audience seated before them and the Argives (gathered together for the first time) standing behind them.

The gender differences that guided the initial blocking have given way to a grouping by bloodlines and city, the two Athenians (mother and son) at the altar, the Argive suppliants (father, mothers, and grandsons) back by the façade. The shift is all the more appropriate, for Aethra now rejects the maxim that women have nothing worthy to say (299–300), and she speaks out strongly not only for her son, but also for the good of the city. Athens should be known for protecting pan-Hellenic norms such as burying the dead, and Theseus should take up the Argive cause as his own. Aethra subverts the idea with which she ended her prologue – 'For women who are wise/it is right to act through men in all things' (40–41) – and sets

125

the stage for the emergence of even more powerful forms of female rhetoric later in the play.

Aethra does more than change Theseus' mind. Her words serve as the catalyst for the first of several overtly political speeches in the play. Using his position at the centre of the orchestra to take in the theatre audience, Theseus gives a short description of Athenian self-government (349–56), emphasizing the democratic nature of the city over which he presides. He will take Adrastus before the Assembly and present the case for intervention on behalf of the Argives, a clear inclusion of fifth-century political practice onto the tragic stage. Only after addressing the audience does Theseus return to the immediate dramatic context, calling for the chorus to remove the suppliant wands that bind Aethra to the altar (359–60). Mother and son exit via one of the *eisodoi*, followed by Adrastus and the sons of the Seven, and the opening act of *Suppliant Women* comes to a close.

We have seen how carefully Euripides plays out the possibilities set up by the cancelled entry, integrating the movements of principals, chorus, and secondary chorus, and exploiting the strength of the orchestra as an acting area. The attention paid to these aspects of the production is not simply technical refinement, but helps to clarify the larger themes of the play – the relationship between men and women in both private and public spheres, the difference between their access to public discourse and their manner of experiencing loss, the nature of civic responsibility *vis-à-vis* outsiders, and the way in which the theatre itself becomes a place to explore the role of democracy, drawing the Athenian audience into the issues of the play.

Left alone in the orchestra, the chorus perform the first stasimon, praising the pan-Hellenic norm of burying the dead, and praying that Theseus' help will lead to a future alliance between Athens and Argos. Their short sixteen-line lyric – two strophes and antistrophes of only four lines each – provides a hiatus that bridges an extraordinarily long 'dramatic' interval, during which we are to understand that Theseus and the Argive men go to Athens, meet with the Assembly, persuade the city to undertake the task, and make their way back to Eleusis. The flexible treatment of space and time is a convention of Greek tragedy, but here Euripides so collapses these elements that the audience gets the impression that Athens and Eleusis have merged. We cease to imagine an off-stage world different from what is visible before us, as if the public world of the Athenian Assembly and the theatre are now one.

Adrastus and Theseus return with plans to recover the corpses, but before Theseus can dispatch his emissary, a Herald from Thebes arrives, rejecting their request in advance. He documents the arrogance of the original Argive expedition against his city, symbolized by Capaneus whom Zeus himself struck down with a lightning bolt. The Herald then launches into a debate on the relative merits of monarchy vs. democracy, referring to the Athenian system as mob rule. Although his tone is condescending and abrasive, the

Herald mounts a telling critique of democracy, stressing the influence of self-serving demagogues over the majority. The common man does not have time to inform himself on issues, and so he gives his vote to the most persuasive speaker (412–25). Democracy only appears to be the rule of the people; more accurately, it is power wielded by a few who manipulate the many through clever speech.[1]

The Herald's most telling indictment involves the patriotic fervour aroused by democracy that blinds itself to the real costs of war:

> When a people vote to make war,
> no one considers that he himself might die
> but turns that harsh fate on to another.
> But if death was *there to behold* when the votes were cast,
> war-crazed Greece would never destroy itself.
>
> (481–85)[2]

Theseus counters by asserting the many advantages of democracy, shaping his defence in terms immediately recognizable to the Athenians in the audience. He praises the annual rotation of officers, a distinguishing feature of political practice in Athens (406–07), and he echoes the phrase that opened each meeting of the Athenian Assembly (438–39). As his mother did before him, Theseus emphasizes the humanitarian aspects of burying the dead, one of the unwritten laws honoured by all civilized people. The debate then degenerates into a boasting and sarcastic stichomythia, and the Herald departs for Thebes to prepare for war. Confident that the gods are on the side of Athens, Theseus exits to make ready his attack, pointedly leaving Adrastus behind. The upcoming battle involves the principle of burying the dead – it has nothing to do with the hatred between Argos and Thebes, arising from a war that Adrastus himself admits he never should have sanctioned (156–60).

The chorus divide into two groups, as they did earlier in their appeal to Theseus, but now they maintain an anxious dialogue with one another. The mothers are alive to the bloodshed to come, having already lost sons in a foreign adventure at Thebes, and they even hope that a 'compromise through discussion' (602) might be reached between the Thebans and Athenians. Their instinctive sense for the anguish of battle, however, gives way to the cry 'Justice calls for Justice, and blood for blood' (614). Caught between the desire to avoid conflict and the appeal of battle as an ultimate tribunal, the women are both the victims of war and the reason that it breaks out again.

As in the previous stasimon, the lyric bridges an enormous passage of dramatic time, covering the invasion of Thebes and the battle to recover the bodies. A Messenger arrives from Thebes with news of the Athenian victory, and an account of the remarkable self-control manifest by Theseus. With the Theban enemy defeated and the way open to seize the city, Theseus refused to press his military advantage, proclaiming instead that 'he did not come/to sack the town, but only to take back the dead' (724–25). The Messenger praises Theseus' moderation with words of particular relevance to the war-torn Athenians of 423 BC:

> Best to pick such a military leader
> who provides in times of trouble the surest defence,
> for he hates the popular tendency towards violent overreaching
>     where, when someone does well,
> he strives to climb to the top of the ladder (*klimakôn*)
> and so destroys the prosperity he had at his command.
>
> (726–30)

The image of climbing too high recalls Capaneus, one of the Argive Seven, who tried to scale the walls of Thebes by ladder (*klimakôn*, 497) and was blasted by the lightning bolt of Zeus (496–99).[3] Capaneus' literal rise and fall epitomize the entire Argive expedition, an exercise in arrogant violence punished by the gods. The Athenian attack against Thebes provides the positive image of that negative adventure. On hearing of Theseus' victory, Adrastus himself admits that the original Argive invasion was unnecessary, that a peaceful and fair resolution had been offered by Thebes, but the Argives had rejected it (739–41). Adrastus sees his own city's error replicated by the Thebans, who refused to give back the bodies and so, also, 'fell victim to their own violent overreaching' (743). The play has reached a point where lessons seem to be learned, and Adrastus echoes the judgement of the Argive women that cities should strive to resolve their disputes by words and not by bloodshed (744–49).

In the process, Theseus emerges as a model of control in the midst of warfare, not afraid of combat but acutely aware of the specific goals for which he fights. His behaviour after the victory is no less exemplary. The Messenger describes how, having recovered the bodies, Theseus initiated their funeral rites, washing the corpses with his own hands and readying the funeral biers, performing the ritual actions normally reserved for the mothers of the dead (762–68). Adrastus is incredulous that Theseus – a man, a general, a leader of the city – would undertake such demeaning duties for dead bodies exposed so long above the ground. It is the kind of work that even slaves would approach 'with abhorrence' (762), 'an awful business, one that is full of shame' (767). We recall that earlier Theseus took the advice of his mother Aethra on a crucial question of policy, reversing his course of action to help the Argives recover their dead (293–341). Now we hear of his willingness to assume the woman's role, caring for the bodies as if they were his own kin. And when the ruler of Athens returns to the stage, it is not in triumph, but as part of a procession bearing the corpses for eventual cremation and burial.

The longest funeral sequence in Greek tragedy (798–954) begins with a *kommos* between Adrastus and the mothers, as the pall-bearers carry the bodies of the Seven into the theatre. After the orchestra fills with corpses and lamentation, Theseus enjoins Adrastus to deliver a full-scale funeral oration for the instruction of 'the young men of the city' (843). The model is the great funeral address (*epitaphios logos*) delivered annually in Athens to honour soldiers who fell in battle that year and received burial at public expense. The practice was instituted earlier in the fifth century and immortalized by Thucydides in Pericles' funeral oration of 431–30.[4] The specificity of Theseus' request would not have been lost on the original audience, and once again Euripides asks them to evaluate the scene on-stage as if it were part of the public discourse of the city.

We can imagine their consternation as Adrastus gainsays the very lessons he had learned before, when he admitted that the Argive expedition was foolhardy and vainglorious, that the deaths could have been avoided, that the gods themselves had punished the Seven against Thebes for excessive pride. The most blatant example of Adrastus' 'mythifying' the past is his re-creation of Capaneus as a moderate aristocrat. Gone is the violent man struck down by Zeus' lightning bolt, the very epitome of violent, overreaching pride (495–99); in his place, Adrastus presents a hero who 'was no prouder than a poor man' (862–63), one for whom 'the mean was enough' (866). To speak of the blasphemous Capaneus as affable and moderate is absurd, and Adrastus compounds his double-speak with an excursus on education. Teaching the young is a process of providing models for behaviour at an early age even if 'they don't fully understand them' since 'whatever someone learns in that way will stay with them/ till they grow old' (915–17). Adrastus' funeral oration turns into a call for the fifth-century equivalent of brainwashing, and the audience are not fooled. As a modern critic asks, 'Could an Athenian citizen really take seriously the advice to bring up his children to be a Capaneus?'[5]

By incorporating a semblance of the Athenian funeral oration into his play, Euripides relentlessly probes its potential for misuse. Although Theseus says nothing to counter Adrastus' speech, the mothers of the dead heroes draw no comfort from it, responding to the glowing words with expressions of grief and despair (918–24). As Theseus and Adrastus lead the bodies out of the orchestra for cremation, the women sing a formally balanced ode of mourning (strophe, antistrophe, and epode, 955–89). At this point Euripides introduces a dramatic rhetoric all his own, a theatrical answer to the public platitudes of the politician and the dignified mourning of the chorus. For suddenly the women spot Evadne, the wife of the dead Capaneus, climbing the rocks above the shrine. From her commanding position on high, Evadne sings an emotionally charged monody, and then, after a brief exchange with her father who arrives to dissuade her, she leaps to her death in the burning pyre of her husband.

Nothing like this scene ever took place in fifth-century tragedy before or after *Suppliant Women*, and we would be hard pressed to find a more theatrically daring moment in the history of the stage. The opera heroine Tosca plummets to her death when she discovers that Cavadarossi has been executed, but Puccini doesn't introduce her for the first time only moments before. With shocking immediacy Evadne interrupts the ritual mourning for the Argive Seven, determined to perform her own ceremony of grief. She mounts the *theologeion* on the roof of the skene so that all can see; she even may have climbed part of the theatre cavea itself, up the side of the supporting wall along one of the *eisodoi*.[6] Wearing her wedding dress, Evadne prepares for a marriage to the dead, singing a monody that conflates erotic and funereal motifs: 'I will mingle in love my body with my husband's, melting in the radiant flames, my skin touching his skin' (1021). When her father Iphis arrives in the orchestra, she rejects his pleas to return with him, preferring to lie with her husband in death.

Significant for the play's Eleusinian setting, Evadne construes her suicide in terms of the Persephone myth, hoping to arrive at 'the marriage chamber of Persephone' (1022). But Evadne re-enacts Persephone's marriage to Hades as if in a mirror. In place of Persephone's ascent into the light and reunion with her mother, Evadne leaps down into the fire to merge wholly and indissolubly with the dead, leaving her father heart-broken. Evadne's journey to Eleusis denies the hope of recovery and rebirth intrinsic to the myth of Demeter and Persephone, and lying at the core of the Eleusinian Mysteries.

Why does Euripides include this *coup de théâtre*, and at this particular point in the play? As we noted before, *Suppliant Women* is overwhelmed with death. The unburied corpses of the Argive Seven dominate the play, and their funeral rites are supplicated for, debated about, fought over, and finally achieved. But with Evadne's self-immolation, the waste of death becomes palpable – someone living is there before our eyes, and suddenly that someone is gone. Death, as it were, is animated, revealing itself as activity, as *dying* and *killing*, rather than something mourned over as a given (the procession of dead bodies) or reported as an off-stage event (Theseus' defeat of the Thebans). The progression from death to dying proves particularly disturbing when the victim is a non-combatant, one who chooses to leave a world already awash with organized killing.

For all its immediacy and surprise, Evadne's suicide is not construed as a private act of grief. When she reveals her intention to throw herself on her husband's pyre, Iphis begs his daughter not to 'say such things before a crowd' (1066), but Evadne insists that from her example 'all the Argives will learn' (1067). Euripides emphasizes that her dying, no less than Adrastus' funeral oration, is a fully public act, and we are asked to compare the lessons she teaches with those offered earlier by the Argive leader. Recall that Adrastus believed in inculcating values of patriotism and military virtue from an early age so they would stay with the young until 'they grow old.' Perhaps this accounts for the devastating surprise of Evadne's suicide, as if only something so shocking and excessive could shake an audience free from the education towards war they have imbibed from their youth. With Euripides' inspired theatrical instinct, Evadne sets off a dramatic explosion that brings home to the audience what the other characters on-stage only talk about, and then forget.

Broken by his daughter's suicide, Iphis leaves the orchestra hoping that his own death will come soon. 'Old age', he muses, 'should make way for the young' (1113). It does so literally, for the secondary chorus of children, bearing urns holding the ashes of their fathers, enter as the old man leaves. Euripides has primed us to attend to the lessons learned by the younger generation, and what we hear is ominous. Joining the chorus in a *kommos* of grief, the boys sing of their orphaned status (1134). One son expresses the hope that as 'shield bearer' he will avenge his father's death (1142–44), and another prays that the gods help him secure 'justice for my father' (1145–46). A third imagines himself personally leading a new Argive assault on Thebes (1149–51).

Given what we know of the original Argive expedition, it is hardly surprising that the boys' cry for vengeance produces an anxious, troubled response from the chorus of women, the boys' grandmothers: 'And this evil still does not sleep./ Terrible events! Too much lamentation,/ too much grief comes at me' (1146–48). Holding the ashes of their fathers who fell in an unnecessary and avoidable battle, the sons resolutely sow the seeds of future conflict.

At this point we should consider the special relevance to the play of one of the ceremonies that preceded the tragic performances at the City Dionysia, outlined in Chapter 2. Orphaned sons of Athenians who had fallen in battle were reared at public expense, and when they reached the age of 18 the young men marched through the orchestra dressed in hoplite armour provided by the city, a gift with which they were expected to defend their benefactress.[7] In the closing section of the play, Euripides purposefully refers to this pre-performance ceremony. Orphaned boys process through the orchestra holding the cremated remains of their fathers, men who were given a funeral oration just as the fathers of the Athenian orphans would have received at their public burial in Athens. The Argive youths long to bear a shield and avenge their war-slain fathers, just as their Athenian counterparts bore the city's gift of armour (including the great hoplite shield) in honour of their forbears.

The unexpected arrival of Athena as *dea ex machina* on the skene-roof adds fuel to the fire. On the one hand the goddess insists on formalizing a defensive alliance between her city and Argos (1183–1212), on the other she gives her blessing to the second Argive assault on Thebes and guarantees its success (1213–26). Athena exhorts the orphans to lead a 'bronze-clad' army against Thebes when their 'beards begin to shadow' (1219–20), again recalling the Athenian orphans who, having come of age, also came into arms.

It is hard to believe (as many critics do) that Athena speaks *for* Euripides when she encourages a fresh outbreak of violence.[8] Athens was engaged in a devastating war with Sparta and her allies, and various aspects of *Suppliant Women* tell us that the Peloponnesian War was integral to the play's composition and its reception at the City Dionysia. Theseus' battle with Thebes over the corpses probably reflects the historical refusal of the Thebans to relinquish the Athenian dead after a military campaign in November of 424,[9] and the Argive–Athenian defensive alliance anticipates the actual agreement achieved in 420, after the Peace of Nicias ended the first part of the Peloponnesian War in 421.

It was the quest for that elusive peace whose influence is felt most strongly in *Suppliant Women*. If the play was first produced in 423, as many scholars believe, then the original performance took place only *a few days before* the Athenian Assembly met to vote on a year-long armistice with Sparta. It is likely that the Peloponnesian delegates had arrived for discussion with the Council before the City Dionysia began and actually were in attendance at the theatre, along with the citizens of Athens who would vote on the agreement.[10] They saw dramatized before them two broad, but clearly opposed, scenarios for their city: to fight – but only as a last resort – in defence of laws and customs that were pan-Hellenic in nature, as Theseus does; or to surrender to the instincts of violence and vengeance, a temptation to which the orphans succumb and Athena actively encourages.

Recall the Theban Herald's observation that 'if death was *there to behold* when the votes were cast,/ war-crazed Greece would never destroy itself' (484–85). Viewing the end of the play with those words in mind, we appreciate the dramatic measures Euripides has taken to present us with images of death 'there to behold'. In the array of corpses that dominate the second half and, above all, in the suicide of Evadne, the play makes every effort to preclude a failure of imagination on the part of its audience, keeping war-generated death forcefully, and shockingly, before us.

With the return of the sons of the dead bearing the urns of ashes, the terrible cycle of violence begins anew. The ripples spread out to the contemporary world when the Theban orphans, eager to arm for war, begin to resemble their Athenian counterparts, outfitted as hoplites and paraded in the orchestra before the performance. Gone are the offerings to Demeter for bountiful harvest that began the play, as well as the wise mother, Aethra, who made them. Gone, too, is the hope of return from death and the underworld symbolized by the figure of Persephone, and institutionalized by the Mysteries in her honour. In their place we have a gathering of ashes, an orchestra full of mourners and future warriors, the patron goddess of the city in her characteristic armour, and, still present as an after-image, the stark and forbidding memory of a wife leaping to join her husband – a theatrical world, in short, firmly wedded to death. Whether that will also be the world of the audience is, I think, the question of the play.

# 9

# EURIPIDES' *ION*

*Ion* is hardly a 'tragedy' in the popular sense of the word. The play treats of recovery and reunion; no one is killed; a foundling finds his real mother; a foreigner learns he was born to the throne. In structure and story-pattern the play seems like a fairy-tale version of Sophocles' *Oedipus Tyrannus*, and critics often label *Ion* (along with Euripides' *Helen* and *Iphigenia among the Taurians*) a 'romance'. In place of the perfectly hinged turning point of Sophocles' tragedy, however, *Ion* requires *three* dramatic reversals to keep the play on track – a dove who drinks the poison meant for Ion, the Priestess who appears in the nick of time to stop him from killing his mother Creusa, and Athena who arrives as a *dea ex machina* at the end. The very energy and invention required to achieve the final result serve to complicate it, as do the experiences of the mother and child who are tossed in the shifting currents of the plot.

Ion himself suggests the problem with a romantic or comic approach to the play when he rejects the apparent advantages of leaving Delphi for Athens: 'Things seen close up are not the same/ seen far away' (585–86). His simple insight mirrors that of the audience, whose perspective on the dramatic events shifts as the play draws them into sympathy with the characters caught in the toils of radical and unpredictable change. By juxtaposing laughable with deadly elements, Euripides keeps the tone of the play ambiguous and unsettling, forcing the audience to look beyond the façade of the happy ending arranged by Apollo into the darker recesses of what that ending wishes to hide.

The play opens with a prologue delivered by Hermes, the 'lackey of the gods' (4), who first provides the background to the story. The Athenian royal couple, Creusa and her foreign-born husband Xuthus, are without a child and have come to Delphi in quest of an oracle. Unknown to Xuthus, Creusa had been raped in her youth by the god Apollo, bore his child in secret, and exposed it in the cave on the Acropolis where the god had violated her. Apollo arranged for Hermes to bring the baby to Delphi where he has grown up and works as a temple attendant, ignorant of his future as founder of the Ionian race. Hermes' review of these events is filled with proper names and

133

places (well over forty in eighty lines), and the god concludes his monologue by formally assigning the name 'Ion' to the young man who follows him on-stage: 'First of all the gods, I / name Apollo's son ION. Name and destiny' (80–81).

Concern with naming and identity proves to be a driving force in the play, propelling the action towards clarification and disclosure much as in *Oedipus Tyrannus*. However, in Sophocles' tragedy the truth exists outside the action, an unseen but omnipresent order that Oedipus finally reveals when he finds the murderer of Laius. In *Ion*, the wilful covering-up of the truth by Apollo, the god responsible for the confusions of the play, never admits a full disclosure, leaving the characters – and the audience – to wonder how stable the underlying order is.

As Apollo's mouthpiece, Hermes outlines the action to come, but his dramatic map for the audience proves faulty: 'Xuthus will enter the shrine, the god will give him / the boy, his own child, saying he's the king's true son. / His mother will not know that he is really hers / until they get home to Athens' (70–73). The god promises a neat, controlled scenario, but the action of the play is hardly so tidy. Terrible crimes are countenanced and nearly committed, and the events as enacted refuse to comply to the hermetic plot arranged in advance, in no small part because the unknowing instruments of Apollo's plans are human beings. The very points at which they fail to operate as expected provide the audience with the moments of greatest emotional engagement. In particular, the qualitative difference between the god's eye view of key events in Creusa's past and the way she herself remembers and relives them on-stage is crucial to the experience of *Ion* as a tragedy.

Consider Hermes' first mention of Apollo's rape of Creusa: 'This daughter of King Erechtheus, the bright-god Apollo yoked in marriage / by violence . . .' (10–11). The line-end suggests a proper wedding (the phrase 'yoked in marriage' was an Athenian commonplace), but the new line highlights 'by violence'. A seemingly formal union turns, with the line-break, into rape. Similarly, a pattern of conflicting images reveals more uncertainty and ambiguity in Apollo's masterplan than Hermes explicitly admits. A shimmering brightness dominates the language of the prologue (indeed the whole play), and Apollo, the sun-god, is named nine times, frequently by his epithet Phoebus ('bright one'). Working against the language of light and clarity, however, are images of darkness and secrecy. Creusa was raped by Apollo in a dark cave under the Acropolis where she returned to abandon her baby, all kept secret from her family (11–17). The priestess who discovers the baby at Delphi assumes it is the 'secret birth' (45) of some local girl, and Hermes tells us that Apollo's motive throughout is to keep his rape of Creusa 'hidden' (73). At the end of the prologue, the verbal tension between brightness and clarity on the one hand and darkness and secrecy on the other generates its corresponding stage action. As Ion enters to 'make the temple steps shine / with his laurel broom' (79–80), Hermes sneaks off to hide in the laurel bushes and watch the story unfold.[1]

Ion brings with him a lyrical purity and innocence as lovely as it is unaware, manifest in his opening description of the sunrise over Parnassus:

> Dawn's shimmering horses raise
> the sun ablaze over the earth
> up through air steeped in fire
> where light on light
> routs the remnant stars
> into the holy dark.
> The unwalked peaks of Parnassus
> flare, smoulder, and take for us
> this day's charge of sun.
> The smoke of desert myrrh
> flutters to the rooftop,
> the shrine of the Bright God.
> (82–90)

Everything is luminous to Ion, but even more striking than his brilliant language is the expressive form he adopts, shifting from anapaests to a fully lyric monody. He sings a strophe to his broom and an antistrophe to the Olympian god he serves, praising the twin realms of earth and sky, of work and worship, that define his young life.

The sudden appearance of a flock of birds prompts Ion to draw his bow and drive them away from the sanctuary. He feels a twinge, however, for the eagles from Parnassus bring omens from Zeus, and the swans provide inspiration for Apollo's own music. Even so, Ion threatens to slay 'the red-footed swans' (162–63) and 'drown their beautiful song in blood' (168–69). The tone remains light, for the danger posed by the birds is hardly serious – they build their nests in the rafters and their droppings pollute the shrine. And yet their natural song, like Ion's own monody, must cease, for 'the sound of the bow will end it' (173). The audience glimpse, in brief, the trajectory of the play – a movement from innocence to experience, the conversion of Ion from broom-sweeping boy to blood-shedding adult.

The invasion of birds is one thing, the arrival of the chorus quite another. Ion puts down his bow and shares the audience's bemusement at this group of Athenian maidens who have come to admire the sights of Delphi. Critics bound by the conventions of theatrical realism imagine an array of architectural and scenic elements that provoke the chorus's wonder. However, the abundance of deictic endings (Greek suffixes that indicate something is pointed at), the imperatives 'look!' and 'see!', the fact that the *parodos* is not sung in unison but broken up into individual and specific utterances, all suggest that the chorus create the sights primarily out of their words and gestures, and the spectators follow

135

the verbal cues to project the sculptured images onto the conventional skene façade.

Specific descriptive details resonate with the chorus of Athenians – and with the original audience – particularly the mythic battle between the Olympian gods and the earth-born giants (206–18). Their patron goddess Athena played a key role in the victory, using her gorgon-shield against the giant Enceladus. They learn from Ion that gorgons also are carved on the *omphalos* that lies at the centre of Apollo's temple, establishing an important imagistic link between Delphi and Athens. But the chorus's thoughts go no further than the surface – 'What we see outside is enough; it charms the eye' (231). Ion will grow to challenge that attitude as events compel him to look behind the temple façade, realizing that its shimmering appearance effaces another, darker story.

That story finds its central character in the figure who now arrives on-stage, the Athenian queen Creusa. The scene develops into the longest section of stichomythia in Greek tragedy (105 lines), a novel way to introduce background information and advance the narrative. The dialogue draws unrecognized mother and son closer and closer together as each identifies with the other's situation – a childless mother and a motherless child – but it stops well short of full recognition. Creusa weeps at the sight of Apollo's temple, and her thoughts continually run back to the dark moments in her past, to the cave on the Acropolis where she was raped by Apollo and later exposed her child. Ion's innocent curiosity about Athens and the Acropolis leads Creusa back to the same dark place, and she deflects his questions or reverts to silence. The process is repeated several times, transforming the dialogue into a form of exposition whose stops and starts are constitutive of its meaning.

The direction of the stichomythia changes for the last time when Creusa introduces her 'fictional other', the third party for whom she ostensibly consults the oracle. When Ion learns that Apollo is the father of this woman's child, he dismisses the claim as incredible, but gradually he comes to sympathize with the unfortunate woman, recognizing the mirror-image of his own motherless upbringing:

Ion:      But what if Apollo took the child and raised him in secret?
Creusa:   No right to act alone! He should share that joy.
Ion:      Your story sings with my own grief.

(357–59)

The dialogue leaves us with a very different Ion from the one we first met. Unlike the birds that flutter down to foul the shrine, the threat to Ion's peace of mind cannot be answered with bow and arrow. Could the god he serves act unjustly? Can a mortal consult Apollo's oracle with questions that incriminate the god himself?

These doubts lead Ion to break out of stichomythia and deliver his first

136

full speech (369–80), counselling Creusa to abandon the quest on behalf of her friend, since the gods cannot be forced to divulge what they do not wish to. Creusa counters with her own request for secrecy, begging Ion not to tell her husband, Xuthus, what has passed between them. He arrives now in great excitement, having received a preliminary prophecy that his wife will leave the sanctuary with a child, answering their need for a son and heir to the Athenian throne. This transitional scene brings together Ion, Creusa, and Xuthus, only to have them go their separate ways unaware of the complex weave that binds their fates together. As her husband enters the temple to consult the Delphic oracle, Creusa is once again an outsider, forced to hear of Apollo's word indirectly, and she exits via an *eisodos*.

Left alone on-stage, Ion delivers a soliloquy that challenges the god he serves. That Apollo should rape women and not take responsibility for the results leads Ion to cry out: 'You've got such power,/ your power ought to serve what's right' (439–40). For Ion, the possession of a god's might entails virtue in its application. Otherwise one has only rape and injustice, a world where evil cannot be condemned because men are simply following the example of their models, the gods of Olympus (442–51).

As the Athenian historian Thucydides tells us, this question of the relationship between power and moral responsibility provoked heated debate in Athens during the Peloponnesian War. The famous Melian dialogue, an account of Athenian designs on the neutral island of Melos, epitomizes the issue. The Athenian envoys argue that the Melians must capitulate: 'You know as well as we do that right, as the world goes, is only in question between equals in power, while the strong do what they can and the weak suffer what they must.'[2] Athens uses the might-makes-right argument to justify subjugating the island, putting the grown males to death, and selling the women and children into slavery. The audience in the theatre of Dionysus may not have recognized in Ion's moral imperatives a reference to this specific debate, but they would have perceived an image of innocence troubled by a question of contemporary – and lasting – importance. The Ion who leaves the stage after these reflections has changed from the young man who, 300 lines earlier, was singing to his broom. The world of Apollo's shrine can never again be cleaned and purified so easily.

The significant action now takes place off-stage in the temple's inner sanctum, where Xuthus receives his prophecy about children. To set that event in its broadest context, the chorus organize their first stasimon around the issue of offspring, appealing to the virgin goddesses Athena and Artemis to help guarantee children for the house of Erechtheus. The women focus on Athena's birth without labour pains (delivered from the head of Zeus), and on the role of Artemis who traditionally helped women in childbirth. Perhaps we are meant to see in these goddesses the counter-image of Creusa, a mortal raped by a god, abandoned in her pregnancy, forced to give birth in secret and without help.

In the antistrophe the chorus raise a paean to the joys of offspring, in which they ask to be granted 'the beloved raising of our own children' (487). The choice of words is precise – the women ask not simply for children, but for the *raising* of children, and not any children but sons and daughters of *their own* (that is, not adopted). The first request has been denied Creusa completely, as she herself tells Ion earlier. As for the second, Hermes has informed us that Apollo plans to present Ion as Xuthus' offspring, not hers. Only later, in Athens, is Creusa to learn the truth. The contrast between the chorus's wishes for themselves and the reality that faces Creusa underlines the anguish of her situation.

In the epode, the chorus describe a strange scene on the Acropolis involving the mythical first family of Athens. The daughters of Cecrops and Aglauros dance in the meadow before the temple of Athena (the Erechtheum) to the music of Pan, the beast-god associated with rampant sexuality. The three spectral daughters are the maidens who leapt off the Acropolis to their deaths at the sight of the snake-baby, Erichthonius, part of the myth of Athenian autochthony that Creusa shares with Ion in their first meeting (265–74). Into this strange atmosphere, the chorus introduce the woman (Creusa's 'third party') who gave birth to Apollo's child in a sunless hollow not far from Pan's cave. Imagining that the child's exposure led to a feast for the birds and wild beasts (503–05), the chorus conclude that they never heard a story in which there was happiness for children born between gods and mortals. At that very moment, Ion – the child of the god Apollo and mortal Creusa – enters to discover if Xuthus has received his oracular response regarding a son.

From the paean for children to a rejection of divine/mortal offspring, the chorus call into question the situation that the play hopes to celebrate. The juxtapositions in the stasimon force the audience to make a series of troubling connections – we must hold together ideas and images of virgin goddesses, families strengthened by legitimate children, licentious sexuality represented by Pan, the myth of Athenian autochthony, the ghosts of dead maidens, an exposed child, the unhappiness fated for the mortal offspring of a god, and the figure of Ion himself. The complexity of associations disturbs any smooth flow of divine revelation and recognition, indicating once again that *Ion* is no simple celebration of Apollonian beneficence. The undercurrents remind us of the dark and potentially deadly side of the story, leading inexorably back to the crimes committed within a sunless cave.

Euripides prepares for the oracular pronouncement in dramatic fashion, bringing Ion back to the stage just in time for Xuthus' grand entrance through the temple doors. We know that the 'recognition' between father and son is skewed, part of Apollo's plan to cover up his own paternity, and yet there is a certain poignancy in Xuthus' joy at finding the son the oracle has promised him. To Ion, however, the affection of the older man seems like the homosexual advances of a pederast, advances that are forcefully –

and humorously – repulsed.³ That Ion must threaten Xuthus with his bow – till now reserved for scaring birds from the temple precinct – marks the inadequacy of his preparation for dealing with the world that will press upon him with increasing force.

The exchange between the two men is delivered in trochaic tetrametre catalectic, a fast and lively dialogue rhythm that Euripides re-introduced into tragedy after it fell out of favour with the death of Aeschylus. We meet this metre in the virulent closing exchange between the chorus and Aegisthus in *Agamemnon*; here in *Ion*, it is used for the first time for undeniably comic effects. Ion at first thinks that Xuthus' claim to paternity is a bad joke, but he slowly understands what the oracle proclaimed – the first person that Xuthus meets coming out of the temple is his son. The tempo of the scene quickens, shifting from line-for-line to half-line exchanges, sustaining the paired thoughts and responses of the two parties. Ion questions the identity of his mother, an issue that Xuthus in his excitement forgot to raise with Apollo's oracle. Together they go over Xuthus' pre-marital affairs, concluding that Ion was conceived one drunken night with a Delphian girl at a Bacchic festival. The cavalier way in which Xuthus tosses off possible pregnancies provides the emotional antithesis for the trauma of Creusa's own 'bitter wedding,/ rape' (505–06), as the chorus describe the fate of the woman who bore Apollo's child in the cave.

Euripides marks the ambivalence of the recognition of father and son by severely truncating their actual reunion, culminating in a stiff and awkward embrace. Ion instinctively addresses his absent mother and not Xuthus who stands before him: 'Mother, wherever you are, I burn to see you/ even more than before, to press you to me' (563–64). For their part, the chorus sympathize with Creusa, whose prayers for a child of her own have gone unanswered: 'We share your happiness, but want our mistress/ to have the chance for children,/ to brighten the house of Erechtheus' (567–68).

Returning to normal dialogue in iambic trimetre, Xuthus proposes that Ion return with him to Athens, but the young man is wary. In his second major speech, he pleads with his new-found father to let him stay in Delphi. Ion focuses on what awaits a 'bastard son of an imported father' in a city whose people pride themselves on being autochthonous and not an 'imported' race (589–92). He reveals an astute awareness of the problems with Athens and Athenians – xenophobia, popular jealousy and envy of success, the prospects of ostracism for public figures, political infighting and power-games, and the cynics' ridicule of those who participate in the political process at all. Ion's analysis reflects the crisis of political involvement that faced the city in the late fifth century, where third-rate politicians rose to power and good men were driven out. Athens is a 'city full of fear' (601), and Ion compares the sovereign rule that Xuthus offers him to a building with a lovely façade, hiding an interior full of pain and sorrow (621–23). Euripides presents a critique of his own city from the mouth of a most disarming critic, an innocent temple attendant who will prove to be the founder of the Ionian people, and as such the guarantor of this very Athens of the future.

As if to confirm Ion's portrait of a city full of insensitive and selfish men, Xuthus brushes aside his heartfelt speech with a single line: 'No more talk like that. You must learn to be happy, son' (650). Xuthus plans to celebrate the discovery of his child with a feast in Delphi, and then bring him back to Athens as if he were a guest or 'onlooker' (656).[4] The rite that Xuthus plans to celebrate is the *genethlia*, usually performed ten days after birth. Keeping with the idea of a birthday, Xuthus names the young man 'Ion', from the participle 'going' (*iôn*), since he met him first when going from the temple (662).[5] In his final two lines (he never reappears on-stage), Xuthus swears the chorus to silence, threatening them with death if they divulge his plans (666–67). Even as Xuthus denies speech to the chorus, Ion prays that his mother turn out to be an Athenian, so that *he* will be entitled to free speech as a citizen born of Athenian parents.[6] Again issues of disclosure and secrecy, self-expression and silence, power and resistance emerge in the action of a play too readily dismissed as a romance.

For the second time the stage clears, and the chorus perform a counter-song (primarily in dochmiacs) to the joyful reunion that Xuthus and Ion go off to celebrate. They sympathize with Creusa who will grieve that her husband has a child while she herself remains barren. Focusing on the fact that the boy's mother is unknown and that Xuthus himself is foreign born, the Athenian women betray the very xenophobia that Ion associated with Athens. In the antistrophe they interpret Xuthus' actions as a deliberate attempt to disenfranchise their mistress and the ancient house of Erechtheus. The tone of the concluding epode shifts radically, beginning with an address to Parnassus and the uplands above Delphi where the Bacchic revels take place, the very circumstance during which Xuthus ostensibly conceived Ion (comparing 550–54 with 714–18). Sharing in the wild dance of the Bacchantes, the women invoke the forces of nature and Dionysus to keep Ion away from Athens, praying that this first day of his new life might be his last. Xuthus' threat to murder the chorus if they speak the truth has now been answered by the chorus's own prayer for Ion's death.

After the lyric describing the Bacchantes with 'their slender feet/ dancing through the night' (717–18), Creusa re-enters the theatre, stumbling down an *eisodos* as she props up the old Tutor of her father. Euripides dwells on the physical difficulties of the old man's entrance, and his rejoinders sound like Attic versions of comic one-liners – 'The foot is slow but the mind is quick' (742, more freely, 'The spirit is willing but the legs are weak'); 'What good is an old man's stick when I can't see where to put it?' (744); and in response to Creusa's encouragement to keep up his strength, 'I feel the same way, but how can I control what I no longer have?' (746).

Critics have tended to view this odd entrance as a piece of protracted, and failed, dramatic realism. We would do better to take our critical cue from a statement of the old Tutor himself: 'The ways of prophecy are certainly steep' (739). Part pun on the precipitous climb to the temple of Delphi (as tourists still can attest), part reference to the false prophecies in the play, the old man's comment is both humorous and on target. Faced with twisted words of the gods, mortals turn to one another for help and sustenance, an idea given visual form with the old Tutor physically supported by Creusa, and acted out in other ways during the scene. Creusa addresses the chorus women more as confidantes than as servants, and the chorus draw the Tutor and their mistress into a shared lyric *kommos*. For the first time someone with the choice to speak out or remain silent opts for disclosure, as the women risk Xuthus' death sentence and divulge the prophecy that Creusa will have no child but that Xuthus has found a son. At the news, Creusa sings of her wish to fly from Greece beyond the Western stars (795–99) – an escape to death – and then falls silent for sixty lines.

Leaving the lyric metres, the old Tutor tries to reconstruct the past out of the fragmentary details presented by the chorus. Discovering Creusa to be barren, Xuthus bore a bastard son, sent him to Delphi to be raised, arranged the ruse of seeking oracular help for infertility, and now plans to take the grown boy back from Delphi and set him up as the ruler of Athens. The Tutor's analysis is reasonable, but dead wrong. On its basis, however, he offers to help Creusa murder both father and son, and the chorus add their voice, eager to join the plot. In their readiness to take violent action, Euripides dramatizes the perverse realization of the idea of mutual co-operation with which the scene began.

If the play to this point has consisted of scenes pressing towards disclosure that always stop short, then Creusa's monody shatters the walls of secrecy. Breaking her long silence, she sings an ode of unparalleled beauty and power, revealing fully the betrayal she has suffered at the hands of Apollo. The catalyst for her song is the way she hears the Tutor's accusations against Xuthus as a pale imitation of the charges she has levelled against the god, and herself.

Creusa re-creates Apollo's epiphany before her, combining images of song, shimmering light, and the beauty of the natural world. But this splendid manifestation turns dark when the god drags her, screaming for her mother, into a cave and shamelessly takes his pleasure. Creusa imagines the birth of Apollo on Delos, where Zeus created a palm and laurel bower to shade the goddess Leto in her labour – an idyllic counter-world to the sunless cave where Creusa herself is ravaged, gives birth in secret, and then exposes her child.

In the details of Creusa's monody, the audience recognize the outlines of another myth of female abduction, the rape of Persephone by Hades and the subsequent anguish of her mother Demeter. Like Persephone, Creusa is swept away by a god while in the fields gathering flowers and then is raped in an underworld setting, the dark cavern of the Acropolis.[7] Creusa invokes the myth again when she finally discovers that Ion is her son: 'I never dreamed I'd find you, but thought you shared/ the earth and darkness with Persephone' (1441–42). Over the course of the play, Creusa comes to embody *both* female roles in the myth – the innocent victim of a god's rape, and the grieving mother whose child has been taken from her.

From the expressive but private mode of Creusa's monody, Euripides shifts to a dialogue of questions and answers that clarifies the events of the past and drives the play in a new direction. The interrogation of Creusa by the Tutor (934–1028) is the second longest passage of stichomythia in Euripides, surpassed only by the earlier dialogue between Creusa and Ion (264–369). Extending the form a second time, Euripides encourages the audience to think back to that earlier conversation, when a sympathetic bond developed between unrecognized mother and son. Now, however, the dialogue concentrates on Xuthus' betrayal and on the Tutor's plan to kill the young man who once had seemed so caring and solicitous.

Creusa moves the murder plot forward by momentarily stepping back into the mythic past. She relates the aetiology of Athena's famed shield-like 'aegis', made from the gorgon that the goddess slew in the battle with the giants, described earlier in the *parodos*. Two drops of the slain gorgon's blood were given to Creusa by her grandfather – one drop cures and the other kills (1013–15) – and Creusa now gives the poisoned drop to the old Tutor to use against Ion. When asked if she keeps the drops separate or together, Creusa responds, 'Always apart. Evil and good do not mix' (1017). Euripides' play, however, demonstrates the impossibility of maintaining such simple discriminations. By enjambing humour with pathos, by overlapping the ludicrous with the deadly serious, *Ion* reveals a world of disturbing complexity. Euripides does not blend the opposites in a palatable mix to be swallowed whole, but rather juxtaposes one mood against the other so surprisingly that we view both the curative powers of the comic and the deadly acts of the tragic as a form of critical re-evaluation – a way of thinking anew the gods, the myths, the politics, and the social mores that inform the world of the play.

With the murder plot in train, the action of *Ion* reverts to secrecy, duplicity, and concealment. The Tutor exhorts the body that barely could bring him on-stage to do its part, and he finds his old legs have grown young at the prospect of vengeance (1041–47). As he races off under his own power, we see the reverse image of the opening entrance when Creusa helped him into the orchestra. The Tutor has been rejuvenated, but the catalyst is the desire for the blood of Ion, the only party in the play innocent of any wrongdoing.

Left alone in the orchestra for the last time, the chorus begin their third stasimon with a prayer to Persephone/Hecate for the success of the murder plot. Eager to ensure that no bastard or outlander ever rules their city, the chorus again exhibit the xenophobia that Ion associated with Athens. The tone of their closing antistrophe shifts, however, as they call for poets to

142

present a fairer treatment of women, and to end the slander that females are sexual culprits when men are really at fault. Reminiscent of the first stasimon of *Medea*, the chorus directly challenge the sexism of their society, revealing a Euripidean sophistication about the problem of representation – who composes the song and sings it, and in whose interest is it sung? The chorus's reflections prod the audience to recall that Apollo controls the 'song' of the play, and that he has designed it to cover up his rape of Creusa.

A Messenger races on-stage to report that the murder plan has failed and that Creusa has been condemned to death. In one of the longest messenger speeches in tragedy, over 100 lines, he recounts the strange events that took place at Ion's birthday feast. More than a quarter of the speech is taken up with a description of the tent that Ion erects for the guests, set up so that all sunlight is kept out (1134–36). The detail is odd, but significant. Just as Creusa was raped and gave birth in a sunless cave (500–02), so Ion's 'rebirth' will take place in a sunless tent. In his case, however, the rays are shut out by artifice, a celestial cosmos woven into the ceiling and walls of the canopy. The artistic equipose of the tapestried heavens provides a counter-image to the world of human passion, violence, and deception that breaks out beneath it.

The Messenger abruptly cuts off his description of the tent and shifts to the world of the banqueters who have gathered in its shade, a picture of social order and community. The Tutor of Creusa ingratiates himself with the guests, procuring the office of wine steward and lacing Ion's cup with the gorgon poison. At the crucial moment, however, one of the crowd utters an ill-omened word, causing Ion to command that the drinks be poured to the ground as a libation and a new round prepared. In a play filled with lies and verbal charades, it is a wonderful touch that Ion should be saved by an unlucky word.

Invading the artificial world of the banquet tent, a flock of doves suddenly flutters in and drinks the wine from the ground. Only the bird that lands at Ion's feet suffers, and the Messenger compares its death-cries to a garbled, impenetrable oracle: 'The bird screeched words/no prophet could ever cipher' (1204–05). The comparison to an enigmatic oracle is apt, given the twisted prophecy that handed Ion over to a false father and made his real mother try to kill him. The dove's death also recalls a time in Ion's life – only that morning – when the sole cloud on the horizon was a riot of birds in the sanctuary. Then he only threatened the 'red-footed swans' (163) with his bow, but now earth-bred Athenian poison kills the 'red-footed dove' (1207–08). The bird's miniature passion symbolizes the death of innocence in the young man, a process that began when Ion first questioned Apollo's morals (429–51), and then took root when he protested going to Athens (585–647). Ion is reborn as a man of action and violence, leaping over the banquet table to force the old man's confession. He then rushes to the Pythian elders and conducts the swiftest prosecution in dramatic history (two lines of direct speech, 1220–21). Within another three and a half lines the court has condemned Creusa to death by stoning (1222–25).

The shot-gun verdict, the abrupt departure of the Messenger, and the brevity of the chorus's subsequent ode set up Creusa's wild entrance pursued by the Delphian mob. Her short exchange with the chorus is in trochaic tetrametres, the same metre used when Xuthus left the temple and embraced his unwilling son (517–62). If that recognition scene was warped, the forthcoming reunion seems even more twisted, beginning as it does with Creusa running for her life from her own child. To make matters worse, the chorus advise her to cling as a suppliant to the altar of Apollo (1255–56), and Creusa finds herself tied to the god who has ruined her life.

The Ion who arrives on-stage is a far cry from the concerned young man the audience last saw some 600 lines before, and almost unrecognizable if we think back to the youth who first greeted the dawn light with a work song and hymn of praise. 'New-born' to murder and violence, Ion rushes on-stage with his sword drawn, followed by a vengeful mob who want Creusa's death. In place of the sympathetic woman he found in their first dialogue, Ion now sees an earth-born Athenian monster, at one with the gorgon-blood she tried to use on him. Particularly unsettling is the attempt that each one makes to outdo the other in establishing a special relationship to Apollo (1282–93). Ion wonders how Creusa could possibly cling to the altar of the god for mercy, and Creusa responds by offering her body to Apollo to protect; when Ion calls himself Apollo's son, Creusa claims an even closer connection to the god. Other ironies abound, as Ion argues he has a right to an Athenian inheritance through Xuthus, and Creusa counters by telling him to go instruct his mother but to leave her alone. For all the verbal play, however, the failed connection between mother and son has reached a crisis, and Ion with his raised sword is on the verge of shedding kindred blood.

The play must take a dramatic turn, and the *coup de théâtre* comes when the doors of the temple, closed for the last 800 lines, suddenly open and the Pythia appears. An earth-bound *dea ex machina*, she speaks not in the oracular voice of Apollo's priestess but as Ion's surrogate mother, and she stops him from spilling human blood at the altar. The Pythia presents the wicker cradle in which she found him as a baby so many years before, and she urges Ion to take it with him to Athens to help him track down his real mother. The hope of discovering his past leads Ion to forget all about the suppliant at the altar, until Creusa herself obtrudes on the action some fifty lines later. The Pythia gives Ion a maternal kiss and re-enters the temple, her touching farewell a prelude to the recognition that is soon to follow between true mother and son.

Again, the story darts off in a radically new direction, ending in a recognition guided by the objects contained in the crib. The physical tokens unite more than mother and son, for they bring together a complex set of images as carefully patterned as any in Euripides. Each object in the crib – the garland of undying olive leaves, the golden snake-clasp for the child, Creusa's unfinished weaving of gorgons fringed with snakes – forges a symbolic link between the abandoned baby and the foundation myths of Athens. The snake-clasp 'retells the tale of Ericthonius' (1427), an important myth of Athenian autochthony and prototype of Ion's own story. As told to Ion in his first dialogue with Creusa (265–74) and referred to in the first stasimon (492–502), Athena entrusted the young Erichthonius into the care of the daughters of Cecrops and Aglaurus, the mythical king and queen of Athens. The goddess commanded the maidens not to look inside the cradle, but they disobeyed and opened the crib. The sight of the snake-child was so terrifying that the girls leapt from the Acropolis to their deaths. Ion also hesitates before opening his cradle, fearful he may discover that he was born a slave, and once again the play teeters on the brink of concealment and secrecy. But the voice of the past no longer can be silenced, and Ion repeats the mythical action of the Aglaurids. He opens the crib and finds a snake-image, but one that provides a clue to his identity rather than leading to his death.

Now Creusa forces herself back into the scene, abandoning the altar of Apollo for she knows she has found her son. Their recognition works as a kind of *ekphrasis*, or verbal description of a work of art. Through stichomythic question and answer, Creusa predicts the contents of the cradle in order to prove her maternity to the incredulous Ion. Earlier in the play, the chorus describe the sculptural programme carved on the temple, and the Messenger details the heavenly scenes woven into the banquet tent. The final *ekphrasis* involves the unfinished embroidery by the young Creusa on the swaddling clothes for the new-born baby, and the modest traces of a girl's hand prove to be the most important in the play. The snakes and gorgon she describes establish Ion's connection to her and to Athens, and Ion equates the presence of the predicted image with finding an oracle (1424). *This* is the prophecy that the play was looking for, not the false revelation that Apollo arranged with Xuthus and Ion. Creusa needs no consultation with the Delphic oracle, but only the chance to break through the secrecy and deception that have kept her from her own past.

In the joy of recognition that follows, Creusa shifts into lyric while Ion remains in dialogue metre. Given their earlier solo-songs, a shared monody was well within the capabilities of the actors playing Ion and Creusa, but Euripides denies Ion a full lyric celebration. Although sharing his mother's joy, he wonders who his father is, and when he hears that Xuthus is not the man, Ion once again has nagging doubts about his parents, questions that eventually lead him to challenge Apollo in his prophetic shrine.

Even Creusa cannot suppress an undersong against Apollo: 'No [nuptial] torchlight streamed me to my bed,/ no wedding hymns or dance/ swept me kindly to your birth' (1476–78). When she refers to the tokens in the crib, they evoke only the hardships of the past: 'Girlish things, my loom's vague wanderings,/ they had to do a mother's work./ I never put you to my breast, never washed you with these hands,/ but in a desolate cave/ left you, blood feast/ for beak and talon' (1489–95). Ion himself abandons his initial enthusiasm at the prospect of a divine father, emphasizing instead the death he nearly suffered from his mother and that he himself nearly inflicted on her.

Ion begins to wonder if Creusa has concocted the story of Apollo's paternity in order to cover up a youthful indiscretion. He attempts to save his mother embarrassment by drawing her away from the chorus, so that she can confess the truth only to his ears. Critics invariably point to these lines as evidence that Euripides found the chorus an obstacle to dramatic realism. They fail to consider the play's ongoing concern with openness and disclosure. By taking Creusa aside and promising to 'bury all of it [her past affairs] in darkness' (1522), Ion re-enacts the processes of secrecy that the play has shown to be futile and potentially fatal.

Although Creusa swears by Athena that Apollo is his father, Ion remains unconvinced and vows to cross the threshold of the temple to ask the god point-blank (1547–48). Early in the play Ion told Creusa that 'No one should ask/ questions that oppose the god' (372–73), but now Ion finds himself ready to confront Apollo with just such a question. As Gilbert Norwood observes, the young man's challenge goes to the heart of the play:

> Apollo has said both that he himself, and Xuthus, is the father of Ion. Which of these statements is true matters comparatively little. One of them must be a lie. The god who gives oracles to Greece is a trickster, and no celestial consolations or Athenian throne can compensate the youth for the loss of what filled his heart only this morning.[8]

The sudden appearance of Athena on the *theologeion* stops Ion from entering the temple. Sent by Apollo, the goddess explains that he thought it best 'not to reveal himself in person, lest he be blamed/ in public for all that's happened' (1556–57). Assuring Ion that Apollo is his father, Athena outlines the glories awaiting the young man as founder of the Ionian race. Far from providing a clean dramatic conclusion, however, Athena herself adopts the discredited mode of secrecy and concealment, commanding Creusa to hide her real relationship with Ion: 'Absolute silence! Breathe not a word/ about how you got your child. Let Xuthus cherish/ his sweet illusion' (1601–03).

The ending of the play remains purposefully equivocal. After the appearance of Athena, Creusa clings to the ring-knockers on the temple door, in sudden rapture at recovering her son (1612–13). Have the wild emotional swings of the play affected her? Does she now not want to leave Delphi? Whatever her bizarre gesture signifies, it calls attention to the simple fact that the temple doors remain shut to Creusa, as they have been throughout the play. For his part, Ion remains sceptical of Apollo's absence, and twice he responds to Athena's assurances of the god's paternity by stating it is 'not unbelievable' (1606, 1608). The use of litotes (affirming by negating the contrary) here and elsewhere in the epilogue suggests that the basic uncertainties in the play remain unresolved.

And yet the ending holds out great promise, both for Ion and for his new city. Athena proclaims that the young man will be the founder of the Ionian race, and his half-brothers will play a similar role in founding the Dorians and Achaeans, the ancestors of the Spartans. Although the date of *Ion* is uncertain, it probably was produced several years after the resumption of the Peloponnesian War between Athens and Sparta in 418 BC. The fact that both the Athenians and their Spartan enemies purportedly rise from the same stock suggests that Euripides has transformed the myth of autochthony from a parochial symbol of Athenian chauvinism to an image of common Greek origin and brotherhood. All Greeks have their roots in violent, earth-bound nature, but as ancestral brothers they also share a common lineage that makes war between them fratricidal and wrong.

Leaving for Athens to father the Ionian race (forerunner of the Athenian empire), Ion represents the future of the city that the audience recognize as their own. In his troubled reflections on life in Athens earlier in the play, and in the fate he nearly suffers at the hands of Athenians, Ion discovers a people caught between introspective xenophobia and outward-reaching power. Euripidean anachronism converts the mythical Ion into a potential victim of the very empire he is destined to found, as well as a symbol of its best hopes. Emerging from the cloistered world of Delphi into the full contingency of adult life, Ion displays to the audience the humorous and deadly, the tragic and the transcendental proclivities of their own nature. A *Bildungsdrama* of individual growth, discovery, and reunion, *Ion* is also a masterpiece of cultural self-inquiry, a tragedy that explores the boundaries of the genre and the critical (and self-critical) capacities of its audience.

# NOTES

## PREFACE

1 Throughout the book the term 'on-stage' means 'in sight of the audience'; it does not imply that the performer is on a raised stage.
2 A. Poole, *Tragedy, Shakespeare and the Greek Example*, Oxford, Blackwell, 1987, p. 12.

## 1 THE PERFORMANCE CULTURE OF ATHENS

1 For the Pnyx, see K. Kourouniotes and H.A. Thompson, 'The Pnyx in Athens', *Hesperia*, 1932, vol. 1, pp. 96–107; and H.A. Thompson, 'The Pnyx in Models', *Hesperia* Supplement 19, 1982, pp. 134–38. For the Council chamber, see W.A. McDonald, *The Political Meeting Places of the Greeks*, Baltimore, Johns Hopkins University Press, 1943, pp. 172–73 and Plates 3 and 4; H.A. Thompson and R.E. Wycherley, *The Athenian Agora*, vol. 14, Princeton, American School of Classical Studies, 1972, p. 34; and Xenophon, *Hellenica* 2.3.50–56.
2 For a survey of lawcourt practices, see J. Ober, *Mass and Elite in Democratic Athens*, Princeton, Princeton University Press, 1989, pp. 141–48; D.M. MacDowell, *The Law in Classical Athens*, Ithaca, Cornell University Press, 1978, pp. 33–40; Thompson and Wycherley, op. cit., pp. 52–72.
3 MacDowell, op. cit., pp. 247–54.
4 R. Garner, *Law and Society in Classical Athens*, London, Croom Helm, 1987, has a useful chapter on 'Law and Drama' (pp. 95–130), although his interpretations of specific tragedies should be read with caution. See also P. Walcot, *Greek Drama in Its Theatrical and Social Context*, Cardiff, University of Wales Press, 1976, pp. 26–27, 37–42. J. Duchemin, *L'Agon dans la tragédie grecque*, 2nd edn, Paris, Les Belles Lettres, 1968, and H. Strohm, *Euripides*, Zetemata 15, Munich, C.H. Beck, 1957, analyse the connections between legal speeches and 'courtroom' debates in tragedies.
5 Plato, *Republic*, 492a–b.
6 K.J. Dover, *Aristophanic Comedy*, Berkeley, University of California Press, 1972, p. 33. For an excellent introduction, see J. Gould, 'On Making Sense of Greek Religion', in P.E. Easterling and J.V. Muir (eds), *Greek Religion and Society*, Cambridge, Cambridge University Press, 1985, pp. 1–33. The number of holidays is not as excessive as it first appears, for Athenian society had no notion of the weekend and its work-rhythms were based on the agricultural season.
7 H.W. Parke, *Festivals of the Athenians*, Ithaca, Cornell University Press, 1977, pp. 18–25, 188–89, offers a good summation of sacrificial practice. Officiating priests usually were paid by a share of the carcasses (skins, hooves, etc.); even the

meat in the butchers' shops came from sacrificial victims, since it was wasteful to slaughter an animal on a purely secular occasion.

8 J. Herington, *Poetry into Drama*, Sather Classical Lectures vol. 49, Berkeley, University of California Press, 1985, pp. 20–31, calls these passages 'lyric dramatizations of lyric'.

9 Plato, *Ion*, 530a–d, 535a–536b; see also Herington, op. cit., pp. 10–15, 51–52, 170–71.

10 For the dramatic qualities of Homeric epic and their influence on the development of tragedy, see S.E. Bassett, *The Poetry of Homer*, Sather Classical Lectures vol. 15, Berkeley, University of California Press, 1938, pp. 57–80, and C.A. Trypanis, *The Homeric Epics*, Warminster, Aris & Phillips, 1977, pp. 59–64, 82–92.

11 E.A. Havelock, 'The Oral Composition of Greek Drama', in his *The Literate Revolution in Greece and Its Cultural Consequences*, Princeton, Princeton University Press, 1982, pp. 262–63. Scholars increasingly question whether the Homeric epics were composed without benefit of writing, but the substance of Havelock's judgement remains valid.

12 Plato, *Theaetetus*, 152e; Herington, op. cit., pp. 213–15, collects and translates the many ancient references to Homer's influence on tragedy.

13 N. Frye, *Anatomy of Criticism*, Princeton, Princeton University Press, 1957, p. 319.

14 As Aeschylus reportedly described his plays, in Athenaeus, *The Deipnosophists*, 8.347e.

## 2 THE FESTIVAL CONTEXT

1 A full bibliography on this question would run longer than this book. Good starting places include A. Pickard-Cambridge, *Dithyramb, Tragedy, and Comedy*, rev. T.B.L. Webster, Oxford, Clarendon Press, 1962, pp. 60–131; G.F. Else, *The Origin and Early Form of Greek Tragedy*, Cambridge, Harvard University Press, 1965; F.R. Adrados, *Festival, Comedy and Tragedy*, C. Holme (transl.), Leiden, Brill, 1975 (org. Barcelona 1972); and R.P. Winnington-Ingram, 'The Origins of Tragedy', in P.E. Easterling and B.M.W. Knox (eds), *The Cambridge History of Classical Literature*, Cambridge, Cambridge University Press, 1985, pp. 258–63.

2 A. Henrichs, 'Changing Dionysiac Identities', in B.F. Meyer and E.P. Sanders (eds), *Jewish and Christian Self-Definition*, vol. 3, Philadelphia, Fortress Press, 1982, p. 158; see also his 'Loss of Self, Suffering Violence: The Modern View of Dionysus from Nietzsche to Girard', *Harvard Studies in Classical Philology*, 1984, vol. 88, pp. 205–40. In the introduction to his edition of Euripides' *Bacchae*, 2nd edn, Oxford, Clarendon Press, 1960, pp. xi–xxviii, E.R. Dodds offers a good overview of Dionysiac religion. For a more literary and structuralist exploration of Dionysiac dualities, see C. Segal, *Dionysiac Poetics and Euripides' Bacchae*, Princeton, Princeton University Press, 1982, esp. pp. 215–40.

3 My account owes much to Henrichs, 'Changing Identities', pp. 143–47. For a more imaginative treatment, see the appendix 'Maenadism', in E.R. Dodds, *The Greeks and the Irrational*, Sather Classical Lectures vol. 22, Berkeley, University of California Press, 1951, pp. 270–82.

4 On cross-dressing, see R.J. Hoffman, 'Ritual License and the Cult of Dionysus', *Athenaeum*, 1989, vol. 67, pp. 91–115; and P. Vidal-Naquet, 'The Black Hunter and the Origins of the Athenian Ephebia', in R.L. Gordon (ed.), *Myth, Religion, and Society*, Cambridge, Cambridge University Press, 1981, pp. 147–85. For

the Oschophoria, see H.W. Parke, *Festivals of the Athenians*, Ithaca, Cornell University Press, 1977, pp. 77–80.

5 For the Anthesteria, see Parke, op. cit., pp. 107–20; L. Deubner, *Attische Feste*, Berlin, Akademie-Verlag, 1932, pp. 92–123.

6 For a discussion of the dithyramb as it relates to the development of tragedy, see Pickard-Cambridge, rev. Webster, op. cit., pp. 1–38, 89–131; and G. Else, *Aristotle's Poetics: The Argument*, Cambridge, Harvard University Press, 1957, pp. 149–63. For the dance of the dithyramb, see L.B. Lawler, *The Dance of the Ancient Greek Theatre*, Iowa City, University of Iowa Press, 1964, pp. 1–21.

7 The Greek *aulos* had a single or 'beating' reed, and the *diaulos* had a double reed, comparable to our clarinet and oboe respectively. The instrument was not (as frequently mistranslated) a 'flute'. See K. Schlesinger, *The Greek Aulos*, London, Methuen, 1939, pp. 45–81.

8 For a convincing reappraisal of the institution of tragic performances in Athens, see W.R. Connor, 'City Dionysia and Athenian Democracy', *Classica et Mediaevalia*, 1989, vol. 40, pp. 7–32, whose argument I follow closely in my analysis. M.L. West, 'The Early Chronology of Attic Tragedy', *Classical Quarterly*, 1989, vol. 39 n.s., pp. 251–54, also discusses the shaky ground beneath the traditionally accepted dates.

9 Thespis was purportedly the first to separate an actor completely from the chorus, and to disguise the face of the performers with white lead or even with wine lees (again, fitting a rural background) before adopting linen masks. However, the sources are late; see Pickard-Cambridge, rev. Webster, op. cit., pp. 79–80.

10 See A. Pickard-Cambridge, *Dramatic Festivals of Athens*, rev. J. Gould and D.M. Lewis, 2nd edn, Oxford, Clarendon Press, 1988, pp. 59–70; W.S. Ferguson, 'Demetrius Poliorcetes and the Hellenic League', *Hesperia*, 1948, vol. 17, pp. 133–35 n. 46; J.T. Allen, *On the Program of the City Dionysia during the Peloponnesian War*, Berkeley, University of California Press, 1938.

11 The idea that women could not attend the theatre in Athens was put forth first by a German scholar in 1796, who invoked eighteenth-century moral prejudices against public licentiousness. Much of the current polemic on the subject reflects the belief that a male-dominated society like fifth-century Athens simply would not allow women in the audience. For a corrective, see A.J. Podlecki, 'Could Women Attend the Theater in Ancient Athens?' *Ancient World*, 1990, vol. 21, pp. 27–43.

12 The League was established a few years after the defeat of the Persians at Salamis in 480 and Plataea in 479. As Athens played a major role in driving off the invaders, she took pride of place in this alliance that eventually became an extension of her empire, accentuated by the transfer of the treasury from the island of Delos to Athens in 454. At the inception of the League, the allies provided a set number of ships annually for common defence, but monetary tribute gradually replaced material contributions.

13 For a discussion of these pre-performance practices, see Pickard-Cambridge, rev. Gould and Lewis, op. cit., pp. 58–59; Parke, op. cit., pp. 133–34; and S. Goldhill, 'The Great Dionysia and Civic Ideology', *Journal of Hellenic Studies*, 1987, vol. 107, pp. 59–64.

14 We might contrast the great Palio in Sienna, where the neighbourhoods within the city compete in a wild horse-race. The event reinforces traditional ties of family and locale going back centuries, an antidote to the rootlessness of modern urban life.

15 For the rural Dionysia and revivals, see Pickard-Cambridge, rev. Gould and

Lewis, op. cit., pp. 42–56; and D. Whitehead, *The Demes of Attica*, Princeton, Princeton University Press, 1986, pp. 212–22.

# 3 PRODUCTION AS PARTICIPATION

1 Recall (Chapter 2, p. 17) that Attic tribes do not imply racial or familial links, but reflect the reforms of Cleisthenes aimed at transferring loyalties to the city and away from the traditional economic and social hierarchies.
2 See N.F. Jones, *Public Organization in Ancient Greece*, Philadelphia, American Philosophical Society, 1987, pp. 48–51; J.K. Davies, *Wealth and the Power of Wealth in Classical Athens*, New York, Arno Press, 1981, pp. 9–38, and his 'Demosthenes on Liturgies: A Note', *Journal of Hellenic Studies*, 1967, vol. 87, pp. 33–40.
3 For a brief summary, see P.J. Rhodes, 'Political Activity in Classical Athens', *Journal of Hellenic Studies*, 1986, vol. 106, pp. 132–44.
4 See V. Gabrielson, 'The Antidosis Procedure in Classical Athens', *Classica et Mediaevalia*, 1987, vol. 38, pp. 7–38.
5 Demosthenes, *Against Meidias*, 16–17; the translation (with minor alterations) is from the Loeb *Demosthenes*, J.H. Vince (transl.), Cambridge, Harvard University Press, 1935, pp. 16–19.
6 The clearest account is by A.J. Podlecki, *The Political Background of Aeschylean Tragedy*, Ann Arbor, University of Michigan Press, 1966, pp. 8–26, 125–29; see also his introduction to Aeschylus' *Persians*, Englewood Cliffs, Prentice-Hall, 1970, pp. 4–11; and the ground-breaking article by W.G. Forrest, 'Themistokles and Argos', *Classical Quarterly*, 1960, vol. 10 n.s., pp. 221–41.
7 M. Lefkowitz, *The Lives of the Greek Poets*, Baltimore, Johns Hopkins University Press, 1981, pp. vi–xi, 67–104, exposes much of the ancient biographical tradition for what it is, a stock of legend and pure invention, mixed with tragic detail and comic parody, and then dished up as fact.
8 A modern parallel might be the great old families of the European circus, where different artists worked under the same tent, but a family of high-wire performers did not produce lion-tamers, and vice versa.
9 Although nearly a century old, A.E. Haigh, *The Tragic Drama of the Greeks*, Oxford, Clarendon Press, 1896, pp. 395–415, 463–81, is worth consulting on the question of playwrights and titles. For lost plays, see T.B.L. Webster, *The Tragedies of Euripides*, London, Methuen, 1967; and D.F. Sutton, *The Lost Sophocles'*, Lanham, University Press of America, 1984. For Aeschylus, see O. Taplin, *The Stagecraft of Aeschylus*, Oxford, Clarendon Press, 1977 (the index under 'Aeschylus/fragmentary plays'); and also the Loeb *Aeschylus* II, H.W. Smyth and H. Lloyd-Jones (eds), Cambridge, Harvard University Press, 1963. For a collection of the tragic fragments, see *Tragicorum Graecorum Fragmenta*, vols 1–4, B. Snell and S.L. Radt (eds), Göttingen, Vandenhoek & Ruprecht, 1971–77.
10 Evidence for the expansion of the tragic chorus to fifteen comes from the anonymous *Life of Sophocles* that credits Sophocles with the change. From what we know of ancient biography, this means that at some point in the production of tragedy the chorus grew to fifteen, and the innovation was credited to one of the three great tragedians. But the date and reason for the change cannot be determined, although they may have reflected the desire to include a larger number of citizens in tragic productions.
11 Advanced by J.J. Winkler, the thesis has taken several forms, including his 'The Ephebes' Song: *Tragôidia* and *Polis*', in J.J. Winkler and F.I. Zeitlin (eds), *Nothing*

*to do with Dionysos?*, Princeton, Princeton University Press, 1990, pp. 20–62. Historically, however, the institutional training of ephebes is not attested in the fifth century, and it is questionable whether such a practice should be read back into the early days of the Athenian democracy. Strong evidence for the thesis is found on the Pronomos Vase, a late fifth- or early fourth-century Attic vase now in Naples (reproduced as Figure 49 in A. Pickard-Cambridge, *Dramatic Festivals of Athens*, rev. J. Gould and D.M. Lewis, 2nd edn, Oxford, Clarendon Press, 1988) that depicts a rehearsal for a satyr-play. However, the fact that the actors are bearded but the chorus members are youths may reflect a vase-painting convention linked with status and have nothing to do with a hard and fast rule about beardless young men serving as chorus members. For example, 82 per cent of all bridegrooms on Attic red-figure vases (wedding scenes were popular) are depicted as beardless. This situation was rarely the case in real life, since men tended to marry at a much older age than women. See R.F. Sutton, 'On the Classical Athenian Wedding', in R.F. Sutton (ed.), *Daidalikon: Studies in Memory of Raymond V. Schoder, SJ*, Wauconda, Bolchazy-Carducci, 1989, p. 344.

12 As we will discuss in Chapter 5, it is not uncommon for actors to join the chorus in a *kommos*, but a monody calls for something special, along the lines of a lyric solo. In Euripides' *Alcestis*, the title character sings a monody and so does her son, Eumelos. However, it is uncertain whether the child's part (otherwise silent) was played by one of the three actors, or more likely by a boy actor, perhaps pulled from the dithyrambic competitions. In Euripides' *Phoenician Women*, Antigone and Jocasta both sing a monody, but the two parts were played by the same actor.

13 See, for example, the scheme for voting proposed by M. Pope, 'Athenian Festival Judges – Seven, Five or However Many', *Classical Quarterly*, 1986, vol. 36 n.s., pp. 322–26.

## 4 THE THEATRE OF DIONYSUS

1 There are no archaeological remains, and various locations have been proposed. The original *orchêstra* probably was situated a bit to the north of Odeion of Agrippa, a roofed concert hall erected in the first century BC, that took advantage of the natural slope of the agora, with seats at the higher, southern end looking down on the stage to the north. See J.M. Camp, *The Athenian Agora*, London, Thames & Hudson, 1986, pp. 46, 89, 183–84; and J. Travlos, *Pictorial Dictionary of Ancient Athens*, New York, Praeger, 1971, p. 8 fig. 5, p. 21 fig. 29.

2 In the Attic *demes* of Rhamnous, Aixone, and Ikaria, the theatre was located in the agora and also served as the meeting place for the local assembly. By the late third century BC, the theatre of Dionysus had superseded the Pnyx as the meeting place for the Athenian Assembly as well.

3 See R.E. Wycherley, *The Athenian Agora*, vol. 3: *Literary and Epigraphical Testimonia*, Princeton, American School of Classical Studies, 1957, pp. 162–63, 220–21.

4 See Travlos, op. cit., pp. 387–92, 537–52.

5 R. Rehm, 'The Staging of Suppliant Plays', *Greek, Roman and Byzantine Studies*, 1988, vol. 29, pp. 276–79. For a sense of what the original theatre may have looked like, see R. and H. Leacroft, *Theatre and Playhouse*, London, Methuen, 1984, pp. 6–15. Even a thorough re-excavation of the theatre of Dionysus in Athens would not resolve the questions about orchestra shape, since the pavement over the dancing floor (dating from the Roman period) rests on bedrock.

6 Aristophanes' *Thesmophoriazusae*, 395, an observation that undermines the claim that seating in the theatre of Dionysus was according to tribes, with the cavea

divided into ten seating wedges. Such a political division may have occurred after stone seating was erected in the second half of the fourth century, but probably not before. Similarly, the reference to the 'seats for the Counsellors' in Aristophanes' *Birds*, 594, may indicate only that this was the section where the Counsellors sat when the Assembly met in the theatre to evaluate the festival after it was over.

7 See Rehm, op. cit., pp. 280–81. For an excellent bibliographical summary on this and other theatre–related questions, see J.R. Green, 'Theatre Production: 1971–86', *Lustrum*, 1989, vol. 31, pp. 7–71.

8 Although we associate Athens with remarkable stone and marble buildings, these permanent structures were erected using sturdy wooden scaffolding and required huge amounts of wood for roofing, especially the temples. A wooden backdrop and skene-building are perfectly in keeping with Greek building practices, where – as with the theatre seats, for example – stone eventually replaced wood construction, referred to as the 'petrification' of the earlier form.

9 A.M. Dale, 'Aristophanes, *Vesp.* 136–210', *Collected Papers*, Cambridge, Cambridge University Press, 1969, pp. 103–18 (org. 1957), demonstrates that a single door is all that is required, along with a window or two, called for in *The Women of the Assembly* and *Wasps*; see also C.W. Dearden, *The Stage of Aristophanes*, London, University of London, Athlone Press, 1975, pp. 50–74; and O. Taplin, *The Stagecraft of Aeschylus*, Oxford, Clarendon Press, 1977, pp. 438–40. K.J. Dover, *Aristophanic Comedy*, Berkeley, University of California Press, 1972, pp. 21–24, 83–84, 106–08, 197–98, and 'The Skene in Aristophanes', *Proceedings of the Cambridge Philological Society*, 1966, vol. 12, pp. 2–17, has made the strongest case for two doors.

10 A.L. Brown, 'Three and Scene-Painting Sophocles', *Proceedings of the Cambridge Philological Society*, 1984, vol. 210, pp. 1–17.

11 Attempts to clarify how this device worked have not met with general approval. See D.J. Mastronarde, 'Actors on High: The Skene Roof, the Crane, and the Gods in Attic Drama', *Classical Antiquity*, 1990, vol. 9, pp. 247–94. I use the term *theologeion* for the platform on the roof, and refer to an appearance of a divinity on high as a *deus ex machina*, whether the god 'flies in' or climbs onto the platform.

12 Pollux, 4.123. See Rehm, op. cit., pp. 279–80; and F.E. Winter, '*Greek Theatre Production*: A Review Article', *Phoenix*, 1965, vol. 19, pp. 106–10. C.P. Gardiner, '*Anabainein* and *Katabainein* as Theatrical Terms', *Transactions of the American Philological Association*, 1978, vol. 108, pp. 75–79, shows that the two terms 'go up' and 'go down' do not imply a raised stage, but rather suggest that the Greeks shared our convention of upstage and downstage for directing actors' movement away from or out towards the audience.

13 See B. Hunningher, *Acoustics and Acting in the Theatre of Dionysus Eleuthereus*, Amsterdam, Noord-Hollandsche Uitg., 1956. Of course, the change in sound intensity decreases the further an audience sits from the action. For those audience members, for example, sitting 200 feet from orchestra centre, an actor would lose only 16 per cent of his vocal production if he moved back 20 feet towards the façade and spoke with the same volume.

14 In the short term, the skene-roof and machine offered stronger areas, but appearances on high were reserved for special occasions.

15 See Rehm, op. cit., passim.

16 N.C. Hourmouziades, *Production and Imagination in Euripides*, Athens, Greek Society for Humanistic Studies, 1965, pp. 9–13, 83–108, argues that Euripides maintains a clear distinction between 'interior' and 'exterior'. However his discussion of the *ekkyklêma* demonstrates that an exposed interior scene frequently

loses specificity and merges with the outside, blurring distinctions between place and boundary.

17 The convention that an exit out the stage-right or stage-left *eisodoi* signalled, respectively, a departure to the country or to the city is of late date, implying a geographical specificity that was foreign to drama in the fifth century.

18 The claim that Greek tragic performances began at dawn is highly impractical (12,000 people finding their way in the dark?), and arises from the mistaken notion that a typical Greek tragedy took two and a half hours to perform. With the addition of a single comedy after the satyr-play during the Peloponnesian War, we would have a performance day of some twelve to thirteen hours, necessitating a sunrise curtain in order to finish before dark. However, played at speed, even the longest tragedies (*Agamemnon* and *Oedipus at Colonus* at about 1,700 lines) would require roughly 110 minutes to perform, while shorter pieces (*Choephori* at about 1,100 lines) would take perhaps an hour and a quarter. Satyr-plays seem to have been shorter still – *Cyclops* has roughly 700 lines, although *Alcestis*, which was performed in the fourth spot usually reserved for a satyr-play, has 1,160 lines. See P. Walcot, *Greek Drama in its Theatrical and Social Context*, Cardiff, University of Wales Press, 1976, pp. 11–21.

19 For an analysis of masks, see F. Frontisi-Ducroux, 'In the Mirror of the Mask', in D. Lyons (transl.), *A City of Images*, Princeton, Princeton University Press, 1989, pp. 150–65; A.D. Napier, *Masks, Transformation, Paradox*, Berkeley, University of California Press, 1986; B.C. Dietrich, *Tradition in Greek Religion*, Berlin, de Gruyter, 1986, pp. 62–79; F.I. Zeitlin, 'The Closet of Masks', *Ramus*, 1980, vol. 9, pp. 62–77; and A. Lesky, *Greek Tragedy*, H.A. Frankfort (transl.), 3rd edn, New York, Barnes & Noble, 1979, pp. 27–46. I have benefited greatly from talking about masks in tragedy with Tony Harrison, and many of his ideas have found their way into my discussion. His views can be found in 'Facing Up to the Muses', *Proceedings of the Classical Association*, 1988, vol. 85, pp. 7–29.

20 F.B. Jevons, 'Masks and the Origin of Greek Drama', *Folk-lore*, 1916, vol. 27, pp. 173–74.

21 The joke is that Cleon's face is too frightening to imitate. However, the mask-makers' fear also may refer to Cleon's unsuccessful prosecution of Aristophanes (or his *chorêgos*) two years earlier, charging that his production of *Babylonians* harmed the city. The fate of this lost comedy and that of Phrynichus' *Capture of Miletus* (discussed in Chapter 3) are all that we know of theatrical censorship in fifth-century Athens.

22 From illustrations on vases, it would appear that the fifth-century mask had a relatively small mouth, and the wide-open mouth dates from c. 300 B.C. What we may have here (as so often) is evidence of changing conventions of visual representation and not necessarily changing masks *per se*. The late testimony from Pollux that various colours of masks represented different temperaments (like the medieval notion of humours) probably reflects Hellenistic innovations. For a discussion of ancient theatrical masks as objects, see T.B.L. Webster, 'The Poet and the Mask', in M.J. Anderson (ed.), *Classical Drama and Its Influences*, New York, Barnes & Noble, 1965, pp. 5–13, and his *Greek Theatre Production*, 2nd edn, London, Methuen, 1970, pp. 35–96.

# 5 CONVENTIONS OF PRODUCTION

1 To use a familiar example, Bertolt Brecht's estrangement- (or alienation-) effect was a concerted effort to confront the audience with contradictions in the social and economic system that were glossed over by the commercial German stage. Brecht's theatrical practice pointed towards possibilities radically different from

those enshrined in the bourgeois theatre and presented there as natural and inevitable.

2 See P. Walcot, *Greek Drama in its Theatrical and Social Context*, Cardiff, University of Wales Press, 1976, pp. 51–53; O. Taplin, *Greek Tragedy in Action*, Berkeley, University of California Press, 1978, pp. 159–71; and, generally, W.B. Stanford, *Greek Tragedy and the Emotions*, Routledge & Kegan Paul, London, 1983.

3 The nature of this 'tragic pleasure' has been much debated – does it imply some intrinsic delight in watching those worse off than ourselves? Does it operate by purging or cleansing our emotions, principally pity and fear? Or does it align these emotions with intellectual perceptions about events that may seem unlikely on the surface, but in dramatic presentation achieve a probable shape and structure? Is the pleasure we take from tragedy a form of clarification, an 'insight experience' that reflects the ordering of highly charged dramatic events so as to convey their importance and relevance? See, for example, S. Halliwell, 'Aristotle's Poetics', in *Cambridge History of Literary Criticism*, vol. 1, *Classical Criticism*, Cambridge, Cambridge University Press, 1989, pp. 158–75.

4 Although ancient Greek was accented by pitch and not stress, we get a rough sense of the way common speech fits into metrical forms by considering a colloquial expression like 'I'd like a coke, a burger, and a shake' which scans as iambic pentametre, the standard blank-verse line in Shakespeare. Greek tragic characters occasionally speak in trochaic tetrameter catalectic, consisting of a line scanned -˘-/-˘-/-˘-/-˘-/, where two short syllables can be substituted for any long syllable. For example, during the argument between Iris and Lyssa in Euripides' *Heracles*, Iris suddenly shifts from normal dialogue trimeters to the tetrameter line, the change indicating the moment of crisis is about to be reached, that talk will soon give way to action.

5 See F. Jouan, 'Réflexions sur le rôle du protagoniste tragique', in *Théâtres et spectacles dans l'antiquité: Actes du Colloque de Strasbourg*, Leiden, Brill, 1983, pp. 63–80.

6 The phrase is from J. Jones, *On Aristotle and Greek Tragedy*, London, Chatto & Windus, 1962, whose study argues that 'the meaning of the ancient drama for ourselves is best fostered by our mustering what awareness we can of its near-inaccessibility' (p. 278).

7 See B. Vickers, *Towards Greek Tragedy*, London, Longman, 1973, pp. 438–94.

8 For his somewhat contradictory model of a hot medium (radio) vs. a cool medium (television), see M. McLuhan, *Understanding Media*, 2nd edn, New York, McGraw-Hill, 1964, pp. 36–45, 259–68. For the problem with McLuhan's metaphors, see K. Burke, *Language as Symbolic Action*, Berkeley, University of California Press, 1966, pp. 410–18.

9 The idea that emptying the stage of actors is the structuring principle of a Greek tragedy derives from Shakespearean criticism, outlined by O. Taplin, *The Stagecraft of Aeschylus*, Oxford, Clarendon Press, 1977, pp. 49–60.

10 For an introduction to Greek lyric metres, see D.S. Raven, *Greek Metre*, 2nd edn, London, Faber & Faber, 1968; and the series of articles on tragic metre, the chorus, and dance by A.M. Dale, *Collected Papers*, Cambridge, Cambridge University Press, 1969.

11 J. Herington, *Poetry into Drama*, Sather Classical Lectures vol. 49, Berkeley, University of California Press, 1985, p. 75.

12 See S. Barlow, *The Imagery of Euripides*, London, Methuen, 1971, p. 25.

13 See, for example, M. Esslin, 'Beckett and the Art of Broadcasting', in his *Mediations*, Baton Rouge, Louisiana State University Press, 1980, pp. 131–32.

14 See R. Lattimore, *Story Patterns in Greek Tragedy*, Ann Arbor, University of

Michigan, 1969, pp. 28–35; and J.-P. Vernant, 'Greek Tragedy: Problems of Interpretation', in R. Macksey and E. Donato (eds), *The Structuralist Controversy*, Baltimore, Johns Hopkins University Press, 1972, pp. 285–87.

15 See B.M.W. Knox, 'Euripidean Comedy' (org. 1970), in his *Word and Action*, Baltimore, Johns Hopkins University Press, 1979, pp. 250–74.

16 Aristotle, *Poetics*, 1454a.37–1454b.2, faults the ending of *Medea* for arising from the machine and not from the plot. For an in-depth treatment of the convention, see D.J. Mastronarde, 'Actors on High: The Skene Roof, the Crane, and the Gods in Attic Drama', *Classical Antiquity*, 1990, vol. 9, pp. 247–94.

17 See B.M.W. Knox's excellent essay, 'The *Hippolytus* of Euripides' (org. 1952), in op. cit., pp. 205–30.

18 See W.S. Barrett, '*Niobe*: P. Oxy. 2805', in R. Carden (ed.), *The Papyrus Fragments of Sophocles*, Berlin, de Gruyter, 1974, pp. 184–85.

# 6 AESCHYLUS' *ORESTEIA* TRILOGY

1 Some editors assign the announcement of the Herald's arrival (489–500) to Clytemnestra, arguing that she reappears from the palace at this point. Since manuscripts do not indicate entrances and exits *per se*, and rarely name a new speaker, editors must make such determinations from the dialogue itself and from their sense of the play. Does a production gain more by having Clytemnestra present and silent during the Herald's speech, or by having her appear suddenly and seize control of the scene after he has finished? The latter seems the better choice; the claim that Clytemnestra must be on-stage to learn that her husband has returned is more appropriate to theatrical realism than to Greek tragedy.

2 The question of Menelaus' whereabouts sets up the satyr-play *Proteus* (now lost) that followed the trilogy, telling of Menelaus' shipwreck in Egypt.

3 The Watchman refers to Clytemnestra as 'like a man in thought' (*Ag.*, 11). We meet Apollo the rapist again in Euripides' *Ion*, discussed in Chapter 9.

4 See R. Seaford, 'The Last Bath of Agamemnon', *Classical Quarterly*, 1984, vol. 34 n.s., pp. 247–54.

5 In *Titus Andronicus* Shakespeare draws heavily on Ovid's treatment of the same myth.

6 If the *ekkyklêma* was used, then the platform holding the bodies of Agamemnon (in his tub) and Cassandra was rolled out, with Clytemnestra standing above them. If the device was not yet available (it may have been introduced later in the fifth century), then servants carried out the bodies and dumped them on the ground, while Clytemnestra took up her position behind them. See O. Taplin, *The Stagecraft of Aeschylus*, Oxford, Clarendon Press, 1977, pp. 325–27, 442–43.

7 See A.F. Garvie (ed.), *Aeschylus, Choephori*, Oxford, Clarendon Press, 1988, pp. 201–23, for an analysis of the stasimon and a discussion of the dramatic device called a priamel, where a series of examples are used as a foil for the point of particular interest.

8 The Greek word is 'parent', but the masculine article implies the father.

9 It is uncertain if the bodies were carried out or revealed on the *ekkyklêma*. See above, note 6.

10 The staging of the opening section has generated endless controversy; the scenario adopted here takes cognizance of the fact that the orchestra was a far stronger playing area than the space back by the façade. It makes clearest sense of the action and enables the prologue of *Eumenides* to forge strong visual links with other key moments in the play and the trilogy as a whole. For a full treatment, see R. Rehm, 'The Staging of Suppliant Plays', *Greek, Roman, and Byzantine Studies*, 1988, vol. 29, pp. 290–301.

11 If Aeschylus had four actors available, as some scholars argue, then Clytemnestra could have been part of the cancelled entry before the prologue, rising from the orchestra floor when it was time for her 'entrance'. A fourth actor also would simplify staging problems in *Choephori*, especially in the final confrontation between Clytemnestra, Orestes, and Pylades, when the servant has just left the stage.

12 To have a stagehand carry on a separate piece of stage-furniture to represent the cult-statue of Athena would disrupt an otherwise smooth transition from Delphi to Athens – the Furies exit at 231, Apollo leaves at 234, Orestes arrives at 235. Those who believe that the *ekkyklêma* was used for the *omphalos* and for Athena's cult-statue fail to consider the problems of upstaging that result, or the fact that such an arrangement pulls the action back to the façade, a relatively weak acting area given its distance from the audience. Moreover, movement is severely restricted if the *omphalos* and the cult-statue are placed on the roll-out machine – the Furies cannot surround Orestes in their binding song, drastically reducing the visual and emotional impact of their dance.

13 A.J. Podlecki (ed.), *Aeschylus, Eumenides*, Warminster, Aris & Phillips, 1989, pp. 17–21, and A.H. Sommerstein (ed.), *Aeschylus, Eumenides*, Cambridge, Cambridge University Press, 1989, pp. 25–32, offer clear and persuasive accounts.

14 The idea that a crowd of spectators, in addition to the jurors, came on-stage is dramatically redundant, given the presence of thousands of Athenians in the audience.

15 Sommerstein, op. cit., pp. 184–85, pictures smaller urns on a table, but such props might be lost in the enormous theatre of Dionysus. Moreover, a solid table would arrest the movement of the jurors when they came to vote. It would be more effective if the jurors could stop between the urns, vote, and then pass through, suggesting the fluidity of the democratic legal process.

16 As a virgin goddess, Athena never subjected herself to sexual domination, a qualification that compromises her apparent subordination to the masculine point of view. R.P. Winnington-Ingram, 'Clytemnestra and the Vote of Athena' (org. 1949), in his *Studies in Aeschylus*, Cambridge, Cambridge University Press, 1983, pp. 124–31, and S. Goldhill, *Language, Sexuality, Narrative: The Oresteia*, Cambridge, Cambridge University Press, 1984, pp. 258–59, offer interesting analyses of the complex and transgressive character of Athena.

17 Athena's prominence indicates that the primary association was the Panathenaia, but resident aliens, referred to as 'metics' (as the Furies are at line 1011), wore purple robes at both festivals.

## 7 SOPHOCLES' *OEDIPUS TYRANNUS*

1 Excellent discussion of this aspect of the play can be found in E.R. Dodds, 'On Misunderstanding the *Oedipus Rex*', *Greece and Rome*, 1966, vol. 13, pp. 37–49; G. Gellie, *Sophocles: A Reading*, Melbourne, Melbourne University Press, 1972, pp. 79–105, 201–08; R.P. Winnington-Ingram, *Sophocles: An Interpretation*, Cambridge, Cambridge University Press, 1980, pp. 150–204; and B.M.W. Knox, 'Introduction' to R. Fagles (transl.), *Sophocles: The Three Theban Plays*, New York, Viking, 1982.

2 Many different ideas have been proposed for the staging of the opening scene. Perhaps the most interesting alternative to the one I suggest is that *no* suppliants accompany the old Priest, and he and Oedipus both use the theatre audience as the crowd who has gathered to seek relief from the plague. Although this scenario handsomely links the plague in the play to the one in Athens around the time of the production (see following note), the Priest orders at least some of the suppliants

to leave with him (142–44), indicating that he is not alone. Obviously, in this staging the chorus come on later in a normal *parodos*. See P.D. Arnott, *Public and Performance in the Greek Theatre*, London, Routledge, 1989, pp. 21–22.

3 On this basis, and the parodies of the play found in Aristophanes' comedies of 425 and 424, experts date *Oedipus Tyrannus* between 429 and 425. For a careful discussion of the play's relationship to the contemporary Athenian situation, see V. Ehrenberg, *Sophocles and Pericles*, Oxford, Blackwell, 1954. The account of the plague is in Thucydides, 2.47–55.

4 Sophocles uses the same word *deina* to open his famous Ode to Man chorus in *Antigone* (332): 'There are many things *deina* in the world, but nothing more *deina* than man.'

5 So, too, the suicide of Lady Macbeth makes it dramatically impossible for her husband to do the same in *Macbeth*, and Svidrigailov's suicide in *Crime and Punishment* tells the reader that Raskolnikov must follow a different path.

6 J. Jones, *On Aristotle and Greek Tragedy*, London, Chatto & Windus, 1962, p. 203, who finds that the process, 'far from being morbid, is the means to restoration, and almost an act of peace'.

7 Recall Lear as he speaks to Gloucester: 'The King would speak with Cornwall. The dear father/ Would with his daughter speak, commands – tends – service' (*King Lear*, 2.4.99–100). Like Oedipus, the shift in verbs suggests that Lear recognizes his changed circumstance, without fully admitting it. Although he does not mention this example, A. Poole, *Tragedy, Shakespeare and the Greek Example*, Oxford, Blackwell, 1987, makes many useful comparisons between the two tragic theatres.

8 Closing lines spoken by the chorus point to Oedipus as once having epitomized good fortune; now he provides the proof that no mortal can be sure of his happiness until his life is over. As with the closing 'choral tags' of other tragedies, however, the lines may be spurious.

# 8 EURIPIDES' *SUPPLIANT WOMEN*

1 Euripides returns to this issue in *Orestes* (902–30, 944–45), and Aristophanes exploits its comic possibilities in the parabasis of *Acharnians* (esp. 631–35) and *Wasps* (698–705, 719–21), and in the running attack on Cleon in *Knights* (41–70, 486–91, 710–809, 1111–20). See also L.B. Carter, *The Quiet Athenian*, Oxford, Clarendon Press, 1986, pp. 82–98; and R.K. Sinclair, *Democracy and Participation in Athens*, Cambridge, Cambridge University Press, 1988, pp. 203–08. Although his work constitutes an eloquent defence of Athenian democracy, J. Ober, *Mass and Elite in Democratic Athens*, Princeton, Princeton University Press, 1989, pp. 112–18, admits the elite status of public speakers in the Assembly.

2 A not uncommon ploy in Greek poetry is to put difficult truths in the mouth of an unsympathetic character, and then arrange events to vindicate the observations. In Homer's *Iliad*, Thersites' comments about the Trojan War are spurned, along with the speaker himself (*Il.*, 2.225–77), only to ring more truly – and more problematically – when Achilles repeats them in the embassy scene (9.315–37, 369–77).

3 The event is referred to obliquely elsewhere in the play (639, 860–61, 934, 1010–11) and described in detail in Euripides' *Phoenician Women* (1172–86). The presence of a ladder identifies Capaneus in the art of the period, and the iconography was so pronounced that the Messenger's reference to the proud man on his ladder might have brought Capaneus immediately to the audience's mind.

4 The classic study of this practice is F. Jacoby, '*Patrios Nomos*', *Journal of Hellenic*

*Studies*, 1944, vol. 64, pp. 37–66; see also W.K Pritchett, *The Greek State at War*, vol. 4, Berkeley, University of California Press, 1985, pp. 94–124, 249–50; and N. Loraux, *The Invention of Athens*, A. Sheridan (transl.), Cambridge, Harvard University Press, 1986, pp. 28–30, 56–72. Pericles' funeral oration is in Thucydides, 2.34–47.

5  J.W. Fitton, 'The *Suppliant Women* and the *Herakleidai* of Euripides', *Hermes*, 1961, vol. 89, pp. 438–39.

6  Some critics argue that Evadne climbed up a special structure (rising behind the temple façade) painted to appear like the crags of Eleusis, but such an anomalous construction would eliminate much of the surprise of Evadne's appearance, since the audience would expect it to be used. Evadne could appear on the *theologeion*, as Athena does as the *dea ex machina* at the end of the play, setting up a meaningful contrast between the overwrought young woman dressed for her wedding and the militaristic goddess with her traditional helmet and shield. However, the possibility that Evadne used the cavea – perhaps leaping off the top of the east analemma (the side wall supporting the slope where the audience sat) towards the area of the Odeion of Pericles – would allow the actor to be observed climbing ever higher as the chorus indicate she does (989), impossible to perform on the *theologeion*. A positive advantage of using a non-traditional area is the spark of pure dramatic surprise as Evadne leaps out of sight (and out of the theatre), a fitting scenario for an unprecedented scene.

7  For a summary of what we know about public support for war orphans, see R.S. Stroud, 'Theozotides and the Athenian Orphans', *Hesperia*, 1971, vol. 40, pp. 288–93.

8  See for example G.M.A. Grube, *The Drama of Euripides*, London, Methuen, 1941, p. 242; D.J. Conacher, 'Religious and Ethical Attitudes in Euripides' *Suppliants*', *Transactions of the American Philological Association*, 1956, vol. 87, p. 26; R.B. Gamble, 'Euripides' *Suppliant Women*', *Hermes*, 1970, vol. 98, pp. 404–05.

9  For the play's date, see C. Collard (ed.), *Euripides, Supplices*, vol. 1, Groningen, Bouma's Boekhuis, 1975, pp. 8–14. V. Di Benedetto, *Euripide: teatro e societá*, Torino, G. Einaudi, 1971, pp. 158–62, offers a good analysis of the political events surrounding the production.

10  For the vote in the Assembly, see Thucydides, 4.117.1–120.1; and A.W. Gomme, *A Historical Commentary on Thucydides*, vol. 3, Oxford, Clarendon Press, 1956, p. 603.

## 9 EURIPIDES' *ION*

1  In a modern theatre a director might have Hermes exit into the audience and take a seat. Gods as both scene-setters and audience are as old as the *Iliad*, where, for example, Athena and Apollo arrange the single combat between Hector and Ajax and then perch in a nearby tree disguised as birds to watch (*Il.*, 7.17–45, 57–62).

2  The translation is Crawley's, *The Complete Writings of Thucydides: The Peloponnesian War*, New York, Random House, 1951, p. 331.

3  See B.M.W. Knox, 'Euripidean Comedy' (org. 1970), in his *Word and Action*, Baltimore, Johns Hopkins University Press, 1979, p. 260.

4  The word *theatês* also is used for 'theatre spectator'. Perhaps Euripides is reminding the audience that the process of 'looking on' in the theatre also implies looking 'into', as Ion does in his soliloquy challenging Apollo (429–51) and here in his speech about Athens.

5  For the *genethlia*, see A.S. Owen (ed.), *Euripides: Ion*, Oxford, Clarendon Press,

1939, p. 115; and J.D. Denniston (ed.), *Euripides: Electra*, Oxford, Clarendon Press, 1939, pp. 131–32. Characters frequently pun on Ion's name – Hermes proclaims the name just as Ion comes on-stage for the first time (81); the chorus announce to Ion that Xuthus is coming out of the temple (*exionta*, 516); Xuthus tells Ion of the oracle proclaiming that the first one he met coming out (*exionti*) would be his son; the chorus comment on the naming (802); and the Tutor convinces Creusa that the name is a blatant cover-up for Xuthus' long-standing plan to foist his bastard son onto the Athenian throne (831).

6 Other Euripidean passages involving freedom of speech include *Electra*, 1049–57; *Phoenician Women*, 391–92; *Bacchae*, 668–69; and *Hippolytus*, 421–23, a passage discussed by W.S. Barrett (ed.), *Euripides: Hippolytos*, Oxford, Clarendon Press, 1964, p. 236.

7 See the Homeric *Hymn to Demeter*, 1–32, 417–33.

8 G. Norwood, *Greek Tragedy*, 3rd edn, London, Methuen, 1942, p. 238.

# SELECT BIBLIOGRAPHY

Arnott, P.D. (1989) *Public and Performance in the Greek Theatre*, London, Routledge.

Bacon, H. (1982) 'Aeschylus', in T.J. Luce (ed.), *Ancient Writers, Greece and Rome*, vol. 1, New York, Scribners, pp. 99–155.

Barlow, S. (1971) *The Imagery of Euripides*, London, Methuen.

Bieber, M. (1961) *The History of Greek and Roman Theater*, 2nd edn, Princeton, Princeton University Press.

*The Cambridge History of Classical Literature* (1985) P.E. Easterling and B.M.W. Knox (eds), Cambridge, Cambridge University Press.

*The Cambridge History of Literary Criticism* (1989) vol. 1, *Classical Criticism*, G.A. Kennedy (ed.), Cambridge, Cambridge University Press.

Conacher, D.J. (1967) *Euripidean Drama*, Toronto, University of Toronto Press.

Connor, W.R. (1989) 'City Dionysia and Athenian Democracy', *Classica et Mediaevalia*, vol. 40, pp. 7–32.

Dale, A.M. (1969) *Collected Papers*, Cambridge, Cambridge University Press.

Deubner, L. (1932) *Attische Feste*, Berlin, Akademie-Verlag.

Di Benedetto, V. (1971) *Euripide: teatro e società*, Torino, G. Einaudi.

Dodds, E.R. (1951) *The Greeks and the Irrational*, Sather Classical Lectures Vol. 22, Berkeley, University of California Press.

Dover, K.J. (1974) *Greek Popular Morality in the Time of Plato and Aristotle*, Berkeley, University of California Press.

Easterling, P.E. (1973) 'Presentation of Character in Aeschylus', *Greece and Rome*, vol. 20, pp. 3–19.

Else, G.F. (1957) *Aristotle's Poetics: The Argument*, Cambridge, Harvard University Press.

——(1965) *The Origin and Early Form of Greek Tragedy*, Cambridge, Harvard University Press.

Flickinger, R.C. (1936) *The Greek Theater and Its Drama*, 4th edn, Chicago, University of Chicago Press.

Foley, H.P. (1981) 'The Conception of Women in Athenian Drama', in H. Foley (ed.), *Reflections of Women in Antiquity*, New York, Gordon & Breach, pp. 127–68.

Gellie, G. (1972) *Sophocles: A Reading*, Melbourne, Melbourne University Press.

Goldhill, S. (1987) 'The Great Dionysia and Civic Ideology', *Journal of Hellenic Studies*, vol. 107, pp. 58–76.

Gould, J. (1978) 'Dramatic Character and "Human Intelligibility" in Greek Tragedy', *Proceedings of the Cambridge Philological Society*, vol. 24 n.s., pp. 43–67.

*Greek Religion and Society* (1985) P.E. Easterling and J.V. Muir (eds), Cambridge, Cambridge University Press.

Grube, G.M.A. (1941) *The Drama of Euripides*, London, Methuen.

Haigh, A.E. (1896) *The Tragic Drama of the Greeks*, Oxford, Clarendon Press.

Harrison, T. (1988) 'Facing Up to the Muses', *Proceedings of the Classical Association*, vol. 85, pp. 7–29.

Herington, J. (1985) *Poetry into Drama*, Sather Classical Lectures Vol. 49, Berkeley, University of California Press.

Hourmouziades, N.C. (1965) *Production and Imagination in Euripides*, Athens, Greek Society for Humanistic Studies.

Jones, J. (1962) *On Aristotle and Greek Tragedy*, London, Chatto & Windus.

Kitto, H.D.F. (1961) *Greek Tragedy*, 3rd end, London, Methuen.

Knox, B.M.W. (1979) *Word and Action*, Baltimore, Johns Hopkins University Press.

——(1982) 'Introduction' to R. Fagles (transl.), *Sophocles: The Three Theban Plays*, New York, Viking.

Lattimore, R. (1969) *Story Patterns in Greek Tragedy*, Ann Arbor, University of Michigan.

Lawler, L.B. (1964) *The Dance of the Ancient Greek Theatre*, Iowa City, University of Iowa Press.

Leacroft, R. and H. (1984) *Theatre and Playhouse*, London, Methuen.

Lefkowitz, M. (1981) *The Lives of the Greek Poets*, Baltimore, Johns Hopkins University Press.

Lesky, A. (1979) *Greek Tragedy*, H.A. Frankfort (transl.), 3rd edn, New York, Barnes & Noble.

——(1983) *Greek Tragic Poetry*, M. Dillon (transl.), New Haven, Yale University Press.

McCaughey, J. (1972) 'Talking about Greek Tragedy', *Ramus*, vol. 1, pp. 26–47.

Murray, G. (1913) *Euripides and his Age*, London, Thornton Butterworth.

Napier, A.D. (1986) *Masks, Transformation, Paradox*, Berkeley, University of California Press.

Ober, J. (1989) *Mass and Elite in Democratic Athens*, Princeton, Princeton University Press.

Parke, H.W. (1977) *Festivals of the Athenians*, Ithaca, Cornell University Press.

Pickard-Cambridge, A. (1962) *Dithyramb, Tragedy, and Comedy*, rev. T.B.L. Webster, Oxford, Clarendon Press.

——(1988) *Dramatic Festivals of Athens*, rev. J. Gould and D.M. Lewis, 2nd edn, Oxford, Clarendon Press.

Podlecki, A.J. (1966) *The Political Background of Aeschylean Tragedy*, Ann Arbor, University of Michigan Press.

Poole, A. (1987) *Tragedy, Shakespeare and the Greek Example*, Oxford, Blackwell.

Raven, D.S. (1968) *Greek Metre*, 2nd edn, London, Faber & Faber.

Rehm, R. (1988) 'The Staging of Suppliant Plays', *Greek, Roman and Byzantine Studies*, vol. 29, pp. 263–307.

Seaford, R. (1987) 'The Tragic Wedding', *Journal of Hellenic Studies*, vol. 107, pp. 106–30.

Seale, D. (1982) *Vision and Stagecraft in Sophocles*, Chicago, University of Chicago Press.

Segal, C. (1982) *Dionysiac Poetics and Euripides' Bacchae*, Princeton, Princeton University Press.

Segal, E. (ed.) (1987) *Oxford Readings in Greek Tragedy*, Oxford, Blackwell.

Simon, E. (1981) *The Ancient Theatre*, C.E. Vafopoulou-Richardson (transl.), London.

Stanford, W.B. (1983) *Greek Tragedy and the Emotions*, Routledge & Kegan Paul, London.

Sutton, D.F. (1984) *The Lost Sophocles*, Lanham, University Press of America.

Taplin, O. (1977) *The Stagecraft of Aeschylus*, Oxford, Clarendon Press.

——(1978) *Greek Tragedy in Action*, Berkeley, University of California Press.

Thompson, H.A. and R.E. Wycherley (1972) *The Athenian Agora*, vol. 14, Princeton, American School of Classical Studies.

Travlos, J. (1971) *Pictorial Dictionary of Ancient Athens*, New York, Praeger.

Turner, V. (1982) *From Ritual to Theatre*, New York, Performing Arts Journal.

Vellacott, P. (1975) *Ironic Drama: A Study of Euripides' Method and Meaning*, Cambridge, Cambridge University Press.

Vernant, J.-P. (1972) 'Greek Tragedy: Problems of Interpretation', in R. Macksey and E. Donato (eds), *The Structuralist Controversy*, Baltimore, Johns Hopkins University Press, pp. 273–95.

Vickers, B. (1973) *Towards Greek Tragedy*, London, Longman.

Walton, J.M. (1984) *The Greek Sense of Theatre*, London, Methuen.

Webster, T.B.L. (1967) *The Tragedies of Euripides*, London, Methuen.

——(1970) *Greek Theatre Production*, 2nd edn, London, Methuen.

Whitman, C.H. (1951) *Sophocles, A Study of Heroic Humanism*, Cambridge, Harvard University Press.

Winkler, J.J. (1990) 'The Ephebes' Song: *Tragôidia* and *Polis*', in J.J. Winkler and F.I. Zeitlin (eds), *Nothing to do with Dionysos?*, Princeton, Princeton University Press, pp. 20–62.

Winnington-Ingram, R.P. (1980) *Sophocles: An Interpretation*, Cambridge, Cambridge University Press.

——(1983) *Studies in Aeschylus*, Cambridge, Cambridge University Press.

Wolff, C. (1982) 'Euripides', in T.J. Luce (ed.), *Ancient Writers, Greece and Rome*, vol. 1, New York, Scribners, pp. 233–66.

Wycherley, R.E. (1957) *The Athenian Agora*, vol. 3: *Literary and Epigraphical Testimonia*, Princeton, American School of Classical Studies.

Zeitlin, F.I. (1985) 'Playing the Other: Theater, Theatricality, and the Feminine in Greek Drama,' *Representations*, vol. 11, pp. 63–94.

# INDEX

Acropolis of Athens 9, 17, 21, 31, 32, 38; in *Ion* 133–34, 136, 138, 141, 145

acting and actors 28–29, 45–51; acting style 48–51; character-building 45–46, 88, 96–97; in choruses 25–26, 54; in Messenger speeches 61; mimetic 10; mute actors 28, 42, 71; playwrights as actors 25, 27–28; presence of 46; rhapsode as prototype 8

Aeschylus 22–27; as actor 27–28; revivals of his plays 23; as theatrical innovator 34, 37; work with specific actors 29; *see also* plays by name

*Agamemnon* 50, 78–92, 115, 139; Agamemnon 50, 79–80, 84–86, 89–90; bath 47, 87; Cassandra 84, 86–90; chariot entrance 84; chorus 56, 60, 79–81, 87 (*kommos*), 90, 92 (*exodos*); Clytemnestra at threshold 83, 84, 97–98; erotic language 83, 90; Helen 77, 79, 81, 83–84, 87, 89, 91; imagery 47, 56–57, 80, 82, 83–84, 90, 91–92 (feasting), 93–94 (inversion of nature); Iphigenia 27, 79–80, 85, 89–91; lyric of Cassandra 27, 57, 86–88; lyric complexity 79; necessity and free will 80; nightingale 89–90; prologue 78; silence 79, 80, 82, 86; tapestry scene 84–86; verbal and gestural hyperbole 85–86; war, horrors of 81–82; wedding and death, conflation of 79, 81, 83, 84, 87, 89; see also *Oresteia*

*agôn* 44, 64–65, 73; *see also* under plays by name

agora of Athens 5, 8, 18, 73; early tragic performances 31–32

*Ajax* 8, 62, 68; *agôn* in 64;

prologue 69; roles, division of 50

*Alcestis: agôn* 64–65; chorus 53, 56; Messenger speech 61; monodies 58; prologue 69; wedding and funeral motifs 7, 66, 67, 88

*Andromnache* 36; funeral cortège 67; monodies 29, 58

*Andromeda* 34

Anthesteria 13–14

*Antigone* 7, 8, 23; costumes 66; *ekkyklêma* 37; Eurydice's role 58; funeral rites and corpses 67; *kommos* 57; male chorus 60; prologue 69; roles, division of 50

Archilochus 14

archon basileus 20

archon eponymous 20, 23, 24, 28

Aristophanes 10, 23, 33, 34; *Acharnians* 17, 19, 25; *Frogs* 24; *Knights* 41; parodies Euripides 66

Aristotle, *Poetics* 14, 34, 46, 49, 50, 70, 110

Assembly, Athenian 4, 5, 16, 17, 18, 73; in *Suppliant Women* 126–27, 132

Athens, reference to contemporary aspects in tragedy 45–46, 59, 64–65, 78, 102–04, 105–06, 108, 131–32, 137, 139–40

audience 30, 39, 45–48, 50; imagination of 37, 100; *see also* under plays by name

*aulos* 6, 14, 21, 25–26, 29, 55

avant-garde 40, 52

*Bacchae* 13, 17, 23, 50; Agave scene 40, 63, 67–68; chorus 57 (*parodos*), 60, 103 (contemporized); drag scene

164